The Irish in Australia and New Zealand

A RESOURCE FOR FAMILY HISTORIANS

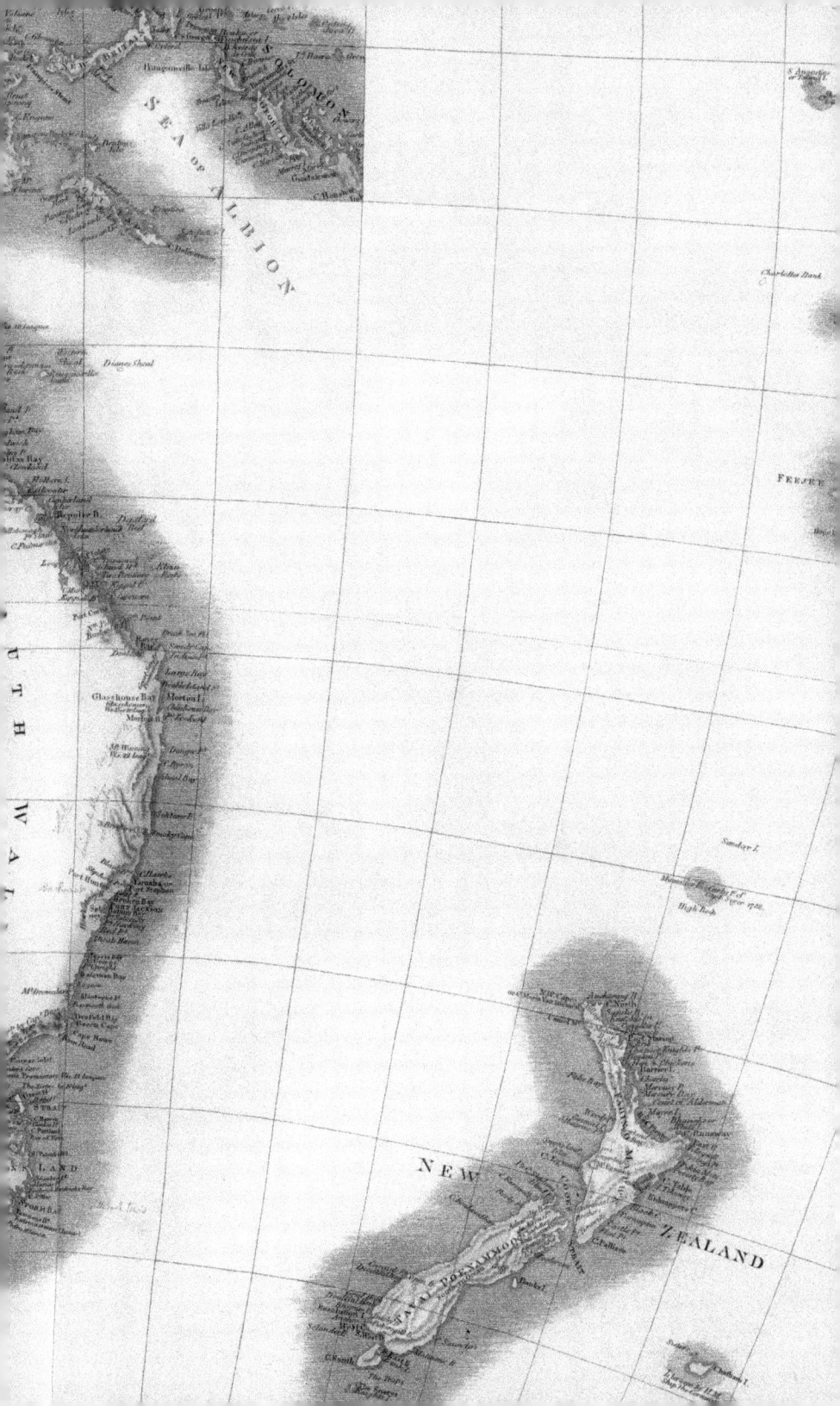

DEDICATION

To the individuals and host societies/organisations who helped to make the Feb.–Mar. 2024 lecture tour of Australia and New Zealand possible: Auckland Council Libraries, Pukekohe; Christchurch Irish Society (Michael Campbell); Collective Community Hub, Johnsonville; Family History ACT; Family History Connections (FHC); Family HistoryWA (FHWA) and the Irish Interest Group; Genealogical Society of Queensland (GSQ); Genealogical Society of Victoria (GSV); Genealogy Sunshine Coast (GSC); GenealogySA (SAGHS); Irish Interest Group of the New Zealand Society of Genealogists (NZSG); Irish Interest Group Lower North Island (NZSG); New Zealand Society of Genealogists, Franklin Branch, Pukekohe; New Zealand Society of Genealogists Library, Panmure; Queensland Family History Society (QFHS); Society of Australian Genealogists (SAG); Toitu Otago Settlers Museum; The Wanaka Genealogy Group and Wanaka Library. We apologise in advance for the omission of any person or group. We wish to thank everyone who helped out.

FRONT COVER

'View of the Heads, at the entrance to Port Jackson, New South Wales' by Joseph Lycett (1824). Courtesy The State Library, New South Wales

BACK COVER

'New Zealand' showing the short-lived names for the islands: 'New Ulster', 'New Munster' and 'New Leinster' used approx. 1841–6, from *The Illustrated Atlas, And Modern History Of The World Geographical, Political, Commercial & Statistical* (1851). The David Rumsey Historical Map Collection

Published 2024 by Ulster Historical Foundation
www.ulsterhistoricalfoundation.com

Except as otherwise permitted under the Copyright, Designs and Patents Act 1988, this publication may only be reproduced, stored or transmitted in any form or by any means with the prior permission in writing of the publisher or, in the case of reprographic reproduction, in accordance with the terms of a licence issued by The Copyright Licensing Agency. Enquiries concerning reproduction outside those terms should be sent to the publisher.

© Ulster Historical Foundation and the individual authors
ISBN 978-1-913993-10-8

DESIGN AND FORMATTING: FPM Publishing
COVER DESIGN: Dunbar Design
PRINTING: SprintPRINT Ltd

Contents

FOREWORD BY TREVOR PARKHILL	viii
ABBREVIATIONS	x

1. The Irish in Australia *by Patrick O'Farrell* — 1

2. The Irish in New Zealand *by Michael Bellam* — 7

3. 'That infant colony': Aspects of Ulster Emigration to Australia *by Trevor Parkhill* — 12

4. The Anglo-Irish Tradition and Anglo-Irish Migration to Colonial Australia *by Gordon Forth* — 35

5. 'Prospects of this New Colony': Letters of Ulster Emigrants to New Zealand 1840–1900 *by Trevor Parkhill* — 62

6. Green Threads of Kinship! Aspects of Irish Chain-Migration to New South Wales *by Richard Reid* — 71

7. Lives moved to New South Wales: Free Passage for Convicts' Families *by Perry McIntyre* — 86

8. Barefoot and Pregnant? Female Orphans who Emigrated from Irish Workhouses to Australia, 1848–50 *by Trevor McClaughlin* — 96

9. Horesman, Pass By ... Irish-Australian Gravestones *by Trevor McClaughlin* — 106

10. Ulster and the Bay of Plenty: The Katikati Special Settlement in North Island *by N.C. Mitchel* — 118

11. The Goldrush to Lamplough, near Avoca in Victoria, Australia during 1859–60 *by Denis Strangman* — 135

12. Family Migration to New Zealand: The Bassett　163
　　Family of Ballygawley, Downpatrick, County Down
　　by John Bassett

13. Sir Samuel McCaughey – Ulster Australian: Irrigator,　170
　　Breeder and Benefactor *by James Thompson*

14. John King – An Ulster Explorer of Australia　179
　　by William B. Alderdice

15. John Ballance – New Zealand Premier, 1891–3:　186
　　Irish Origins and influences *by Tim McIvor*

Foreword

It is estimated that eight million men, women and children emigrated from Ireland in the nineteenth century, of whom some five per cent, a not-insignificant proportion, found their way to Australia and New Zealand. Just as significantly, *The Oxford Companion to Irish History* (1998, p. 31) considers that Irish migrants 'made up nearly a quarter of all immigrants [to Australia] during that period'.

The timely alignment of the Australian bicentennial in 1988 and the commemoration only two years later in 1990 of the sesquicentenary of the Treaty of Waitangi proved to be a suitable focus for a wholly new departure for many interested in researching – from a personal, genealogical or academic perspective – the Irish diaspora. The significance of the historic links between Ireland, particularly the nine counties of the historic province of Ulster, and Australia and New Zealand, has featured regularly and with telling effect in the pages of *Familia: Ulster Genealogical Review*.

The first edition of the journal was published in 1985, just as historians in Ireland were becoming, in the context of the links between Ireland and Australia that were so presciently anticipated by the work of the late Patrick O'Farrell in the Dublin Castle transportation archives in the early 1970s, more fully aware of those links. Indeed, it was O'Farrell himself, in the first issue of *Familia: Ulster Genealogical Review* (1985, pp 37–41) who wrote with authority: 'In no other British settlement were the Irish so central to the composition and character of a new nation' than that of Australia. He went on to point that that 'about a third of Australia's present population of fifteen million have some Irish ancestry'. From the New Zealand perspective, Michael Bellam in the same issue (pp 41–3) provided an equally informed contextual summary for New Zealand, saying that 'the role of the Irish in New Zealand history has been largely overlooked' in spite of the fact that 'about ... 14 per cent of the total [1981] population can claim Irish ancestry'.

What became clear from the outset to researchers on this side of the world was the quality of the Antipodean immigration sources, particularly in Australia, that was now being brought to our attention in Ireland by a brigade of authoritative researchers and authors. The result was an epiphany of awareness that inquiry into Australian sources for researchers in Ireland was, or could well be, altogether more promising and satisfying than had been the case for the many who had tried, more often than not fruitlessly, to follow up the migration of their family or community members on arrival in the United States, for so long the focus of the great human haemhorrage from Ireland throughout the nineteenth century. Just as effectively, sources in Ulster, including letters retained over many years by local families whose sons had migrated there in the nineteenth century and which featured in the archives held in the Public Record Office of Northern Ireland, added to the human stories that became such a feature of the Ireland–Australia/New Zealand emigrant trail.

The first issue of *Familia* contained Barry Kirkwood's recounting of the Capper family letters 1862–78, available for consultation in PRONI. This story of the sons of a reasonably prosperous County Armagh family chasing the allure of gold in the mining fields of Ballarat demonstrated the extent to which the Capper family's example, as relayed in their letters home, served as a magnet for many like-minded young men in post-Famine Ireland faced with ever-diminishing prospects. The powerful effect of family migration to Australia is also an issue followed up by Denis Strangman's account of his family's involvement in the Lamplough gold rush 1859–60, his great-grandfather having followed the lure of gold there from County Cork.

Perhaps one of the most intriguing features of the new research thrown up by Australian archival sources were the stories of the female orphan children sent out from the workhouses in Ireland 1848–50 to take up a new life in Australia. Richard Reid's and Trevor McClaughlin's research evident in *Familia* (1987) not only outlined the concept and the reality of what at first sight appeared to be a barbarous experiment but also set the scheme in the context of the Great Famine, whose sesquicentenary was being commemorated in the mid-1990s. McClaughlin's subsequent research of course painted a slightly more wholesome account of the individual stories of females whose lot in Australia turned out to be altogether different – in most cases vastly improved life chances – than would have been the case had they stayed incarcerated and utterly without prospects in an Irish workhouse. He also assessed (in *Familia* 1998) the impact of the transportation to Van Diemen's Land of women convicts during the Famine. Additionally, *Irish Women in Colonial Australia*, a significant consideration of the role of women in shaping settlement in Australia, which McClaughlin co-edited and containing contributions by David Fitzpatrick, Richard Davis, Portia Robinson, Pauline Roche, Eric Richards and Anna Herannis, was reviewed in *Familia* 1999. In this same issue, the theme of the impact of the Famine on settlement in Western Australia is well evidenced in Jennifer Harrison's case study of the Poor Law Inspector, Sir Arthur Edward Kennedy, who became Governor of the state.

Chain emigration, in which families have forged ahead and have subsequently arranged the passage and initial settlement in their New World of others, sometime family members, sometimes neighbours, has been almost traditionally associated with the migrant stream from Ireland to North America in the nineteenth century. In *Familia* 2019 David Hume's research narrates the story of a twentieth-century example of family-assisted migration to Australia: the Barry family who migrated in the early 1920s from Magheramorne, County Antrim. As was the case with many emigrants, James and Susan Barry had been encouraged to consider Australia by another immigrant from County Antrim, Bob Wilson. He had settled near Loch in the South Gippsland region of Victoria and recommended to the Barrys that they would find a new life of relative hope and prosperity in Australia. In turn James Barry acted as 'sponsor' or 'nominator' for others from the Ballycarry area, including Sam Hunter, who arrived in 1925 and his parents Adam and Agnes Hunter (née Killen), who arrived the following year. Hume's article also carries a 'whatever happened to' account of the seven children of James and Susan and their always meaningful contribution to the society of their adoption.

The case for elaborating Ulster links with New Zealand, the focus of *Familia* 1989 was led by Don Akenson, one of the foremost authorities in the recent and ongoing re-interpretation of the pathways of Irish migration. It was accompanied by the stories of the

Bassett (County Down) and Ballance (County Antrim) families, the immigration of the latter, of course, paving the way for the innovative and forward-thinking premiership of John Ballance (1890–93).

Familia has always carried a strong and well-informed 'reviews' section, in which books on topics relating to genealogy, migration and settlement abroad are considered by reviewers who are themselves experts in their field. In the 1995 issue of *Familia*, Brenda Collins' review of the late David Fitzpatrick's *Oceans of Consolation* (1994) – fourteen families' sequences of letters 1840s–1900s narrating as it does powerful evocations of the stories of emigrants to Australia, stands out. More recently Collins' review (2014) of Elizabeth Rushen's *Colonial Duchesses: The Migration of Irish Women to New South Wales before the Great Famine* and Perry McIntryre's assessments (2012 and 2013 respectively) of Richard Reid's brilliant *Farewell My Children: Irish Assisted Emigration to Australia 1846–1870* and McCarthy and Todd's *The Wreck of the 'Neva'* have brought their considerable experience to bear on publications of some significance.

Recent issues have appropriately reflected the merited current preoccupation with the First World War, particularly the role of immigrants fighting in ANZAC divisions. The part played by Irish immigrants is neatly illustrated in Hugh Farren's account (*Familia* 2013) of his uncle and namesake, who was, as the subtitle aptly summarises: 'Born in Derry, died in France fighting for New Zealand'. The ongoing research in this area is amply demonstrated by Jeff Kildea's painstaking research, evident in *Familia* (2015), 'The Irish Anzacs Project', the availability of whose data about participants should prove to be very beneficial to individual searches.

Kildea's 2017 book, *Hugh Mahon: Patriot, Pressman, Politician – Volume 1, the years from 1857 to 1901*, the first part of a biography of a journalist-turned politician who arrived in Australia in 1882 trumpeted as 'a sterling young Irishman, a victim of British tyranny', is warmly reviewed by Richard Reid in *Familia* 2018. And it is worth noting that there have been reviews in recent issues of *Familia* of no less than five titles on aspects of female migration to Australia from Ireland, issued by the redoubtable Anchor Press, whose authors include Kathlyn Gibson, Jennifer Harrison, Perry McIntyre and Elizabeth Rushen,

FOREWORD

Indeed *Familia* and the work of the Ulster Historical Foundation, particularly its publications programme, could well make a modest claim for being an effective vehicle for making more widely accessible the knowledge and information of the historic links between Ireland and Australia and New Zealand that are continually being uncovered.

TREVOR PARKHILL
Editor, *Familia*

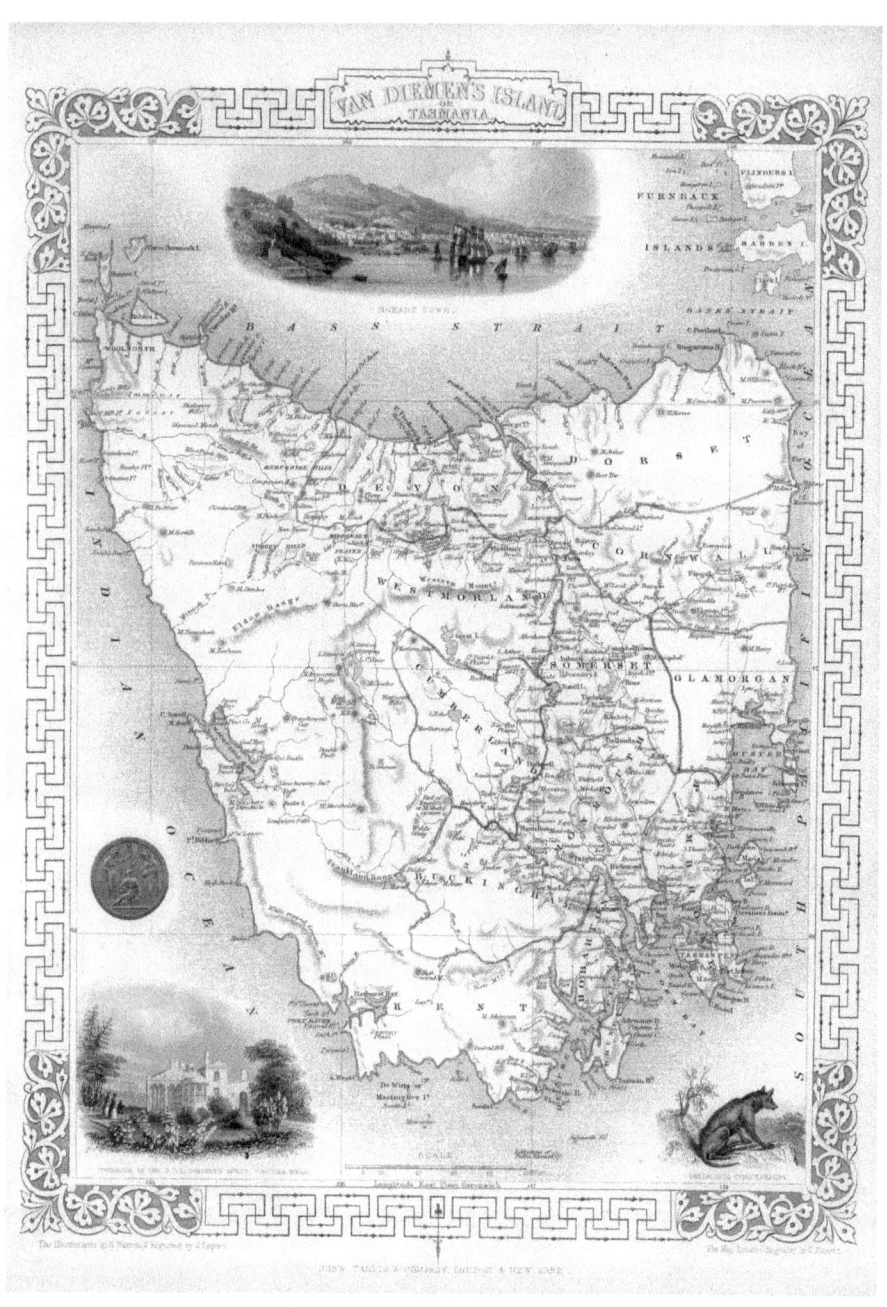

'Van Diemen's Island or Tasmania'
from *The Illustrated Atlas, And Modern History Of The World Geographical, Political, Commercial & Statistical* (1851).
The David Rumsey Historical Map Collection

1
The Irish in Australia

Patrick O'Farrell

Australia without its Irish aspects is simply unthinkable. In no other British settlement were the Irish so central to the composition and character of a new nation than they were in the making of Australia: about a third of Australia's present population of fifteen million have some Irish ancestry. Moreover, unlike America, where the Irish were one of a number of nationalities that contributed to the melting pot, in Australia they were the sole significant element of ethnic diversity, the only major non-English culture. So, since the foundation of settlement in 1788, it was the Irish minority alone that questioned and challenged the exclusive dominance of the majority's English-orientated culture and religion.

The resulting interaction moulded Australia's history away from that of being a stagnant prison (and later, a respectable little Britain of the south) toward becoming an open, tolerant, egalitarian and plural society. In this creative process, until recently the Irish have been *the* traditional dynamic factor, that is, the galvanising force at the centre of the evolution of Australia's national character. Now, by the 1980s the descendants of those Irish immigrants have become so much part of what is seen as the dominant Australian establishment and culture, that the newer migrant groups that have come to Australia since the Second World War refer to Australia's mainline culture not as English, but as Anglo-Celtic. This term, first used widely in 1902 by E. W. O'Sullivan, an Irish Australian who was a New South Wales Government minister, to describe what he saw as his own background, captures the two related faces of Australian's origins. Now everywhere in Australia, those of Irish ancestry are at the national process, long interwoven integrally into all aspects of national life and character.

This position was not won easily: 'We are Englishmen', thundered the *Melbourne Age* in 1883, 'and this is an English colony ... we do not intend to let a handful of "foreigners" ... impugn our loyalties to the hard-won traditions of race'. The 'foreigners' were the Irish: many in the Australian colonies demanded that the Irish reject their consciousness of distinctive national origins and the consequences of their differing religion – or in other words, abandon their identity. That they refused to do. And hence the controversy that surrounds their history. What they were prepared to do – happily – was to compromise, to accept their new environment and fit into it. But not entirely on terms dictated by the English – orientated majority: the Irish would not accept Australia defined as a tiny southern shadow of England. No: they demanded a definition of Australia broad and flexible enough to include them as they were, which would embrace or accept, at least to the degree of tolerance, those aspects of their character and loyalties they held to be most important.

So there is a sense in which Australia has had two histories, those of the English majority and the Irish minority, only recently blending, but in the process of two centuries of interaction, tension and abrasion, gradually producing modern Australia. The direct Irish contribution to Australian liberties has been very great, but perhaps even more vital, though less tangible, is the effect of their activities and opinions on liberalising and humanising the climate of Australian life. Vital too has been their injection of colour, and their vigorous refusal to accept either exclusion or injustice as they saw it.

Indeed, the greatest contribution of the Irish in Australia, as the only powerful and distinct minority until recent times, was to raise, and raise again and again, and keep on pursuing, that crucial question: what kind of society would Australia be?

The dominant assumption was, it would be a small replica of England. The Irish challenge to that became, not divisive, but the main unifying principle of Australian history. What held this country's people together, in a creative and productive social and political relationship, was a continuing debate, always vigorous, sometimes bitter, even violent, about what kind of country this should be. That debate compelled Australia's inhabitants, of all kinds, to take stock of their society.

The centrality of the Irish to this process of national self-examination and growth is obvious when one lists the major contests and disputes in Australian history. In all, the Irish and their descendants have been prominent. Most of these great issues have been generated by the Irish, centred around them, and were about matters vital to them. Here these major issues are: the largest continuing divisive issue in Australian history – state aid to Catholic education; the contentious matter of religion in politics, beginning in the 1840s and going on until the split in the Australian Labour Party over the role of the Catholic Action Movement in the 1950s; the great matter of the access of small farmers to Australia's lands, from the 1820s, with, for example, the involvement in Duffy's Land Act of 1862 of Charles Gavan Duffy, Irish Premier of Victoria; the most bitter and divisive conflict in Australian history, over the Conscription Referenda of 1916–17, with Melbourne's Irish Archbishop Mannix at the centre of the victorious 'No' campaign; the long debate over immigration, beginning with vehement hostility to free Irish immigration in the 1830s, but appearing again in relation to the Irish for the next fifty years, and reappearing thereafter in relation to the Irish for the next fifty years, and reappearing thereafter in relation to other groups, most recently Asians. Two other areas of debate should be added to this historical list – the sectarian issue, the continuing battle until recent times, between Protestants and Catholics; and arguably the greatest enduring contest of them all, labour verses capital, where the contribution of Irish Catholics to the support and composition of the Australian Labour Party is one of the commonplaces of Australian political history.

A glance at these decisive issues, and the centrality of the Irish and their descendants in all of them makes the inescapable point – where the action was in Australian history, there also were the Irish. To sum up, the total creative effect of this combination of questioning, challenges, protests, insistence on the validity of minority views and values, the demand for tolerance and acceptance, was to mould a distinctive Australian identity – that curious equilibrium of Irishness protesting against the extremes of Englishness, that odd blend of radicalism and conservatism that reflects the Irish position – not so much against the system as against efforts to exclude them from it.

Emphasis on the dramatic and colourful aspects of the Irish role in Australia should not blind one of their quieter contributions – to the diversity of hard-working colonial life, to the arts and to popular music, to their introduction into Australia of a vigorous sense of family and community, lacking or little developed in the primitive penal colony. Nor should we overlook the diversity among the Irish themselves. The protestors, the sources of radicalism, social unrest and agitation were mainly Irish Catholics. But the Anglo-Irish and Ulster Protestants also made significant and substantial contributions to national life and character, long neglected in Australian history and only now being appreciated. Ulster Protestants made up about 10 per cent – at some periods to 20 per cent – of Irish immigrants to Australia. Some few – like some few of the Irish Catholics – brought their extremism from Ireland, in the form of the Loyal Orange Lodge, but most preferred to leave such antagonisms behind them, and to put their superior skills and enterprise into commerce, the trades, and farming. Their Protestantism allowed them to blend in smoothly with the prevailing colonial ethos. So did the Anglo-Irish whose contribution was at the top of Australian society, particularly in administration and the professions: the most common university degree held in early-and mid-nineteenth century Australia tended to be that from Trinity College, University of Dublin. The prominence of the Anglo-Irish in Australia sprang initially from their large representation in the imperial administration, those who ran the British Empire overseas. In that they tended to be reforming liberals, like Sir Richard Bourke, Governor of New South Wales 1831-7, favouring a tolerant, open society with freedom of local initiative and development: their influence at all levels of Australian colonial administration was a liberalising one. The importance of Anglo-Irish professional men – lawyers, doctors, engineers – is particularly notable in Victoria, from the 1850s to the 1880s, where all aspects of the formation of that young colony, down to the adoption of an Irish railway gauge, and up to the establishment of the University of Melbourne, came under Anglo-Irish influence. Victoria too, from its foundation, was now home to various members of the landed Anglo-Irish aristocracy and gentry who determined the character of the colony's elite social life.

So, from top to bottom, the Irish of all kinds were part of Australia's life and history, more influential in some states – Victoria and Queensland – less in others – South Australia and Tasmania. But in numbers they were concentrated at the bottom, and one major strand in Australian history is the story of their pushing their way up from positions of inferiority and disadvantage to equality, using in particular the Catholic education system as the vehicle of their ambition to ensure that the children had access to opportunities superior to those of their parents. Their story is closely linked with that of the church of the Irish majority, for the Catholic Irish lacked lay leaders and relied on the priesthood to provide such leadership.

That story – the Irish move upward in their Australia world – is the story of both individuals and a social group. It begins with the Irish as convicts, many transported as a result of the 1798 rebellion. Then, from the 1830s to the 1880s, the Irish poured in as immigrants always unwelcome, following the gold rushes, looking for work as labourers or domestics, saving to buy a farm, or wandering as nomads, shearing, navvying on the railways. Then from the 1880s to the First World War, they were led by their church in the pursuit of integration and respectability, joining the Labour Party, the public service, trying to educate their children, all in what amounted to an Irish Australian sub-culture. And then, from 1915 to 1921, led by Archbishop Mannix, and with the Easter Rebellion of 1916 being used as a means to brand them disloyal, they became involved in major social conflict convinced that they were being isolated from and penalised by Australian society, as defined by the then government of W.M. Hughes. They sought then, successfully, to defend themselves and their liberal idea of Australia, against what they saw as oppression, ultra-English imperialism, exploitation, Tory ascendancy. Their victory was a turning point in Australian history, deciding the future for a liberal Australia, an open society. Between 1915 and 1921, Irish Australian forces, led by Mannix, successfully asserted the claims of difference and insubordination against the powerful legions of hierarchy and conformity, led by W.M. Hughes.

Thereafter aggressive Irishism in Australia rapidly declined: it had served its positive Australian purpose of ensuring a plural society in which the descendants of the Irish – and any later diverse comers to the present day – could live easy, with dignity, as themselves.

Published in *Familia: Ulster Genealogical Review*, no. 1, 1985, and at that time had been reproduced with permission of *Ireland Today*.

Purse family headstone, Ballyhalbert, Co. Down, including reference to 'Hugh Purse, Whitechurch, who died at Maorie Point, Otago, New Zealand the 11th Sept 1864'. Interestingly this headstone sits in a family plot consisting of nine memorials spanning a period of *c.* 160 years, from 1739 to 1898, for this relatively rare family name.

2

The Irish in New Zealand

Michael Bellam

New Zealand represents the far-flung edge of the Irish diaspora. The role of the Irish in New Zealand history has been largely overlooked and an examination of this topic is long overdue.

About 450,000 (1981) New Zealanders or 14 per cent of the total population can claim Irish ancestry. It appears that about 75 per cent of the Catholics in New Zealand are of Irish descent. The history of the Catholic Church in New Zealand is largely the history of the Irish in that country. Because the number of Irish immigrants was very low in absolute terms and because they were widely dispersed throughout New Zealand, unlike the United States, Irish city neighbourhoods and Irish dominance of urban politics did not emerge in New Zealand. Also, New Zealand was different from the United States in that significant proportions of Irish immigrants married outside their group from the earlier years, and went into mining and farming. Today there are still distinct New Zealand-Irish rural communities in, for example, Southland, South Canterbury and Taranaki. As was the case elsewhere, most of the immigrants in the past came from the depressed areas of the west and south of Ireland (counties which seem to have been strongly represented in New Zealand were Cork, Kerry and Galway), and were escaping eviction, famine, poverty and alien rule.

The Irish were present in New Zealand from the very beginning of the colony. Indeed the first Governor (1840–42), William Hobson, and the Head of the first Executive in 1854, James Edward Fitzgerald, were Irish as were the 'Fencibles', a group of Irish ex-soldiers who were settled on the outskirts of Auckland in the late 1840s to act as a buffer between the colonists and the Maoris. However, the first big inflow of Irish immigrants came with the Otago and the West Coast gold rushes in the 1860s. A substantial number of New Zealand-Irish are descendants of these immigrants who came mainly via Australia. In fact, the Californian, Australian and New Zealand gold rushes were part of a sequence, with some of the miners participating in all three. According to a contemporary judge, 'the miners were a vigorous and manly breed of men. Their code was simple – courage, generosity and honesty were the cardinal virtues'. On the West Coast, 30 per cent of the gold rush community were Irish at a time when less than 13 per cent of the New Zealand population as a whole were Irish. In the view of historian Philip Ross May, in some ways the gold diggers, who were unassisted immigrants, were better than the general run of immigrants having undergone a process of selection more rigorous than any English immigration agent would apply.

This influx was followed by Premier Vogel's large scale immigration thrust of the 1870s. This programme brought in particular a significant number of Irish women destined for domestic service. Other Irish came as indentured labourers to work on the new farms.

Irish immigration fell off relatively in the first half of the twentieth century and thus New Zealand links with Ireland were somewhat attenuated. However, there was another large influx from Ireland in the 1950s which was a period of prosperity and labour shortage in New Zealand. Today few Irish are coming to New Zealand partly because of tighter New Zealand restrictions on immigration and partly because of improved economic conditions at home.

The New Zealand Irish, although relatively limited in numbers, have had a disproportionate impact on New Zealand society. This is evident if one looks at, for instance, their role in the churches, politics, literature and education. However, unlike Australia, the New Zealand Irish have not had a particularly marked influence on national character and popular culture.

As in the USA and Australia, the Catholic Church in New Zealand acted as a focal point for the Irish Catholic community and separate Catholic school and social welfare systems were established at great cost. In 1984 there were over 56,000 Catholic school pupils and over 50 Catholic hospitals and other charitable institutions in New Zealand. Up to about the 1920s sectarian conflict was fairly prevalent and the Catholic insistence on its own schools particularly gave offence to the Protestant majority. With the passage of time such religious ill-feeling gradually declined and is now largely non-existent. Since 1979 all Catholic schools have been integrated with the state system and they now receive considerable government assistance.

The Irish impact on the New Zealand Catholic hierarchy has been substantial with two-thirds of the bishops historically being either Irish born or of Irish descent.

Most of the Catholic clergy and religious also have been largely New Zealand-Irish. This led to a distinct Irish imprint on the New Zealand Catholic Church, especially in the nineteenth and early twentieth centuries. This imprint brought a strong spirituality and sense of discipline and commitment. On the other hand it has been argued that a certain anti-intellectualism tended to hold back the advancement of the Catholic community, and that for some time the Church was not attuned sufficiently to the needs of the indigenous Maori population.

In the nineteenth century many New Zealand politicians had Irish connections and Irish politics were closely monitored. Numerous Irish nationalist leaders visited New Zealand on their antipodean tours. The Irish influence on New Zealand politics remained considerable up to the early 1920s. However, most New Zealand politicians of Irish descent are essentially New Zealanders who consider that Irish political questions are no longer relevant to the New Zealand political scene.

New Zealand Prime Ministers with an Irish background range from Sir George Grey (Prime Minister from 1877 to 1879, his mother was born in Co. Westmeath), to, in recent times, Sir Robert Muldoon (Prime Minister from 1975 to 1984). Other New Zealand-Irish Prime Ministers include John Ballance (Liberal Prime Minister from 1906 to 1912 and from 1928 to 1930), William Ferguson Massey (Conservative Prime Minister for varying periods between 1912 and 1925, born in Co. Derry) and Michael Joseph Savage (the first Labour Prime Minister, 1935 to 1940, born in Australia of Irish parents, a populist leader who was the 'darling of the left').

Historically, the New Zealand-Irish tended to form a largely lower income group, and voted for parties of the left, firstly Liberal and then, when it was formed, Labour. A significant segment of the first Labour cabinet had Irish links. Although mostly poor, the New Zealand-Irish valued education highly and this was to be the vehicle for substantial upward mobility after World War II. Today there is no such thing as an Irish bloc vote, and although figures are lacking, it appears that, with increasing affluence, more New Zealanders of Irish descent vote for parties of the right, especially in the rural electorates.

The Irish contribution to New Zealand literature begins with poet/journalist/politician Thomas Bracken (1843–98), a native of Clones, Co. Monaghan who wrote the New Zealand National Anthem 'God Defend New Zealand'. In the twentieth century, two New Zealand-Irish women made a strong mark on New Zealand literature. The first was Nelle Scanlan (1882–1968) whose parents came from Co. Kerry and Co. Cork. She was the only woman ever to be editor of a daily New Zealand newspaper and introduced, through her famous Pencarrow series, the best-selling novel into New Zealand. The second was Eileen Duggan (1894–1972) whose parents came from Co. Kerry. Miss Duggan was New Zealand's first internationally acclaimed poet. Her Irish ancestry was an important influence on her work. She was an intensely spiritual writer who had a deep empathy with the Ireland of her forebears.

In the post World War II period New Zealand-Irish writers of accomplishment include Dan Davin (1913–), Maurice Duggan (1922–74) and Vincent O'Sullivan (1937–). In the opinion of O'Sullivan, Duggan is 'far and away the best New Zealand prose writer since Katherine Mansfield'. O'Sullivan himself, whose father came from Co. Kerry, has been described by one critic as New Zealand's best contemporary writer. He has written poetry, short stories, plays and criticism. O'Sullivan has a deep understanding of Yeats – like him, he is very conscious of country.

As in other countries with a substantial Irish population, the Irish in New Zealand made a significant contribution towards education at every level. Reference has already been made to the Irish involvement in and commitment to education in the New Zealand school system. The Irish also left their mark at the tertiary level. It was an Irish-born politician, Sir Maurice O'Rorke, who at one stage was Speaker of the House of Representatives, who was largely instrumental in founding the University of Auckland. He served as Chairman of the University's Council from its inception in 1883 until his death in 1916. Dr Watters, another Irishman, was among those who founded Victoria University, Wellington.

In sum, as in the rest of the New World, the history of the Irish in New Zealand is essentially a success story. Today many New Zealand-Irish are prominent in the professions (especially the law and the civil service) and business, as well as in the Churches. A recent survey, in fact, indicated that they may be better educated and wealthier than the population as a whole. Clearly this group is in the mainstream of New Zealand society.

Published in *Familia: Ulster Genealogical Review*, no. 1, 1985, and at that time had been reproduced with permission of *Ireland Today*.

3
'That infant colony':
Aspects of Ulster Emigration to Australia

Trevor Parkhill

A study of migration from Ulster to Australia has a genealogical value in that it helps to identify individuals who settled there, either willingly or unwillingly, in the formative years of its colonisation. It also illustrates the variety of means which were used to assist removal from an intensively agricultural economy to one which, even though it was on a vastly different scale, was certainly an attraction for migrants with experience of both pastoral and arable farming. Researchers in both Australia and Ireland have been well served by a number of recent publications which have drawn attention to, and suggested the research possibilities of, a range of sources to use to genealogical study.[1] Helpful as these have been at the national level, the Irish migratory experience benefits – as a number of published works[2] have shown – from a regional consideration, not least because the immigrant's place of origin was a major factor in determining how he emigrated, his first place of residence and subsequent movements in Australia, the sort of employment he would have found and, most intriguingly of all perhaps, how he responded to the challenge of his new environment. The sources available for an Ulster study include the writings of immigrants, the value of which has been exemplified in O'Farrell's work.[3] In particular, letters received from emigrants who left the west and north-west of Ulster not only throw some light on the noticeable stream of migration from Londonderry and north Antrim, Fermanagh and Tyrone in the two decades on either side of the Great Famine (1835–60) but also enable a plausibly representative impression of the immigrants' progress to be reconstructed.

The general mid-nineteenth century view of Australia from afar is well represented in Lewis Carroll's jibe: Alice, as she fell down the rabbit hole, feared that she would fall right through to 'The Antipathies'.[4] By the time *Alice's Adventure in Wonderland* was first published in 1865, the popular conception of Australia in Ulster was greatly influenced by the arrival of messages of buoyant confidence in the new country: James Johnston, writing in 1860 from Creswick Creek in Victoria, some 100 miles from Melbourne, enthused: 'I often dream of going home but still dream of going back again [to Australia]. I think if I was not at home I would not be content. I have plenty of money and friends and good health, and feel thankful for it and is well content ...'. By then, the number of free settlers, whose passages were assisted by a variety of officially-sponsored schemes, had restored some balance to the extent of the forced migration which dominated the flow for Ulster – and elsewhere – to Australia in the half century following the departure of the *Queen,* the first Irish convict ship which sailed from Cork in April 1791, to arrive at Sydney on 26 September. The *Queen* sailed in the Third Fleet; and there had of course been a proportion – estimated at 4 per cent[5] – of Irish convicts transported on the First and Second Fleets who had been tried in and transported directly from England. But of the 148 convicts who comprised the first emigrants direct to Australia from Ireland, one-sixth (24) had been tried and convicted at assizes in the nine counties of Ulster,[6] a modest enough criminal achievement bearing in mind the unsettled times the whole of Ireland, but particularly Ulster, found itself in in a period – the 1790s – of turbulent political and social disturbance. Both Shaw and Rudé[7] have drawn careful distinctions between the different categories of prisoners who occupied the holds of the prison ships – political, social and ordinary criminals. In all these categories, and in the other form of enforced migration – of female orphans from the workhouses – there was always an appreciable Ulster representation.

This was particularly manifest in the 'political' category of convicts who were sentenced for involvement in the attempted rebellions at either end of the period being here discussed – 1798 and 1848. The intellectual origins of the 1798 Rebellion, and a good deal of the violence which erupted in the months of May and June of that year, had their roots in Ulster. Much of the leadership and articulation of the United Ireland movement was to be found in Ulster: the *Northern Star,* the newspaper of the movement, was published in Belfast on a regular basis from 1792 until destroyed by General Lake's forces in 1797.[8] Of the estimated several hundred specifically political prisoners removed to Australia by the early years of the nineteenth century,[9] and of the further group of estimated 1,800 social rebels by 1815, there are sufficient identifiable individuals from Ulster to confirm the province's tempestuous decade of upheaval and disaffection.

The case of William Orr, a watchmaker and native of the parish of Antrim, who was sentenced to transportation in 1799, demonstrates something of the social background from which Ulster transportees were sent. And, although there is no doubt that Orr and his family were clearly part of the radical Presbyterian tradition which featured prominently in the political disaffection in Ulster, Orr's story suggests caution before classifying convicts as 'political' or 'social' prisoners. Orr's defence statement asserted that 'the crimes with which I am charged are many and the evidence to support them rests entirely with one man'. He further claimed that, following the burning of his mother's house by the army 'my brother being suspected of being concerned in the insurrection', he left home and hoped to emigrate to America, 'where he still intends to go if acquitted'.[10] In the event, William Orr was charged with robbery, convicted and transported in 1799 but, after representations had been made on his behalf, he was allowed to return to Ireland in 1805 when the Lord Lieutenant of Ireland adjudged, as he did in the cases of many of the transported United Irishmen, that 'there is reason to believe that Orr was unjustly charged with the offence for which he was transported'.[11]

There was similarly clear and strong Ulster representation in the political prisoners transported after the failure of the 1848 Rebellion. Of the seven Young Irelanders who led the abortive rising and who were then transported to Van Diemen's Land, two – John Mitchel and his brother-in-law John Martin – were of Presbyterian stock from south Down (Mitchel was, in fact, the son of a Non-Subscribing minister and is buried in the Non-Subscribing graveyard in Newry). Both Mitchel and Martin kept diaries of their imprisonment which confirm them to be inheritors of that libertarian Presbyterian tradition which characterised the late eighteenth century Ulster radical movement.[12] It is Mitchel's better known and widely read – both then and now – published *Jail Journal* which conveys much of the rather gentlemanly – certainly in comparison with the treatment experienced by ordinary felons – custodial lifestyle they were obliged to observe. In an unpublished letter, to Dublin in 1852, he deplores his imprisonment, 'It would be uncandid to pretend that with all the furtherances and appliances we have we are content ... Disguise itself as it will, Slavery is a bitter draught ...'.[13] And he resents the reports he has heard of 'the vulgar rogues of newspaper men in Ireland upholding me as the happiest man of modern times ...'. Yet Mitchel's writings cannot help but reveal an attraction for practically every aspect of his existence, apart from his confinement. He records: 'have had a serious consultation with John Martin as to whether I should allow at length my wife and family to come out to Van Diemen's Land ... To escape ... clandestinely would indeed be very easy for all of us at any time, but it is not to be thought of. It is grievous to think of bringing up children in this island, yet by fixing my residence in this remote, thinly-peopled and pastoral district engaging in some sort of farming and cattle feeding, and mingling in the society of the good quiet colonists here, we might almost forget at times the daily and hourly outrage that our enemies put upon us in keeping us here at all ... in short, I do so pine for something resembling a home ... and I have written this day to Newry, inviting all my household to the antipodes'.[14]

This is a sentiment which is echoed in the response of more mundane felons who were transported from Ulster but who developed an affection for, and saw possibilities in continuing a life in, their adopted country. Ticket-of-leave prisoners, or emancipated transportees were at liberty to ask to have their families to join them. A series of their communications both to their families and to the authorities in Dublin Castle remains and enables some suppositions to be made about the prisoners who settled in Australia, the qualities of a significant number of them to be adequate and progressive citizens in a developing environment, and the role convicts themselves had in establishing a chain of immigration to Australia from Ireland. *The Report of the select committee into education in Ireland*,[15] which preceded the establishment of a national system of schooling in 1831–2, had found that, of the four provinces, Ulster was the best provided for in terms of a ratio of schools to population and that, in the English language at least, Ulster men and women were the best educated in Ireland. So it is no surprise to find that some of the more discursive and, from the research point of view, informative communications relate to prisoners' families being encouraged to leave Ulster to join their reformed parent.

Alexander Boyce, writing from Wollongon, New South Wales, 25 January 1835, to his wife and children in Belfast, exhorts his

> Dear love, on receipt of this letter [he had similarly written three years previously but had received no reply from her or her authorities] ... address a Memorial to his Excellency the Viceroy of Ireland stating the then cause of you not coming and that you are now ready to join your husband ... granting you and your children a passage ... there has been many similarly situated and none ever had been refused ... [16]

And, although the three years of silence may betoken Mrs Boyce's disapproval of her husband as a convict, and she may as a consequence have kept the letter to herself, generally speaking letters from abroad were circulated and known about. Had the letter been read by others in Belfast – a port where the departure of emigrant ships for the United States and Canada direct across the Atlantic or via Liverpool had made the prospect of emigration a real and practicable proposition – there can be no doubt of the effect of Boyce's assertion that

> there is no part of the world where an industrious man can do better. He can earn from 5s to 7s 6d per day ... [and] he can take a piece of land on a clearing, lease for 7 years without any rent, all he grows is his own, free from tythes or taxes ... there is another [scheme] – you can place yourself on a piece of government land which you may occupy until government may require it for sale and if you had bid 5s per acre you can get as much as you want ... .[17]

O'Farrell confirms that this was a means of emigration for some if not many, and understandably refuses to lay too much stress on its importance. 'The magnet effect did operate from Australia as emancipated convicts sought to persuade family and friends to join them – but weakly – they were too few and Australia [was] too far away to compete for Irish migrants with the stimulus of free or cheap passage'.[18] The general part played by the receipt of letters from

Australia in developing the dynamics of emigration to that part of the world – as American letters to Ulster had done throughout the eighteenth century and continued to do in the nineteenth – will be discussed in due course.

What the prisoners' testimonies, contained in the Free Convicts Papers, confirm is the unlikely contribution male and female emancipated convicts made to the Australian settlement, from the point of view of becoming respectable citizens, skilled craftsmen, hard-working farmers, responsible wives and mothers. For instance, Alexander Boyce in his letter to his wife refers to 'a neighbour of mine here most respectably married named Sarah Cramshee who, at the time of her being transported, left a boy child ... in the poorhouse ... she is most anxious to get him out to her living as she is well off ... she has been a kind friend to me'.[19] An account in the *Belfast News Letter* of March 1825 reports that Sarah Cramsie – 'she was come of decent people' – attacked one John McQuillan: 'the prisoner Boyle held him by the arm while Cramsie took his notes out of his pocket – both guilty; transported 7 years'.[20] O'Farrell also observes that 'In Australia ... the emancipated convict Irish soon developed modest but significant entrepreneurial qualities'[21] and this is borne out in letters to Ulster from emancipated convicts such as Robert Boyd, writing from Modbury County, New South Wales: 'I am happy to inform you that I am master of sixteen head of cattle which I have bought at difrent times with money earned after doing my governmental work'.[22]

Between the rebellion of 1798 and the end of the Napoleonic Wars, much of the rural disturbances and 'social' crimes occurred elsewhere in Ireland than in Ulster. Clarke and Donnelly have commented on, and tried to explain, 'the comparative tranquillity of the north in the early nineteenth century'.[23] The post-Napoleonic War slumps in Ireland, however, affected Ulster particularly severely for a number of reasons. It was the region whose agriculture was given over most intensively to tillage, so the post-war fall in prices for foodstuffs affected the Ulster tenant farmer badly, all the more so since there was no commensurate fall – the opposite on some estates – in the levels of rents, an impasse which made the spectre of arrears of rent inevitable. Ulster's economic prosperity in the later eighteenth century had been as much based on the development of linen spinning and weaving as on agricultural produce: this prosperity had seen a population increase whose 'biological carryover' into the depressed years after 1815 created, in Crotty's phrase, 'the cauldron of social and economic pressures which characterise Ireland during these years'.[24]

It was against this background of population pressure and economic depression that the increasing number of transportations from Ulster to Australia after 1815 must be seen. According to Shaw, 'from 1817 to 1829, more than a fifth of the 9,500 male Irish convicts transported came from Dublin, and nearly one quarter (some 2,300) from Ulster'.[25] And a study of the assize books of courts in Co. Antrim suggests that the 'comparative tranquillity' of Ulster which Donnelly and Clarke saw in their study of agrarian violence was counterbalanced by the number of larceny offences for which transportation was adjudged an appropriate punishment.[26] For example, of the 130 convictions at the Co. Antrim assizes in Carrickfergus in 1827, 80 were for grand larceny – that is theft of goods to the value of more than 12 pence – 40 of whom were sentenced to transportation. No other crime had more than seven convictions and those associated with Shaw's classification of 'social' or 'political' crime – arson, riotous assembly, houghing if livestock, murder, etc – had insignificant numbers. A scrutiny of newspapers in Ulster for the period 1830–45 has noted a total of 1,190 cases of sentence by transportation, which must be an underestimate by at least 50% of the total.[27] However incomplete, this survey has a usefulness in showing the geographical spread of transportation – 25% from Belfast, 13% from Co. Antrim, 12% each from Co. Londonderry and Co. Tyrone, 7% each from Co. Donegal and Co. Armagh, and 2% each from Co. Down and Co. Fermanagh. Of the 1,190 transportees from Ulster, 25% were women, or twice the proportion of the British convicts'.[28] Consequently, says Shaw, three-eighths of female prisoners in Australia were Irish, whereas only one quarter of all male convicts were Irish.

The predominant image of Australia in pre-Famine Ulster, it would appear from a modern standpoint, must have been exclusively related to its penal role, but the Free Settlers Papers suggest that although, if anything, the removal of erstwhile convicts' families to join them reinforced the association of the colony with those whom Ulster had expelled, the stigma of transportation was not sufficient to deter families joining husbands and fathers (although one wife in her reply refers to the disgrace her husband has brought on her). It would be easy to make too much of typicality of the convicts' communications and their readiness and ability to prosper from a seemingly hopeless position. But they must have done a good deal to correct the notion of the permanence of transportation and to begin the process, which would be later echoed in shipping advertisements, published letters giving details of loans and free passage schemes, and letters from emigrants themselves, of conveying the message that Australia *did* provide opportunities for enterprising individuals.

All that, however, was for the 1830s and later. Until then, it tended to be men of some substance who were favoured by free land grants that served to make them leave the fruits of success they had already achieved in Ulster. Henry Osborne left his father's substantial Co. Tyrone farm in 1828 and invested the £1,000 his father gave as a farewell gift in Irish linen which, on arrival in Sydney, he is reputed to have sold at a fine profit.[29] Osborne received two land grants, each of 2,560 acres at Marshall Mount, some 12 miles south of Wollongong in the finest dairy country to be found in the Illawara district.

Osborne's experience on the land in Ireland – the quality of land on the family farm in Dernaseer, parish of Dromore, suggests he would have been well acquainted with a mixed pastoral and arable farming – plus the right to about 30 convict labourers with his first grant, helped put his farming venture in Australia on a sound footing. He later acquired vast tracts of land between the Murrimbidgee and Murray rivers, and continued to acquire land as one of the stockowners who forced the New South Wales government to extend the 'limits of location' of pasture land to the extent that by 1850, 73 million acres of Crown land were leased to less than 2,000 farmers – an average leasehold of 30,000 acres. By 1854, Osborne himself held 261,000 acres at less than one-fifth of a penny per acre per year, including land which contained valuable coalfields at Newcastle and, by 1856, three years before his death, he was referred to in a Sydney newspaper as 'among the wealthiest of our country gentlemen'.

Tasmania, for which there was no escaping the stigma of a penal settlement, also attracted enterprising Ulster settlers endowed with capital. Samuel Dawson wrote to his father-in-law in Belfast, Dr Robert Tennent – who may well have been the source of Dawson's means – from Claremont, Tasmania, in 1835: 'although my property here is of considerable value, and yearly increasing therein ... as yet all has been outlay with me but thank God I have now conquered most of the difficulties attending a settler, so that I may reasonably work for some return for all my great labour and expenditure of capital upon my farm ... at Tempo [one of his two estates, named after the Tennent estate in Co. Fermanagh] I have about 300 head of cattle and several valuable horses, the increase from which must, by and bye, be considerable'.[30] Case histories such as Osborne, the Wilson family from Broughshane, Co. Antrim and, in the 1870s, Sir Samuel McCaughey from Ballymena – all of whom arrived from Ulster in Australia and built land and commercial business empires – are exceptional in every sense but not so rare or unique as to be discounted.

Just as exceptional, at least in terms of the adaptability they brought to the developing settlements, were the immigrants from throughout Ireland whose passages to and establishment in Australia were directly aided by the colonial authorities: Fitzpatrick has commented on the eagerness with which the Australian Irish exploited government nominated schemes.[31] Ulstermen took advantage of the various assisted passage schemes which operated from the early 1830s to New South Wales and, later, to South and Western Australia, including a loan system for skilled tradesmen and their families 1832–6, a Bounty System 1836–45 and the remittance or nomination system 1848–86.[32] The Ulster proportion of Irish people who benefitted by assisted passages is uncertain. O'Farrell says that 'a further distinctive strand of Irish migration to Australia was that of Protestants from Ulster, an element fluctuating between 10 and 20 per cent of the Irish total'.[33] However, for the pre-Famine period certainly, the percentage of Ulster people in the gradually accelerating stream of free emigrants to Australia must have been much greater than 20 per cent. W. F. Adams, in his seminal work on Irish emigration to North America between 1815 and 1845 estimated, as precisely as the sparse pre-1851 statistics allowed, that one million people emigrated from Ireland.[34]

More recently, Clark and Donnelly have put the Ulster contribution to this figure as high as 40 per cent, and there is no reason to assume that the Ulster proportion of Irish emigration to Australia before 1845 numbered less than 40 per cent, given the extent of the traffic suggested by sources here and in Australia.

Among the sources which assist with a study of pre-Famine Ulster emigrations are the Ordnance Survey Memoirs, compiled in the 1830s.[35] The Memoirs contain information garnered from each locality but it is only for the Ulster counties of Londonderry and Antrim that the information and details on the subject of emigration are at all helpful to research. Three parishes in Co. Londonderry – Coleraine, Kilcronaghan and Maghera – are noted as having members who left for the new colonies. In the case of all 10 immigrants, comprising one family group and the rest young single males, average age 22, they were bound for Van Diemen's Land. From the Co. Antrim parishes of Ahoghill, Killead and Templepatrick, a further 10 individuals are noted, eight of whom went to Van Diemen's Land and two (apparently a father aged 50 and son aged 22) to Sydney. One of the individuals in the parish of Templepatrick is noted as a 'farmer with £100 capital', in all probability raised from the sale of his tenant right.

There are other instances scattered in estate papers of the raising of capital by the sale of a tenant's 'right' to receive compensation for improvements he may have made to his property during his tenancy. On the Stuart estate in Co. Tyrone a rental contains observations in the agent's hand such as 'James and R. Alcorn held about 33 acres ... by lease at £24.12s.6d; they went to Australia and sold with my consent to John Perry for £315'.[36] There are other references to the landlord's consent to the 'sale' of the land: the land, since it was his, was not being sold; it was the tenant's interest in it for which the incoming tenant was paying about £10 per acre. The Devon Commission, a parliamentary enquiry on landholding in Ireland which took evidence in centres throughout the island in the early 1840s, found that in many areas of better quality land, tenant right could sometimes raise a tenant up to £30 per acre. There is a significant number of references in the inquiry's evidence to the value of Tenant Right in assisting emigration and, although only North America is mentioned specifically in this respect, the sale of Tenant Right on a substantial farm was clearly sufficient in some cases to be applied to a farming family's passage to Australia. Lord Dungannon's agent felt that there was a detrimental side to the Ulster custom '... it is carried to too great an extent ... the tenant, in some instances, sells at an enormously high price and he puts the money in his pocket and emigrates to America or some other part of the world and takes it with him.'[37]

In the case of emigration to Australia, even where an intending emigrant and his family were having the bulk of their passage paid for by the colonial government, it remained the case that no emigration, by whatever scheme of assistance, could be contemplated without sufficient ready money to meet the expenses of the various stages of a family on the journey – from Ireland to London and thence to Plymouth followed by the lengthy 14–20 week voyage to Australia. The burden of the costs incurred in emigrating to Australia was sufficient to provoke Vere Foster in 1854 to subtitle one of his pamphlets on emigration to America – in which series he gave detailed practical advice for intending emigrants on the best means of travel – 'The advantages of emigration to America rather than to Australia'.[38]

He listed a variety of 'advantages' in favour of the traditional emigrant's route, including the better prospects of work in the cities: 'in America a very large number of emigrants are much more sure of finding employment owing to there being a much larger resident population to give employment'. Foster was principally concerned, however, to alert migrants to the equation that 'the same money which is required for the passage of one person to Australia being nearly sufficient to carry five to America'. The advertisements for sailings to Australia which appeared in the Irish press were always at pains to assure readers that the waiting time for the departure of sailing ships – a perplexing aspect of emigration which travellers to North America had found expensive since they were obliged to stay in lodging houses in the ports, having travelled there from their place of origin, until the ship was full, or the tide was right or whatever – was minimal. The advertisements which began to appear in Ulster newspapers in the 1830s took care to assure that 'persons from all parts of the Three Kingdoms can join these vessels [bound for Australia] at a small cost at London or Plymouth where they can embark with certainty on the days stated, and avoid all further expense ... a limited number of married mechanics, agriculturalists and shepherds will, on certain conditions, be allowed a free passage by these ships'.[39]

The increasing availability of assisted or sponsored passages from the 1830s went some way towards overcoming the difficulties of the cost of transport. At a local level in north-west Ulster, there were more specific 'packages', designed to attract people with farming and artisan experience and their families, advertised in the *Londonderry Sentinel* throughout the 1830s. Those named in the lists of emigrants for Van Diemen's Land and New South Wales in the Ordnance Survey Memoirs may have been early beneficiaries of a scheme thus advertised. The *Ellen*, 600 tons burthen, was advertised from July to September 1836 with the attraction that 'her Majesty's government in order to encourage the emigration of industrious young married couples to the Australian colonies will now grant towards the expense of their passage a bounty or free gift of £20 for each married couple without regard to their trade or occupation ... thus a man and wife who are possessed of £18 may be conveyed free to Van Diemen's Land or Sydney with all provisions for the voyage ...'.[40]

In the later 1820s and 1830s, the north-west of Ulster, including the counties of Londonderry, Donegal and Tyrone, had been badly affected by the accumulating difficulties facing agriculture throughout Ireland and, more crucially, by the downturn in the economic viability of the domestic linen industry which had become more and more a dependent source of income. The industrialisation processes which affected the spinning of yarn especially, from the late 1820s, had forced a large number of small holders to entertain emigration as an alternative to the quandary of reduced income, increased rents and sizable families to feed. The same newspapers which advertised Australia's advantages had also from 1828 carried regular notices inserted by the Canada Land Company – whose London agent was A.C. Buchanan, himself a native of Co. Tyrone – for farmers and labourers with families on the premise that family units would be a more stabilising and reliable form of immigration than young mobile single people. It was with this class of tenant in mind that the notice in the *Londonderry Sentinel* for the *Ellen* also had a specific message for the 'overseers of parishes and others [who] now have an opportunity [of ameliorating] a condition of the poor classes by transferring the surplus to New Holland which contains an immense track of rich land and the climate which is so healthful as 'tis lovely, where the expense of living is scarcely equal to one-third of what it is in Ireland and where there is full employment for all at higher wages'.[41]

It was this sort of rhetoric – which also aimed to combat the image of the penal colony – that David Fairley, a young carpenter in the city of Derry, and his wife responded to in the mid-1830s. They emigrated armed with recommendations sufficient to meet the requirements of the Bounty scheme for free passage to New South Wales from his clergyman and employer which praised Fairley 'as a young man understanding his trade, under the age of twenty-six and most desirable as a person calculated to meet the views and plans of Government in providing and inducing young tradesmen to emigrate to New South Wales and settle in that infant colony'.[42] Generally, it is letters from immigrants sent home and detailing their observations on their new life which have proven to be most useful source materials. David Fairley did write home as soon as he landed in Sydney, and his letter was, unusually, published immediately in the *Londonderry Sentinel*.[43] When his brother James replied to it, he remarked 'Mr Stark was very glad to hear of your welfare and came for the letter and he kept it for 2 weeks. The most of all the gentlemen in Derry had it and thought [it] the greatest wonder ever witnessed'.

Rodney Green, in his essay on emigrant letters published in 1969,[44] stressed the value immigrants' letters home had in maintaining the impetus of emigration. Their example continued to be a source of curiosity and inspiration to those who remained at home. There can be no doubting that the publicity of an emigrant's letter, both by hand within a local circle of friends and to a broader readership throughout the whole north-west of Ireland, including Tyrone, Londonderry and Donegal which the newspaper served, demonstrated to many the practicability of a root and branch family emigration. Fairley's published letter pulled no punches: he refers to 'a very favourable passage but a great many deaths – twenty-five children and five adults, 4 women and one man'. But the combined effect of the emotional appeal of the letter – 'It would give me great pleasure to see all my brothers and sisters here, where there is some reward for labour and industry' – and the practical detail on wages and living standards – 'I joined the government work with the rest of my shipmates, as a bricklayer, at two guineas per week, which is regularly paid every Saturday. A great many of the carpenters went to country gentlemen at the same wages but [also] found in house and fuel ... where we are employed in the Governor's botanic gardens ... we could reach almost off our scaffolds to the lemons and oranges, fig trees, pomegranates, peaches, etc. and the parrots sitting on the trees beside us in flocks ... all differing from the northern part of the globe' – must have influenced the inclination to emigrate of a considerable number of families in north-west Ulster.[45]

Just as helpful, from the point of view of determining a clearer picture of the conditions in Ireland which emigrants were leaving and the perennial question – were they pushed by those conditions or, rather, were they pulled by the prospects of this new country? – are what Rodney Green has termed 'reverse' emigrant letters. James's letter to his brother in Sydney is just such an example. It says that 'There's a great number going out by the *Parland* ship this year. James Bradley, a carpenter, is going out ... there is three carpenters going from this town to Sydney ... and William McCullough the shoemaker with whom we send this letter. You may tell Mr Presday's friend that he is well and is a high up man in Derry'.[46] For several years in the decade prior to the Famine, a number of ships bound for Australia, among them the *Parland* which James Fairley refers to and which clearly plied the Australian route regularly, carried tradesmen and farmers with their families who were going to join, at least in the first crucial days on arrival, brothers, relatives, friends, work colleagues. This form of chain migration had already been established from Ulster to North America and it was its own guarantee of keeping the emigration movement to New South Wales going.

Although O'Farrell says that 'very few Famine refugees came to Australia from Ireland',[47] the constant trickle from the west of Ulster which has already been identified in the pre-Famine period was seen to continue in no small measure throughout the 1840s and 1850s. But the Ulster emigrants to Australia were more displaced persons than refugees. Displaced by economic and social factors – pressure of population and rents, removal of the crutch of domestic industry – the experience gained through more than a century of reactive emigration became apparent in the carefully staged migration to Australia of family and close friends.

Fitzpatrick's view is that chain migrations not only assisted family, but also community emigration.[48] This sense of community migration is evident in, for example, the 'Removals from Portaferry Congregation to Australia' extracted from registers for the Co. Down parish.[49] The ratio of 70 emigrants bound for Australia and 52 for North America in the years 1852–60 not only reflects the directional trend but also supports the notion of a fairly integrated communal drift towards Australia, even if there is no evidence of a similarly close knit pattern of settlement on arrival. The Australian immigration sources – which are generally more helpful than their American counterparts in recording an immigrant's precise place of origin – reveal, in the period from 1848 and continuing into the 1860s, a regular stream of immigrants from a broad arc in south and west Ulster, taking in Lisnaskea, Enniskillen, Lowtherstown, Kesh, Strabane, Derry City and Donegal. The extent to which farming communities, both Roman Catholic and Protestant, particularly in counties Tyrone and Fermanagh, transferred themselves to relatively compact areas of New South Wales suggests a very strong communal tide. The re-creation of a 'home from home' in a new country of settlement was a feature of Irish settlement in urban America, illustrated in the lists of names contained in emigrants' letters home of people the writer has seen and who would be known at home. There is a sense of this already happening in Australia in David Fairley's letter of the late 1830s but there is not the same continuation in later letters of this 'urban village' idea. O'Farrell prefers the Canadian model for comparative purposes, where 'the Irish chose not to live in villages of the close kind but to live apart from each other'.[50] Emigrants of Ulster origin generally did not remain in groups even when they emigrated with friends and relatives, or with people from the same region.

The Ulster migration to Australia, at its most dense from the west and south of the province, continued throughout the 1850s, a period for which there are more sources to make generalisations about the character of the emigrants themselves. O'Farrell makes the point that the 'mass Irish population (come) from the 1850s ... in search of gold, land, fortune, and adventure; they were a much more accomplished, venturesome and happy lot than those the Famine had dumped on America'[51] and the letters back to post-Famine Ulster tend to have a ring of confidence not only in their description of success but also in their readiness to disclose doubts, uncertainties and misfortune and to overcome them. James Johnston, who earlier professed himself as being very content with his new life in Australia, had emigrated in 1859 or 1860 from the family holding of some 30 acres in Crevinish, near Kesh, Co. Fermanagh. He is representative of the migration from western Ulster in most respects except that he travelled singly and with no intention apparent in his letters to assist other members of his family to join him. As it did for many, the lure of gold proved irresistible: 'I have a good mind to try my fortune at the digging for a while. I never saw anyone from home that I knew yet'.[52] It was the Munster-Irish who dominated immigration into Victoria – from where Johnston was writing – in the 1850s and 1860s, while the Ulster immigrants tended to gravitate towards New South Wales. Having served notice of his fortune-hunting, James Johnston's next surviving letter, some four years later from Hardie's Hill, Victoria, reports: 'We have been pretty lucky in speculating since we started it. We are in weighty (?) now in four different mining companies; if they turn out well, which they are seeming to do well, we will be able to go home ... they cost us a deal of money but any speculation we make we can pretty near double our money, but the right time is not come yet. If a man has money here he can make money without it he can do nothing'.[53] This success story has a poignant ending, however: having assured his parents that 'we will both go home together again if things go well again this year ... I send my respects to Father, Mother, Belle, Mary and William and hopes soon to meet again if not here I hope in a better world where toils and trials is no more'. The next chronological item in the collection is a short note, an obituary of sorts, to the effect that James Johnston had died of gangrene poisoning after a perfectly innocent knife-wound he received while opening a sack of grain.[54]

There were examples of other Ulster gold diggers who also made good, if not by turning up the yellow nuggets at least by eventually establishing for themselves a way of life and means of earning a living that was to a large degree dependent on the trades and skills they took with them to Australia. Among these are Hugh Maguire, of Strabane, Co. Tyrone and James Getty of Ballymoney, Co. Antrim who both found themselves in Melbourne in 1852–3 and whose correspondence relates their separate workings in the gold fields and their frequent return trips to the base of Melbourne. Maguire is soon confessing his lack of progress: 'as for my own success upon the diggings I must candidly say that up to the present time it has fell far short of what I expected. I was fourteen months in the diggings ... yet I have been only able to come to Melbourne with about sixty-five pounds sterling'.[55] And, although he affirms 'I do not mean to give the diggings up, however, as I hope by perseverance to outhector fortune and yet return a lucky Gold Digger', by 1860 his letters home suggest his employment, which he has clearly been in for some time, is as a traveller for a clothing firm (he himself had been apprenticed to the drapery business in Strabane). James Getty trained as a millwright in Ballymoney, Co. Antrim and the letters he received from his family while in Melbourne between 1853 and 1859 make it possible to reconstruct his progress in the coalfield and then at his original trade in Melbourne.[56] These collections make it clear that the possibility of removal to Australia is merely an additional string to the bow which played the refrain at the emigrant's wake: both the Maguire and Getty collections refer to migration to the United States (where some family members have clearly been long established) as well as to Australia – and there is even reference made to a family which, having left for America, then found its way to Australia. Although there is no direct evidence in either of these collections of named individuals being nominated for assisted passages, there is a raised sense of expectation in the families of joining Maguire and Getty, and this is strongly evident in the 'reverse' emigrant letters of the Getty family: ... 'would I not make as good a partner as any you have got yet. If you think so, I will go [to Australia] for it is losing time stopping in Ireland for you can make more money in one month than we can all make in one year'.[57] And, although the general pattern of post 1850 emigration to Australia is one of increasing betterment migration, the changes in circumstances in Ireland which impelled Irishmen abroad, or the improved fortunes they met in their new environment, were generally not dramatic.

The social and economic difficulties of the 1840s saddled landlords and tenants alike for years after with the bequest of arrears of rent. So it was not merely philanthropy which was behind the assistance offered to tenants on the Shirley estate in Co. Monaghan in 1849 when their passages to South Australia were arranged. Major Shirley had, in fact, been assisting passages for tenants to Canada from the mid-1840s, even (apparently) before the full onset of the Famine. In fact, the ticket stubs containing the names, ages and addresses of the beneficiaries whose emigration to South Australia was being aided were originally to be used on the Canada passage, and only manuscript lists of families confirm that, in the end, a tightly knit rural community was transplanted to Australia, helped as much by the colonial authorities' schemes as by the munificence of landlords such as Shirley in Co. Monaghan, Caledon in Co. Tyrone and others.[58] In all probability the Shirley tenants' passages were assisted by the South

Australian government; the landlord may have assisted with their outfitting, or journey to the point of embarkation. And there were other schemes, not government sponsored, to help with emigrants' passages to Australia.

One of the most prominent of these in the later 1850s and 1860s was the Donegal Relief Fund. It raised money from the growing numbers of Australian-Irish with the specific purpose of helping to alleviate the distress which continued to be experienced on the west coast of Ulster and, in 1859 alone, it is reported to have been responsible for the passages of one third of the 2,544 Irish who landed in New South Wales under the government's assistance scheme.[59] In all, five shiploads of Co. Donegal migrants arrived in New South Wales and Victoria, the most renowned carrying refugees of what was to become known as the Derryveagh evictions. In 1861 47 families on the estate of John George Adair in Co. Donegal were evicted on his orders, in the belief that a number of them had somehow been involved in the murder of his steward.[60] The consequent bitter scenes attracted much interest and it was the response of the Donegal Relief Committee to pay for the passages of 143 young men and women – mainly single people, there were only four families among them – who had not been reinstated on the Adair estate.[61] They landed, on the *Abyssinian,* in May 1862, the majority of them to take up jobs as servants and farm labourers, although the first task for many of these native Irish speakers would have been to improve their command of the English language.

Of the various assisted passage schemes in Ireland and in Australia, there is one which remains to be considered and which, although it was the shortest-lived, was and is the most controversial – the female orphan scheme.[62] From the Australian viewpoint, it was of course designed to help alleviate a labour problem and to try to provide a better balance between males and females. The extent of the imbalance by the 1840s was in the order of two males to one female in the cities, and eight to one 'beyond the boundaries'.[63] On the Irish side, the emigration of female orphans from some workhouses had in fact been taking place, from Ulster to Canada, from the mid 1840s. The administrators of workhouse policy were Guardians of the public purse as well as of the inmates, and their task was to make economic use of the poor law rates levied to fund the workhouse. In their view, and in that of the Poor Law Inspectors, orphans had to be considered residents and, therefore, long-term drains on public money. The Poor Law Commissioners had recommended, before the female orphans to Australia movement was instituted in 1848, that local Guardians should 'send as emigrants to Canada, at the cost to the Electoral Division, anyone of the able-bodied inmates of the workhouse, especially females ... In this mode (continued Mr Edward Senior's memorandum) some of the permanent deadweight in the workhouse may be got rid of at a cost to the E[lectoral] D[ivision] of about £5 or about one year's cost of maintenance'.[64]

The emigration of female orphan paupers had, therefore, been in operation from a number of workhouses in the north-west of Ulster, Londonderry, Coleraine, Limavady, Strabane, Ballymoney among them. This had, of course, been the area trawled in the 1830s and early 1840s by the Canada Land Company, so it is no surprise to see A. C. Buchanan's name mentioned in the discussions in the workhouse minute books. And, although the Guardians were not obliged to pay the cost of the passage to Australia, the outfits with which the orphans needed to be furnished did not make the Australian emigrations significantly cheaper for the workhouses. Joseph Robins and Trevor McClaughlin have described the female orphan emigration movement in detail; my only concern is to make appropriate observations on the Ulster contribution.[65] Of the 4,000 odd orphans which Trevor McClaughlin of Macquarie University has calculated were sent, nearly 900 (under 23%) came from Ulster, so in numerical terms at least Ulster was, if anything, under-represented.[66] But it was the Belfast contingent on board the *Earl Grey* who attracted most attention, not least in the New South Wales Commission of Inquiry and Report, and in the editorials of the *Sydney Morning Herald*, for their allegedly raucous and licentious behaviour, the allegations mainly emanating from Henry Grattan Douglas, the *Earl Grey's* surgeon who, like many ships' surgeons before him – and there had always been a continuing Ulster tradition among the ships' surgeons on Australian-bound ships – had his eyes on a land grant. Of the 186 orphans on board the *Earl Grey,* over 60 were from the Belfast workhouse, 56 of whom were subsequently sent on – banished – to Maitland and Moreton Bay, Brisbane. The inquiry into the *Earl Grey* affair chose to offer a redemptive explanation for the Belfast orphans' behaviour, attributing it to 'the peculiar circumstances of that town, wherein there is a great and constant demand for the labour of young girls in factories, the effect of which is to expose them at an early age to the contamination of evil example, and to familiarise them with the use of improper language'.[67]

But it should be remembered that several other workhouses had sent orphans via the *Earl Grey,* and practically every workhouse in Ulster dispatched young girls under this scheme. And it was not Belfast or even areas most severely affected by the privations of the Famine, including Donegal, who sent most orphans, although as has previously been pointed out, workhouses from the north-west of Ulster tended to send orphans to Canada as to Australia. And it was not always orphans who were Canada-bound; very often they were young single mothers with one or more children. One of the allegations made about the *Earl Grey* complement was that orphans they may have been, but young they were not. However, a study of orphans on board some of the later ships shows that, in practically every case, their given age at least was between 13 and 18. It is also worth noting that the Enniskillen workhouse sent the most orphans – 107 – of all the workhouses in Ireland, except for Dublin and Skibbereen. Other workhouses in the west and south of Ulster, and on the borders of that area, sent significant numbers: Armagh (57); Sligo (68) and Lisnaskea (44) predict the strong links between south and west Ulster that is evident in the New South Wales immigration records in the post 1850 period.[68]

A further wave of Ulster immigration into Australia was to come in the 1880s and 1890s. This article has sought to show the various types of emigrants, and the schemes which assisted emigration, from the early days of settlement until the more traditional pattern of emigration was established in the 1860s. Before that, political prisoners, ordinary felons, tradesmen, already-established business and farming figures, orphans and what O'Farrell has described as 'the rank and file of the migrant army' from Ulster have left behind evidence in a variety of forms and which is useful in a number of ways. It paints a slightly more informed picture of the social and economic conditions in Ulster which prompted a widespread and serious consideration of migration. It also helps an understanding of the process of emigration and the central roles of assistance both from the state and friends. It may be said that the evidence is, in the main, that of achievers but enough examples have been instanced from it to demonstrate the constructive part immigrants from Ulster – political prisoners, convicted felons, orphans, assisted migrants and free settlers – had to play in establishing the Australian colony, even if it was in the very modest form of adapting their agricultural and manual crafts and pioneering skills in making a relative success of their own lives.

Published in *Familia: Ulster Genealogical Review*, no. 3, 1987.

Notes

1. See, for example, Nick Vine Hall, *Tracing Your Family History in Australia: A Guide to Sources,* Rigby (1985), and Trevor McClaughlin, *From Shamrock to Wattle: Digging Up Your Irish Ancestors,* Collins (1985).
2. See, for example, R. J. Dickson, *Ulster Emigration to Colonial America 1718–1776,* Ulster Historical Foundation reprint (1982); Sholto Cooke, *The Maiden City and the Western Ocean* (1952), which are of particular relevance to Ulster.
3. Patrick O'Farrell, *Letters from Irish Australia 1825–1929,* NSW University Press and Ulster Historical Foundation (1984).
4. Lewis Carroll, *Alice's Adventure in Wonderland* (1965).
5. PRONI, T3602/1.
6. A. G. L. Shaw, *Convicts and the Colonies,* Melbourne Univ. Press (1977), p. 166.
7. G. Rudé, *Protest and Punishment: the story of the political and social protesters transported to Australia, 1788–1868,* Clarendon (1978).
8. PRONI, N11.
9. Shaw, op. cit. p. 182. See also Edith Mary Johnston, 'Violence Transported: Aspects of Irish Peasant Society' in *Ireland and Irish-Australia: Studies in Cultural and Political History,* (eds.) Oliver MacDonagh and W. F. Mandle, Croom Helm (1986).
10. PRONI, T1956.
11. Ibid.
12. John Mitchel, *Jail Journal;* and PRONI, D560, Diary of John Martin
13. PRONI, T413/2, 4 Oct., 1852 to 'Miss Thomson' Dublin.
14. Mitchel, op. cit., p. 245.

15 H.C. 1826–7 XII.
16 PRONI, T3650, quoted in B. Trainor 'Sources for Irish-Australia Genealogy in PRONI' in *The Irish Australians,* Ulster Historical Foundation and Society of Australian Genealogists (1984).
17 PRONI, T3650, 25 Jan. 1835.
18 P. O'Farrell, *The Irish in Australia* N.S.W. Univ. Press (1986) p. 62.
19 PRONI, T3650, 25 Jan., 1835.
20 *Belfast Newsletter,* 29 Mar. 1825.
21 O'Farrell, op. cit., p. 63.
22 PRONI, T3650/7.
23 Samuel Clark and James S. Donnelly Jr., *Irish Peasants: Violence and Political Unrest 1780–1914,* Manchester Univ. Press (1983), p. 149.
24 R. Crotty, *Irish Agricultural Production: Its Volume and Structure,* Cork Univ. Press (1966), p. 39.
25 Shaw, op. cit., p. 179.
26 PRONI, ANT2/2A/1.
27 Compiled by Nigel McCarley, ACE researcher for the Ulster Historical Foundation 1985–6. I am indebted to him and to Dr B. Trainor for permission to consult this work.
28 Shaw, op. cit., p. 183.
29 O'Farrell, op. cit., pp 24–6. See also Pat MacDonnell 'The Land that Osborne Left', *Familia: Ulster Genealogical Review* Vol. 2 No. 3 (1987), Ulster Genealogical and Historical Guild.
30 PRONI, D1748/B/1/51/1–5.
31 D. Fitzpatrick, *Irish Emigration 1801–1921,* Economic and Social History Society of Ireland (1984).
32 For a summary of the various schemes see Richard Reid, 'From Ballyduff to Boorowa – Irish Assisted Emigration to N.S.W. 1830–1896' *The Irish Australians,* UHF and Society of Australian Genealogists and Trevor McClaughlin, *From Shamrock to Wattle* (1985).
33 O'Farrell, op. cit., pp 100–102.
34 W. F. Adams, *Ireland and Irish Emigrations to the New World 1815–45,* Genealogical Publishing Co. Inc., Baltimore (1980).
35 PRONI, MIC6. Originals in Royal Irish Academy, Dublin.
36 PRONI D847/57/7.
37 Devon Commission pt. 1, p. 604, 1 Apr. 1844, Q37.
38 PRONI, D3618/D/9/14.
39 *Belfast Newsletter,* 17 Apr. 1838.
40 PRONI, N12/1/1, 23 July 1835.
41 PRONI, N12/1/1.
42 PRONI, T3635/1/1.

43 *Londonderry Sentinel*, 24 Feb. 1838.
44 E. R. R. Green, 'Ulster Emigrants' Letters' in *Essays in Scotch-Irish History*, RKP (1969).
45 Letter from David Fairley, *Londonderry Sentinel*, 24 Feb. 1838.
46 PRONI, T3635/2/1.
47 O'Farrell, op. cit., p. 63.
48 Fitzpatrick, op. cit., pp 21–22.
49 PRONI, D2709/2/4. I am grateful to Miss Cathy Wilson, Queen's University, Ontario and Institute of Irish Studies, QUB, 1986–7, for drawing this source to my attention.
50 O'Farrell, op. cit., p. 62.
51 O'Farrell, op, cit., p. 63.
52 PRONI, T3602/1.
53 ibid.
54 ibid.
55 PRONI, D1420/2.
56 PRONI, T2052-1-4.
57 PRONI, T2052/1.
58 PRONI, D3531/P/1–5; also described in Nigel McCarley, 'Where did they go?' *Familia: Ulster Genealogical Review* Vol. 2, No. 2 (1986).
59 O'Farrell, op. cit., pp 69–70.
60 W. E. Vaughan, *Sin, Sheep and Scotsmen: John George Adair and the Derryveagh Evictions, 1861,* Appletree Press and the Ulster Society for Irish Historical Studies (1983); see also W. E. Vaughan, *Landlords and Tenants in Ireland, 1848–1904,* Economic and Social History Society of Ireland (1984), pp 10–12.
61 O'Farrell, op. cit., pp 69–70.
62 For a fuller treatment of this topic see Joseph Robins. *The Lost Children: A Study of Charity Children in Ireland 1700–1900,* IPA Dublin (1982); and Trevor McClaughlin, *From Shamrock to Wattle: Digging up Your Irish Ancestry,* Collins (1985).
63 Trevor McClaughlin, 'Barefoot and Pregnant: Female Orphans who Emigrated from Irish Workhouses to Australia', *Familia: Ulster Genealogical Review* Vol. 2 No. 3 (1987).
64 PRONI, BG5/A/2.
65 Joseph Robins, op. cit.
66 I am grateful to Trevor McClaughlin, Senior Lecturer, Dept. of History, Macquarie University, for a preview of the results of his research on the female orphans.
67 NSW Legislature Report and Proceedings, June 1850.
68 These calculations are based on Trevor McClaughlin's work.

4

The Anglo-Irish Tradition and Anglo-Irish Migration to Colonial Australia

Gordon Forth

In December 1840, George Winter, a gentleman squatter, visited the recently founded settlement of Port Phillip. It was on this occasion that Winter clashed bitterly with a fellow Ascendancy colonist, Augustine Barton, in the presence of the diarist and leading member of the 'Irish Cousinage' Charles Griffith. In the course of an 'unpleasant altercation' Winter denounced Barton's conduct as 'very colonial', a statement which Griffith considered 'expresses what we call at home going very close to the wind'.[1] Some months later, Griffith and no doubt other Port Phillip gentlemen were struck by the appearance of George Winter's younger brother Samuel as he rode through the settlement. A confident and experienced bushman of twenty-five, full-bearded, tall and strikingly handsome, the younger Winter reminded Griffith of 'one of the knights errant in the days of chivalry'.[2] On such occasions it was apparently Winter's custom to have an Aboriginal page in livery mounted up behind him and to be escorted by several retainers of foot.

In attempting to play the eighteenth-century style grand seigneur, Winter may well have been influenced by romantic images from his Ascendancy background. In a modified colonial fashion, he was possibly striving to emulate the likes of John Fitzmaurice, later Earl of Shelburne, who a century earlier had received official guests resplendent in brilliant feudal regalia attended by mounted retainers. Such unusual as well as less remarkable behaviour on the part of Australia's Ascendancy colonists can often be linked to their Old World Irish background. As representative of a separate national subgroup, these Anglo-Irish brought with them to Australia distinctive and commonly held attitudes and customs. Both consciously and unconsciously, this Anglo-Irish tradition influenced the responses of these Ascendancy to their new and changing circumstances in the Australian colonies.

As a small, scattered and rapidly assimilated migrant group, it is hardly surprising that Anglo-Irish colonists in early Australia have received so little recognition from historians. Yet at least during the first half of the nineteenth century, the Anglo or Ascendancy Irish were an influential as well as distinctive element in Australian colonial society. An Anglo-Irish presence was particularly noticeable in pre-goldrush Tasmania and the Port Phillip District (later Victoria) of New South Wales during the 1840s. As senior government officials; military officers in charge of penal settlements; Anglican clergyman; gentlemen pastoralists and founding members of the professions, the collective influence of the Anglo-Irish on early colonial society was considerable. Often outspoken and independently minded, these colonists, though not always identified as Anglo-Irish, featured prominently in the establishment of Australia's legal, political, religious, educational and cultural institutions. Influenced by their distinctive Old World tradition, generally speaking the Anglo-Irish in early Australia strove enthusiastically and with a fair degree of success to improve the crude and often brutal penal-pastoral society in which they found themselves. By examining the ways in which the Anglo-Irish tradition influenced the aspirations, attitudes and behaviour of a small but influential group of colonists this paper seeks to reconcile a generally positive assessment of the Ascendancy Irish in Australia with the widely accepted view of Ireland's Protestant gentry as a particularly selfish and reactionary class.

The Anglo-Irish tradition had its origins in the particular situation of the Protestant landed class established in Ireland following Cromwell's defeat of the Catholic Loyalist forces. Though the English (Norse-Welsh) had established a foothold in Ireland by the end of the eleventh century, the Anglo-Irish were largely the descendants of English settlers who took advantage of Cromwell's victory to acquire the defeated Catholic's confiscated estates. Based on entries in Burke's *Landed Gentry of Ireland,* Curtis concludes that the overwhelming majority of this class settled in Ireland during this period.[3] Under the 1652 Act of Settlement a majority of Catholic landowners were deprived of their estates and required to move to designated areas west of the Shannon. Cromwell's soldiers who had fought in Ireland, and adventurers who helped finance the campaign, were entitled to apply for grants of land from the Catholics' forfeited estates. With the greater part of Ireland's more fertile lands distributed amongst them, the Act of Settlement saw the creation of a new class of Protestant gentry, the Irish Ascendancy.

The violent manner in which this Protestant élite was established in Ireland greatly influenced the kind of landed society that developed subsequently. By the early eighteenth century the descendants of these settlers, the Anglo-Irish, held attitudes and had developed a lifestyle regarded as typical of their class. Though having much in common with the longer established English gentry, whom they strove to emulate, their situation as an alienated and isolating ruling class and their exposure to Gaelic culture resulted in important differences. As well as unconsciously held beliefs and attitudes by the Anglo-Irish brought to Australia a conscious awareness that they were the descendants of a conquering military caste: that their family's gentry status had involved the defeat, dispossession and continued suppression of the Catholic majority. The behaviour of the Anglo-Irish in Australia was also influenced by their knowledge of the Ascendancy's historic role as civilising colonisers both within Ireland and abroad. The nature of the British occupation of the Australian continent provided the Anglo-Irish with little by way of opportunity for military conquest. Distance and a harsh environment rather than armed resistance from a scattered native population proved the main obstacles to the expansion of European settlement. However as influential members of the ruling elite in what was generally a brutal society where Aborigines and convicts were often subject to cruel abuse, Ascendancy colonists had ample scope to play their part as civilising colonisers.

Though usually from relatively humble backgrounds themselves, the newly established Protestant gentry possessed the typical colonist's contempt for the native Irish. Regarding themselves superior on account of their proven military prowess, religious orthodoxy, English blood and more advanced culture, few Protestants mixed freely with the Celtic Catholic population. With most Catholic gentry having either fled abroad or been exiled to Ireland's barren west, the victorious Protestants presided over a demoralised and largely leaderless native population. This was still basically the situation a century and a half later when the first Ascendancy Irish began arriving in Australia. In Ireland and abroad, these Anglo – or establishment Irish possessed the deeply ingrained attitudes of an established ruling class and were thus well suited, at least in this respect, for membership of pre-goldrush Australia's penal-pastoral hierarchy.

The first generation of Cromwellian settlers in Ireland though far from secure assumed the arrogant and self-confident stance of a dominant landed caste. In spite of Cromwell's crushing victories and the fact that the Catholics had largely been deprived of their capacity for effective armed resistance, the newly established Protestant gentry faced the prospect of losing their estates. Following the restoration of Charles II in 1660, former Catholic proprietors confidently applied to the English court to have their estates returned. As a concession to his Catholic supporters Charles required certain Protestants to give up a portion of their estates to former Catholic proprietors who had been judged innocent of involvement in the initial insurrection of 1641. Though Charles eventually confirmed the great majority of Protestant landowners in the possession of their estates, the possibility remained of a future English monarch making further concessions to Catholic claims. Hated and feared by the Irish they had dispossessed they also faced losing their lands and lives in the event of a future uprising. Isolated on their estates, resident Protestant landlords, their families and employees remained vulnerable to attacks upon their persons and property.

Not until after the comprehensive Williamite victory over the resurgent Catholic forces at the Boyne in 1690 were Ireland's Protestant gentry really free from the threat of dispossession by military or legal means. The Ascendancy's dominance now acquired legal sanction through the passing of penal laws designed to prevent the possibility of a future Catholic uprising. Rather than seeking to retain their landed property by conforming, many influential Catholics responded by seeking service with sympathetic rulers abroad. The completeness of their victory and the fact that the Catholic peasantry were deprived of their natural leadership enabled the Protestants to consolidate their position of dominance over a demoralised Catholic population. Yet even then the Protestants, though well armed and organised into local militia, relied heavily on continued British military support. Unwilling or unable to assimilate with the native Irish, these Protestants remained colonists psychologically, permanently attached to English culture and institutions. Though staunchly imperialist and monarchist, the Anglo-Irish remained ambivalent in terms of their national allegiances, not feeling fully Irish yet often disliking and being highly suspicious of the English.

Insecurity resulting from their position as an imposed ruling caste led to the adoption of a garrison mentality amongst the Protestant gentry: an attitude which persisted long after the reasons for it had ceased to be important. More than anything else, it was the fierce desire to retain their landed property which united these Protestants into a particularly close-knit and resilient community. The Anglo-Irish then came to Australia not only with the usual gentry emigrants' desire for land, but with particular sensitivity to any move which threatened their continued possession of it. Though eventually secure in the possession of their estates, Ireland's Protestant gentry recognised that few amongst the Catholic majority recognised the legitimacy of their position. Memories of the violent fashion in which they had been dispossessed, continued religious persecution and exploitation as cheap labour maintained the Catholic's deep sense of grievance and ensured that the Protestants remained isolated and alienated. Though masked by outward displays of pride and arrogance, suspicion and guilty fear of the oppressed Catholic population remained features of the Anglo-Irish tradition. Apart from its sharp division on religious lines, the most striking feature of Irish society at the beginning of the eighteenth century was just how successful the Protestant landlords, often magistrates as well as the major local employers, were virtually a law unto themselves. During the eighteenth century rapid population increase and extensive enclosure of agricultural land for pastoralism meant that while more labour was available in Ireland, significantly less was required. In much of Ireland an increasingly desperate peasantry had to pay exorbitant rents and provide low-cost labour for a few acres on which to grow potatoes, or face the prospect of beggary and starvation. The power of landlords over the Irish peasantry was total. According to one contemporary observer, the Ascendancy wit, lawyer and politician, Jonah Barrington, 'no English nobleman could have ruled so absolutely over his tenantry as did any Irish gentleman'.[4]

The liberal-minded Arthur Young, appalled by the power of Irish landlords, claimed that 'a landlord in Ireland can scarcely invent an order which a servant, cottar or labourer dares to refuse to execute. Nothing satisfies him but unlimited submission'.[5]

In pre-goldrush Australia, Ascendancy settlers on their remote holdings also found themselves subject to little direct government control. Yet they were for the most part not as free as Protestant landlords in Ireland to treat 'inferiors' (Aborigines, assigned convicts and free farm servants) as they wished. For a start the law in Australian colonies, being centrally administered, was more impartial in its applications than in Anglo-Ireland. Those who assumed immunity from the law on account of their status as Irish gentlemen and openly flouted government regulations were likely to find themselves deprived of official favour or facing prosecution. One such case involved William Bryan, formerly of Spring Valley, County Meath who during the 1820s managed to establish his own pastoral tenantry by entering into an illegal agreement with two of his assigned convict servants. As a consequence of this action and his subsequent intemperate behaviour, Bryan was singled out by senior officials including Governor Arthur, and in April 1834 was forced to flee to England to avoid arrest.[6]

More importantly, Ascendancy settlers who sought to oppress their farm servants in the worst traditions of Irish landlordism faced possible retaliation, or at the very least the potentially ruinous desertion of workers. This is precisely what happened in the case of George Winter whose failure as a pioneering squatter was largely due to the fact that 'no man would stay with him for more than a week owing to the way he treated them'.[7] For while chronic unemployment and widespread poverty produced a large and servile workforce in Ireland, labour remained scarce and independently-minded in the colonies.

Throughout the eighteenth century Ireland's southern Protestants justified their continued domination of the Catholic native Irish by proclaiming the superiority of their Anglo-Saxon culture, the orthodoxy of their Anglican faith and the innate inferiority and unreliability of the native Irish. Far from involving any denial of Irishness, the Ascendancy saw themselves as the true Irish. Yet in spite of the often arrogant and self-assertive manner in which such claims were made, the Anglo-Irish were never free of the guilty fear that those they had so brutally oppressed would eventually rise and revenge themselves for past humiliations. Wellington's biographer Phillip Guedalla suggests that because 'Anglo-Irish magnates knew themselves observed by long rows of Irish eyes ... the silent watchers made and kept them prouder than ever'.[8] This deep seated sense of insecurity influenced the manner in which the first generations of Protestant landlords utilised their Irish estates. Owing to the uncertain bases on which members of this class initially held their grants, many looked to their Irish estates for short term profits rather than as longer term investments. Seeking quick returns, many Irish landlords granted tenants perpetual leases following the payment of a cash sum. As well as gaining a quick return from an as yet uncertain investment, Irish landlords were influenced by the need to have a tenant in possession to consolidate their claim to ownership. During the eighteenth century, perpetual tenants, who were in fact landlords themselves, took advantage of increased land values to raise rents paid by sub-tenants on short-term fixed or determined leases. Deeply etched into the Ascendancy's psyche was the view that land was an asset to be exploited, rather than developed or improved, to provide them with the means of a genteel, leisured existence. Their short-term aspirations as emigrants plus the speculative nature and general insecurity of landholding in pre-goldrush Australia reinforced this view amongst Ascendancy colonists. Like their Cromwellian forebears in Ireland, Australia's Ascendancy settlers initially viewed their colonial holdings and stock as short-term investments: speculations with the potential to provide a quick and substantial return on capital invested. For most, landholding in Australia represented the most promising option available that would enable them to achieve financial independence and eventually resume their place in Ascendancy society.

If landlordism was the basis of Anglo-Irish landed society, absenteeism was one of its more distinctive features. The difficulties and dangers of living and travelling in Ireland and the fact that many landlords owned more than one estate contributed to the extent of absenteeism. Whilst most English gentry permanently resided on, or at least regularly visited their country estates, many major Irish landlords never or only rarely visited theirs. Though probably not as widespread or damaging as had often been claimed, absenteeism contributed to the depressed living standards of the peasantry and seriously undermined the reputation of Ireland's Protestant gentry. Large scale absenteeism in Ireland resulted in the flow of much-needed capital from the Irish countryside often to support the absentee's extravagant lifestyle in London, Bath or Dublin. Yet there is no conclusive evidence that the absentee's tenants were, generally speaking, worse off. Some were excellent landlords, with others only absentees because economic circumstances forced them to close up their large country houses and find cheaper accommodation elsewhere. Though certain notable absentees spent substantial amounts improving their estates, the practice overall deprived Ireland's backward agriculture of the desperately needed capital. The absentee mentality also encouraged many of Ireland's most able people to live and work abroad. Allegations concerning the greed and indifference of Ireland's absentees, (many were of course English) has done much to damage the Ascendancy's reputation. Ireland's Protestant gentry have considerably been portrayed as a class of irresponsible landlords who ruthlessly exploited Ireland's fertile lands and people for their own selfish ends.

Absenteeism also encouraged the practice, common amongst Irish landlords, of successively subletting and subdividing their estates. Generally the greater part of an estate was let to substantial tenant farmers or agents (middlemen) on long term leases at moderate, fixed rents. Middlemen subdivided their leased land into small agricultural holdings sublet for the highest possible rents. This practice obviously reduced an individual landlord's sense of responsibility for the proper management of an estate and the welfare of people who lived and worked on it. Lack of alternative land meant that many Irish peasants were forced to pay exorbitantly high rents for small potato plots. The ruthless practices of 'rackrenting' middlemen has done much to damage the general reputation of the Irish gentry. That most astute observer of rural Ireland in the late eighteenth century, Arthur Young, angrily denounced 'middlemen' as '... the most oppressive species of tyrant who not satisfied with the screwing up of rent to the uppermost farthing ... are rapacious and relentless in the collection of it'.[9] Young is highly critical of these 'squireens' for their seedy, pretentious lifestyle, referring to them as 'the masters of a pack of wretched hounds with whom they wasted both time and money'.[10]

Colonial Australia offered few opportunities for large landowners to establish themselves as landlords. Consistent labour shortages, relatively high wages and the availability of cheap farmland made it difficult for landowners to attract and retain agricultural tenants. Ascendancy colonists seeking to replicate the Irish land rental system in Australia such as William Bryan in Northern Tasmania and William Rutledge at Port Fairy were unlikely to succeed, at least in the longer term. Perhaps the most successful of Australia's Anglo-Irish landlords was William Rutledge, formerly of Bawnboy, County Cavan who between 1843–65 had many tenants on his 'Farnham Park' estate near Koroit in Western Australia.[11] Yet for those who did become large landholders, conditions of pastoral pioneering in the colonies certainly encouraged absenteeism. For as in Ireland a century before, Ascendancy settlers on their remote farms and pastoral runs in early colonial Australia, frequently experienced loneliness and harsh living conditions, difficulties in travel and the threat of native or outlaw attack. Not surprisingly, those who could arrange it, like Samuel Pratt Winter at Murndal in Victoria's Western District, employed resident managers while remaining for the most part in more civilised locations. Samuel Pratt Winter for example, only visited his Spring Valley run for about a month each year during the 1840's, preferring to live mainly on his small Cluan estate in northern Tasmania.

Irish laws and customs relating to the rental of farming land also contributed to the backward state of Irish agriculture and the low living standard of the Irish peasantry. Unlike England, where landlords were responsible for basic improvements, Irish tenants, Ulster excepted, received their lands bare, and most were not compensated for improvements completed during their lease. Those who undertook substantial improvements faced the prospect of paying increased rents as a result. For when a fixed term lease 'fell in', the tenant in possession had no special claim and the lease was auctioned to the highest bidder. An obvious disincentive for much needed improvements, this practice resulted in some tenants deliberately wasting their plots towards the end of a lease to make it less attractive for competitors.

Lacking education, capital and the incentive to improve their holdings, Ireland's peasant farmers remained poor and ignorant. In most accounts it is Protestant landlords rather than the Irish land rental system which have been singled out as the principal cause of the peasantry's distress.

The second half of the eighteenth century, saw a marked deterioration in the situation for the poorer classes of Irish peasantry. Widespread degradation of land due to poor farming practices and the greater profitability of pastoralism resulted, in some counties, in the wholesale eviction of smallholders as leases expired. Denied legal redress and with little prospect of alternative employment, desperate Irish peasantry increasingly turned to systematic agrarian terrorism as their sole defence against evicting or otherwise oppressive landlords. In Munster and parts of Leinster, resident landlords, their families and employees and even non-conforming tenants became subject to attack. The terrorist activities of Catholic guerrilla bands such as the notorious Whiteboys and Steelboys and the savage retaliation these attacks provoked, formed part of Ireland's still unresolved tradition of mutilation and murder.

Only a small proportion of Australia's Anglo-Irish would have themselves been the victims of agrarian terrorism in Ireland or have actively participated in punitive expeditions against suspected Catholic terrorists. However, many, who had grown up on country estates had experienced a turbulent, violent atmosphere with 'the bullet, the sabre and bayonet lash and halter, being met by the pike, the scythe, the blunderbuss, the hatchet and the fire-brand'.[12] Few questioned the necessity of rigorously suppressing outrage whenever it occurred. During the first decades of white settlement in Australia, settlers and officials in remote regions also faced the prospect of native or out-law attack. With their Old World background, Anglo-Irish colonists such as William and Samuel Bryan in Tasmania, were as one might expect prominent in local initiatives to repel such attacks and punish those responsible. However, should such measures involve illegal actions which became public knowledge, Anglo-Irish colonists were more likely to face prosecution than Protestant gentry in Ireland undertaking similar reprisals. For example, when George Winter and several of his men fired on and killed five Aborigines and then failed to report the incident, Superintendent La Trobe did everything he could to have Winter arrested and charged with murder.[13]

Though he might with relative impunity apply his whip to the backs of peasants blocking his path or burn the wretched cabins of suspected Catholic rebels, the Ascendancy landlord usually enjoyed only limited rights over 'his' landed property. As well as being bound by the detailed provisions of existing mortgages and leasehold agreements, most had to abide by the complex feudal style arrangements governing property rights within Ascendancy families. Having inherited rather than acquired estates, Irish landowners were normally required to make specific provisions for both living and future family members. The standard, traditional provisions of settlement and wills were designed to keep landed property intact within families. About half of the Irish estate owners were in fact mere life tenants with limited powers over what was in reality family property. Having acquired land themselves, Anglo-Irish landowners and landholders in Australia were free of many of the legal and customary restraints which traditionally governed land ownership and utilisation in Ireland.

In Ireland, disputes over property matters between and within Ascendancy families were sufficiently common to be a feature of the Anglo-Irish tradition. Legal complications and the general confusion which accompanied the Cromwellian resettlement of Ireland often led to protracted and often quite senseless property litigation. The Bowens of Bowen's Court, County Cork were one Ascendancy family whose fortunes suffered due to one family member's penchant for property litigation for quite futile ends.[14] Fortunately, not all such disputes involved recourse to the courts. Where wiser counsel prevailed, quarrels could sometimes be more economically and amicably settled by referring disagreements to a trusted relative or mutual friend for arbitration.

Most Anglo-Irish who arrived in Australia would have possessed some detailed knowledge of Old World property laws and customs and probably an inclination towards litigation. In colonial Australia, the rapid and largely unsupervised nature of the pastoral expansion resulted in a high incidence of property disputes between landholders and stock owners. As settlers or officials in remote areas, the Anglo-Irish were involved in often bitter and protracted disputes over such matters as the proper location of boundaries, the ownership of unbranded stock and the employment of 'runaways' (absconding workers). Though in general, the principles of British law applied, knowledge of Old World property laws and procedures was often of little use in such situations. Without appropriate local laws and customs to guide them, most settlers also lacked reasonable access to senior officials, courts or even trusted mutual friends to whom they might refer disputes. To succeed in the competitive and largely unregulated world of pastoral pioneering, these Ascendancy colonists had basically to rely on their own resources.

Proud, close-knit and litigious, the situation of the Protestant gentry in Ireland also encouraged an indolent and indulgent lifestyle. Lacking education and with little opportunity to exercise civic responsibility, the Irish gentry acquired a reputation for dissipation and extravagance. John Loveday in 1732 observed that 'The Irish gentry are an expensive people continually feasting one another'.[15] Lord Chesterfield, Viceroy of Ireland, claimed that 'nine gentlemen in ten in Ireland are impoverished by the vast quantities of claret which from mistaken notions of hospitality they think it is necessary should be drunk in their houses'.[16] Arthur Young, later in the century, criticized the 'numbers of brothers, cousins and younger sons found swarming in gentlemen's houses with nothing better to do than to chase after hares and horses'. Young roundly condemned these '...fellows with round hats edged in gold who hunt in the day, get drunk in the evening and fight the next morning'.[17]

This leisured gentry lifestyle was possible for a high proportion of the Ascendancy because of relatively lower costs in Ireland. With land cheap and servants plentiful, even the pettiest squireen could supply his own basic provisions, including illegally distilled whiskey. For many, entertainment consisted entirely of feasting and field-sports. A high proportion of Australia's Ascendancy would have experienced firsthand, even if only as guests or dependent relatives, the Irish gentry's privileged lifestyle. In this respect the Old World background of Ascendancy settlers contrasted sharply with that of the Scots' experience of frugality, piety and hard work.

In pre-goldrush Australia, though wages were higher and servants much harder to find, circumstances were similar to those which encouraged the Irish gentry to lead such wasteful and dissolute lives. In both societies alcohol provided a ready palliative to isolation and boredom. Like Anglo-Ireland, oppression and brutality were common-place in penal-pastoral Australia. However while a large and servile peasant population supported an essentially parasitic gentry in

Ireland, shrewdness and consistent endeavour were usually required in Australia for material success. Though a gentry background provided important advantages, considerable adjustment was required on the part of most Anglo-Irish if they were to succeed as colonists in Australia.

Whether grand magnate or petty squireen, the Ascendancy's lifestyle depended on the continued possession of landed estates. Though many landlords neglected or mismanaged their estates, the importance of land-ownership in Ireland can hardly be over-stated. Even more than for the rest of Britain, the continued possession of landed estates was virtually a requirement for gentry status in Ireland. Where this was not possible, the Anglo-Irish responded enthusiastically to opportunities offering in the New World to acquire cheap farming land. Career and other investment opportunities were important, but the prospect of acquiring pastoral land was central to the motivation of those Ascendancy who chose pre-goldrush Australia as their New World destination.

The possession of a landed estate as well as providing status and a rising income, conferred important benefits on Ascendancy families. Life on a well situated country estate provided family members, their relatives and friends with ample opportunities for hunting, fishing and shooting. Experience with horses and guns, of outdoor life generally, proved useful training for the sons of Irish gentry intent on a military career. Such experience and a lack of employment opportunities in Ireland (rather than the Ascendancy's alleged inbred fighting qualities) resulted in high proportion of Anglo-Irish officers in British regiments. Pre-emigration experience of country life may have encouraged Ascendancy emigrants to take up pastoral pioneering in Australia. Yet on balance these apparent advantages were more than offset by Ascendancy settlers' softgentry origins. As members of a rural leisured class, young Irish gentlemen may well have developed rare skill in riding over fences at breakneck speed in pursuit of a fleeing stag or in wringing woodcocks in rapid succession. However, should his hunter lose a shoe or his gun jam, most such young gentlemen had little idea and less inclination to effect even minor repairs. Similarly, while living on a country estate provided ample opportunities for observing Old World farming practices, few of the young Irish gentlemen who arrived in Australia brought with them any detailed knowledge or practical experience of the work involved. In spite of the obvious advantages of an Ascendancy background which usually included some access to family capital, influential connections and experience of country life, the average young Ascendancy gentleman was hardly a prime candidate for success as a settler in pre-goldrush Australia.

Another highly prized aspect of estate ownership in Ireland was the extent to which it conferred a sense of intellectual and social independence on individual landlords. With a general lack of customary and legal restraint, estate ownership in Ireland encouraged independence of thought and action which in the case of certain Irish gentry took the form of outspoken and eccentric behaviour. Isolated and on their country estates with relative freedom to speak and act as they pleased, the Irish gentry were less selective in their choice of acquaintances than their more class-conscious English counterparts. With little by way of constructive activity to occupy their time, some Irish gentlemen indulged in wayward or even violent behaviour. Though tolerated in eighteenth century Ireland, such behaviour, as certain Anglo-Irish colonists were soon to discover, was far less acceptable in early nineteenth-century Australia.

Mindful of the extent to which their future economic security and gentry status depended upon the continued possession of landed estates, Ascendancy families sought at least to preserve and where possible extend their holdings. To this end the rule of primogeniture strictly applied. The negotiation of satisfactory marriage alliances with other Ascendancy families involving mutually acceptable financial and property arrangements was also vitally important. As heir to at least the family's principal estate, the eldest son or nominated male relative was expected to acquire additional property through marriage. Though designated owner of certain estates, the terms of inheritance usually limited the heir's powers over 'his' property. Under the provisions of his parents' marriage settlement and wills, the favoured eldest son was usually required to adhere to specified financial arrangements for other legitimate family members and his own future issue. Anglo-Irish colonists who acquired rather than inherited landed property in Australia were obviously not bound by such family and dynastic considerations. Many had come to Australia in the first place because of their position as younger, potentially property-less sons.

Through emigration they had effectively removed themselves from their extended family circle and direct moral responsibility for other, less well-off family members. Most were therefore free to dispose of their colonial property as they thought fit. Even so, as members, albeit long absent ones, of extended Ascendancy families, many still felt obliged somehow to assist less fortunate relatives and friends at home. For certain Anglo-Irish in Australia this meant encouraging and financially assisting friends and relatives in Ireland to take full advantage of better employment and investment opportunities in the colonies.

Eligible young Ascendancy men besides marrying within their own propertied, Protestant class, were under some pressure to marry close relatives and neighbours. The Irish gentry's somewhat belated concern over racial purity, logistics and even property considerations all contributed to this practice. According to Curtis '... it was because the Anglo-Irish suspected a degree of ethnic mixture in their veins, yet prided themselves on purity of race that they paid themselves the highest possible compliment by marrying cousins'.[18] Commenting on the extent of intermarriage between neighbouring usually interrelated families, Edith Somerville explains that 'each estate was a kingdom and with the impossibility of locomotion, each neighbouring potentate acquired a relative importance quite out of proportion to his merits; for to love your neighbour – or, at all events to marry him was almost inevitable when marriages were made by a map'.[19]

Religious and ethnic considerations were important, while difficulties involved wider travel certainly encouraged intermarriage between neighbouring families. Both parties would also have been aware of the advantages of linking adjacent estates to form larger, more economic units. For whatever reasons, this tendency of the Irish gentry to marry neighbours and relatives meant that 'Anglo Ireland was not just a class of landowners strewn over the countryside ... It was a congeries of familiar families, tied together by marriage, by mortgages, history, creed and a myriad of mutual interests'.[20]

Individual Anglo-Irish came to Australia as members of close-knit, extended families to which most intended returning as soon as financial circumstances permitted. Such powerful kinship ties meant that once established, many Anglo-Irish in the colonies sought to persuade friends and relatives at home to join them. Multiple chain migration of related Anglo-Irish was to result in the formation of several Ascendancy enclaves in Australia, the most notable being the 'Irish cousinage' of Port Phillip in the 1840s.

Life for most Irish gentry by the late eighteenth century had become more comfortable and secure following a period of persisting peace and relative prosperity. In many cases their rambling fortress-style houses had been replaced by elegant Georgian or Italianate mansions, sited with prospect rather than defensive capability in mind. As well as serving as family residences, these impressive 'Big Houses' and the surrounding demesne represented an outward expression of the Protestant gentry's sense of power and permanence. Usually accommodating numerous staff, guests and dependent relatives, the Anglo-Irish 'Big House', as T.R. Henn points out, served as 'a centre of hospitality, of country life and society, apt to breed a passionate attachment'.[21] In rural Ireland the local Big House also served as an administrative and legal centre where rents were paid, quarrels reconciled and old debts arbitrated. For Henn, the construction and maintenance of such impractical and often ruinously large expensive houses represented the Ascendancy's 'search for beauty and stability in the midst of poverty and defeat'.[22] As with the possession of landed estates, the ownership of such country houses was necessary to establish a family's status within the ruling Protestant hierarchy. For an impoverished peasantry in their smoke-filled, ramshackle cabins the Big House became a reference point and source of envy. Most of Australia's Anglo-Irish colonists aspired to become eventually master or mistress of their own Big House, preferably in Ireland, but alternatively in Australia. Circumstances in pre-goldrush Australia were hardly conductive to the replication of this distinctive feature of Anglo-Irish society. Their own initial short term aspirations as colonists, the uncertain profitability of pastoralism, and the general lack of surplus labour or a potential tenantry discouraged attempts to recreate the physical and social environment of the Irish Big House.

With the Big House, the other focal point for an often scattered Southern Protestant community was their local Church of Ireland. However, for many, active membership of the Church of Ireland by the end of the eighteenth century had become more an expression of Protestant solidarity than genuine religious commitment. During the eighteenth century Ireland's Southern Protestants looked less to their

Anglican orthodoxy to justify their continued domination of the Catholic majority. Having failed to convert the Catholic masses through systematic coercion, there followed a marked softening of attitudes amongst the Anglo-Irish. Unlike Ulster's hardline Presbyterians, the Ascendancy's collective memory of massacre and pillage faded with the passing of the generation that experienced it. Many now recognise the absurdity and injustice of continuing to persecute countrymen whose sole crime consisted of maintaining a different doctrinal interpretation of Christian theology. It was significant that Catholic Emancipation was supported by a majority of Anglo-Irish members years before it was eventually passed in the British Parliament.

Increased toleration was also reflected in growing apathy and religious indifference amongst the Ascendancy. Elizabeth Bowen commenting on the Ascendancy's need to '... make a social figure of God' suggests that because of their circumstances 'nothing ... gave the soul any chance to stand at its full height'.[23] As far as Ireland's Protestant gentry and religion were concerned Bowen argues 'that to enjoy prosperity, one had to exclude feeling, or keep it within prescribed bounds'.[24] By the end of the nineteenth century apathy and emigration had resulted in a moribund Church of Ireland attended by a dwindling and ageing congregation of drably respectable, often nominal Protestants.

This gradual drift towards spiritual impotence was interrupted by the evangelical revival which spread from England to Ireland following the Act of Union. By zealously propagating the study of the scriptures, ardent evangelicals sought to revitalise their fellow Protestants as well as convert Catholics. Though not particularly successful in either area, the movement provided Anglican laity with new opportunities to become actively involved with the work of their Church. The Church of Ireland remained the natural channel for airing the views of the Anglo-Irish community as a whole. McConville suggests that due to evangelical influence, 'rakes, bucks and eccentrics ... faded as a subspecies' during the first half of the nineteenth century when 'the Anglo-Irish knuckled under to the conformist respectability that flowed from Victorian England'.[25] Though many clergy remained ineffectual and indifferent, the Church of Ireland produced its share of effective evangelical reformers.

The Anglo-Irish who arrived in Australia, however, were more likely to be nominal/Anglicans or freethinkers than inspired evangelicals. In colonial Australia as in Ascendancy Ireland the Anglo-Irish benefitted from their association with a privileged Anglican Church. In both societies Catholics, though eventually no longer subject to penal sanctions, were distrusted and openly discriminated against by the dominant Protestants. Bitter sectarian feeling remained a feature of Australian colonial society yet few prominent Ascendancy colonists became active in the anti-Catholic majority had produced an insular and aggressive Protestantism. In Australia, the Anglo-Irish could become part of the religious, cultural mainstream. In any case, by the time the Anglo-Irish began arriving in Australia strident anti-Catholicism was no longer such a distinctive feature of their tradition.

Though a majority generally supported the gradual repeal of anti-Catholic penal laws, few Ascendancy seriously questioned the morality of their continued domination of Ireland. Most Ascendancy intuitively recognised that any substantial move towards wider political representation or the more equitable distribution of land threatened the very bases of their society. For this reason Nora Robertson believes that 'the Anglo-Irish could not recognise that deep down, the normal native Irishman was obsessed by his longing for national freedom and the ownership of land'.[26] Because of their situation in Ireland, many Ascendancy who in England would have been Whigs or even liberals, remained staunchly and inflexibly Tory.

In Australia, individual Anglo-Irish were obviously less threatened by moves towards more democratic forms of government or a more equitable distribution of farming land. However, it was not simply the changed circumstances of their colonial situation that encouraged prominent Ascendancy emigrants in Australia to support progressive causes. Though mostly unwilling to make significant concessions to the Catholic majority in Ireland, within their own ranks the Anglo-Irish practised a kind of aristocratic egalitarianism. In an inherently unstable Anglo-Irish society, land ownership and achievement rather than lineage determined status. To ensure their survival, the ruling Protestant minority saw the need to foster talent among their own caste. Ambitious young Protestants from humble backgrounds could gain admission to Trinity where sizar-ships were available to assist the most able. With students coming from a wider range of backgrounds,

Trinity was something of a liberal institution compared with the Tory backwaters of Oxford and Cambridge. Though it remained largely Protestant, Trinity in 1793 became the first British University to readmit Catholics. Trinity's liberal atmosphere was reflected not so much in the formal courses of study but in the nature of the College's student societies.

Within Ireland's resident gentry class, isolation, interdependence and the need for company discouraged class distinction. Necessity also encouraged the adoption of democratic practices in the Ascendancy's civilian militia, the Volunteers. Formed in the late eighteenth century as a response to a threatened French invasion, the Volunteers elected their own officers, a practice then unthinkable for the rest of Britain. Within both the civilian and military sphere, the possibility of such advancement for Protestants of humble origin was characteristically Anglo-Irish.

The idea of Ireland's Protestant gentry being somehow liberal minded or democratically inclined hardly tallies with the widely held view of this class. In the traditional picture of Anglo-Ireland, 'the most familiar figure' according to J.C. Beckett, '... is that of the greedy tyranical landlord squeezing the last penny out of a starving tenantry and spending the proceeds in the fashionable world of London or Bath or in riotous living at home'.[27] At the wider level, the more extreme Irish nationalists have generally dismissed the Ascendancy as West Britons, agents of a foreign power and apostles of a foreign culture. Historians have for the most part supported the nationalists' view that the Anglo-Irish were somehow responsible for much of the pre-republican Ireland's often violent and miserable past. For example, in commenting on the Cromwellian resettlement of Ireland, Paul Dubois asserts that 'never has a more savage design been put into execution ... than the project of destroying one nation and putting another in its place'.[28] In 1945, T.J. Kiernan, a former Irish ambassador to Australia, went so far as to liken Anglo-Irish landlords to the Nazis. Referring to the disastrous consequences of the Great Famine, Kiernan held the Ascendancy responsible for the legalised extermination of one million people.[29]

Recent scholarship provides a more balanced, less emotive view of the historical role of the Ascendancy. In *The Anglo-Irish Tradition* J.C. Beckett suggests that where the Anglo-Irish are concerned, 'historians have been inclined to accept at face value allegations which have long been accepted as self evident truths'.[30] Revisionist histories of the Anglo-Irish refer to misuse of contemporary sources to provide an unjust and basically inaccurate view of the Protestant Ascendancy. Some of the most damning criticism of Ireland's Protestant gentry has taken the form of quotations by leading Ascendancy writers. For example, frequent use has been made of Swift's assertion that in Ireland 'every squire, almost to a man, is an oppressor of his tenants, a jobber of all public works, very proud and generally illiterate'.[31]

What the Ascendancy's critics rarely mention is that Swift was writing in a highly satiric fashion. Similar use has been made of carefully selected passages from Jonah Barrington's *Personal Sketches*. Essentially a wit and satirist, Barrington, a lynx-eyed observer of eighteenth-century Ireland, offers a basically comic view of his fellow Ascendancy. Yet his desultory mélange of recollections has obviously misled many into supposing that these were the common characteristics of his class. Maria Edgeworth's fictional account of a particularly unattractive Ascendancy family, the appropriately named Rackrents, has provided even richer fare for those who would condemn without qualification Ireland's Protestant gentry. In spite of the writer's unambiguous assurance when Castle Rackrent was first published in 1800 that 'the race of Rackrents has long been extinct in Ireland'[32] it has widely been assumed that the fighting Sir Kit, the slovenly Sir Condy and the drunken Sir Patrick were contemporary, representative figures. In all, eighteenth-century Ascendancy writers with their satire and colourful characters have helped perpetuate the misleading impression of a society 'compounded of whiskey, rot, decay, guttering candles, damp, horses and dust: or in more abstract terms of improvidence, stupidity, cupidity, pride, subservience, animosity, sentimentality, brutality and perversity'.[33] To entertain and possibly appeal to the anti-Irish prejudices of their English readers, leading Ascendancy writers have frequently emphasised the humorous and colourfully distinctive aspects of the Irish gentry's lifestyle. In Edgeworth's case, it should in fairness be pointed out that she was a sincere reformer who sought to shame less responsible members of her own class into following the example of her own worthy father. The model of an improving landlord and sincere country gentleman, Richard Lovell Edgeworth was reputed to have 'honestly and unostentatiously used his utmost endeavours to obliterate all that could lead to perpetual ill will in the country'.[34]

This tendency to portray the Ascendancy as a basically irresponsible and rather eccentric class is present in several recently published works on the Anglo-Irish. Barrington's jaundiced view of his fellow Ascendancy re-emerges in coarser form in J.P. Donleavy's bawdy novel, *The Destinies of Darcy Dancer, Gentleman,* which describes the amorous escapades of an impetuous young Ascendancy rake. While having an obvious and valued place in comic literature, such exaggerated accounts of Ascendancy life are less acceptable in otherwise scholarly histories of the Anglo-Irish. In seeking to entertain as well as inform, Michael McConville's *From Ascendancy to Oblivion* and Mark Bence Jones's, *Twilight of the Ascendancy* reinforce misleading stereotypes.[35] Concentrating mainly on the eighteenth century, McConville seeks to offer a 'welcome counter to the polemicists who try to reduce Ireland's inherited complexities to us and them, good and bad'.[36] Viewing the Anglo-Irish as 'a rich source of comedy' McConville describes the eccentric, often violent behaviour of such certifiable misfits as the infamous 'Fighting' Fitzgerald, 'Fireball' McNamara, and 'Hairtrigger Dick' Martin. As well as murdering several of his peers, Fitzgerald once chained his elderly father to a live pet bear and later imprisoned him (the father) in a cave on the family estate. Explaining Anglo-Ireland's seemingly endless supply of eccentrics, McConville refers to the effects of persisting peace and a bored gentry's need to find outlets for energies previously expended on warfare. Bence-Jones's description of the decline and eventual demise of the once powerful Ascendancy is liberally spiced with gossipy anecdotes describing the often quite bizarre antics of a decaying and impoverished gentry. Again the overall impression is misleading. Insufficient attention is paid to less colourful but more representative landlords such as the Martins of Ross and Pakenhams of Pakenham Hall.

Yet in seeking a more balanced view of the Irish gentry, too great a reliance should not be placed on the memoirs and family histories produced by some of the more literate members of the Ascendancy. Such basically sympathetic accounts of this class include the genteel, witty reminiscences of Somerville and Ross[37] the novelist Elizabeth Bowen's thoughtful history of her own Cork family, and Nora

Robertson's often astute account of Anglo-Irish society this century. Usually humorous and sharply observant, such accounts are frequently tinged with a deeply felt sense of regret for the passing of the world they describe. Written when the Ascendancy's once-impregnable world was beginning to crumble or had all but disintegrated, these writers express a subtle yearning for times past when life for Ireland's gentry consisted of a more or less continual round of social and sporting events. Happier times are recalled when a devoted tenantry lit bonfires (outside rather than inside the Big House as was to become the custom) to celebrate the birth of a male heir or the landlord's long awaited return from abroad. In her account of what were in 'most ways ... fairly ordinary Anglo-Irish country gentry' Elizabeth Bowen refers to 'a lively and simple spontaneous affection between the landed families and the people around them'.[38] She attributes the strength of this bond partly to the foster system which involved the gentry's children being wet-nursed and mothered by Catholic servant women. Violet Martin commenting on the landlord-tenant relationship at Ross wistfully recalls that the 'personal element was always in it and the hand of affection held it together'.[39]

Yet, thoughtful and insightful, rarely do the authors of such cosy rural reminiscences rise above the privileged, insular world they describe. Most avoid confronting the unpleasant truth that the maintenance of the Ascendancy's lifestyle necessarily involved the continued exploitation and suppression of the Catholic majority. Brian Inglis in *West Britain* reflects on the nature of the landlord-tenant relationship in Ascendancy Ireland. He suggests that 'we loved them as a landowner in the Deep South loves his negro servants – because they knew their place and stayed in it'.[40] The rising tide of Irish nationalism experienced at the local level is described in terms of tenant disloyalty conveniently attributed to the influence of a few, misguided extremists.

Lacking the zeal, aggressive militarism and ruthless acquisitiveness of their Protestant forbears, these writers seem unwilling to concede that the position of their class, now untenable, was never morally defensible. As with most of their fellow Ascendancy, they seem unable to recognise Ireland as a nation of people capable of governing themselves without the supervision of an hereditary ruling caste. This view of themselves as a class born to rule may help explain why so many Anglo-Irish sought and obtained positions as governors and other senior positions in Australia.

The truth concerning the common attitudes and behaviour of Anglo-Irish, during the century when representatives of this class emigrated to Australia, remains elusive. Identifying the important features of the distinctive Old World tradition which the Ascendancy brought to colonial Australia involves somehow reconciling contrasting accounts of the Anglo-Irish: the exaggerated, highly coloured accounts offered by satirists and novelists; the politically motivated, polemical accounts of the nationalists; the romanticised, nostalgic accounts of the apologists; and recently published revisionists histories of the Ascendancy period.

Perhaps it is sensible to begin by rejecting extremes. Improving landlords were not as common as members of the Kildare Street Club like to think, or rare as the nationalists would have us believe. On balance, available evidence seems to support the view that Ireland's Protestant gentry were neither as unpopular or a wickedly irresponsible as depicted by the nationalists. Anecdotal evidence, and the fact that a relatively small number of Protestants were able to retain power with minimal military force, support Professor Maxwell's carefully qualified conclusion 'that on the whole, setting aside the general and often theoretical dislike of the people for English and Anglo-Irish, and for particular landlords who definitely ill-treated them, it would seem that the Irish gentry were not so very unpopular'.[41]

Though, as Beckett readily admits, 'the Anglo-Irish were not good managers', neither were they '... cruel and grasping tyrants, wringing the last penny of rent from a starving and terrified tenantry'.[42] While the Protestant gentry in Ireland as a class have much to answer for, it is simply unjust to hold them primarily responsible for the impoverished state of the Irish peasantry. In the first place the situation of most Irish peasants during normal times was not particularly grim when compared with the conditions of other rural populations in the poorer parts of Europe. In this respect it was England, not Ireland, in the late eighteenth century that was singularly and phenomenal. During the second half of the eighteenth century agricultural prices rose more sharply than rents, with the increase going mainly to the tenant. In spite of their monotonous diet of potatoes, their appalling housing and ragged dress, Irish peasants were often observed to be happy and capable of considerable exertion. In fact, the backward state of the Irish peasantry had more to do with Ireland's lack of natural resources and the depressed state of the Irish economy than the rapacious practices of Protestant landlords. The landholding system in Ireland (as in much of Europe) was patently unjust, involving the mass exploitation of a hungry peasantry, yet other factors were more significant. A potentially disastrous rate of population increase coupled with the peasantry's dangerous dependence on a single crop; England's restrictive policies which effectively discouraged the growth of Irish trade and manufacturing, all contributed to a deteriorating situation which culminated in the disastrous famine of 1845–9. Probably more than any other single factor, it was the Great Famine which fixed in the minds of the Catholic population as a whole the idea that the Protestant landlords were somehow the major enemies of Ireland. Yet despite evidence to the contrary, the nationalist myth persists that 'English' landlords (the Anglo-Irish) were directly responsible for the deaths and suffering of millions of Irish Catholics. In fact, the great majority of Irish landlords, whether resident or absentee, were relatively powerless to cope with a disaster of the magnitude of the Great Famine. Many faced ruin themselves, due not only to a sharp reduction in income as rents remained unpaid, but also as a result of their own considerable efforts to assist a stricken population.

The Anglo-Irish tradition was neither stable nor uniform. Like their Catholic Celtic countrymen, each generation of Anglo-Irish emigrants brought with them a different experience of Ireland to the New World. On the whole the Ascendancy Irish who emigrated to Australia were better educated and more liberally minded than generations that preceded or succeeded them. By the late eighteenth century when the first Anglo-Irish began to arrive in New South Wales and Tasmania, a period of prolonged peace and prosperity had resulted in Ireland's Protestant gentry becoming more civilised and tolerant. The Anglo-Irish who arrived in Australia during the first century of European settlement represented a society that had peaked intellectually and culturally but was soon to enter a period of stagnation and decline. By the late nineteenth century when Anglo-Irish emigration to Australia had all but ceased, the Ascendancy had become classbound and intellectually rigid. Reflecting on Anglo-Irish attitudes at this time, Nora Robertson recalls that 'the heads of leading Protestant families were, generally speaking less intellectually minded than their grandfathers'.[43] Commenting that fewer Ascendancy families now sent their sons to Trinity, Robertson attributes the Irish gentry's intellectual decline to the increased influence of the British military in Ireland.

To conclude – it is possible to reconcile the generally favourable impression of the Anglo-Irish in early Australia as able and energetic and on the whole liberal minded colonists with far less flattering descriptions of Ireland's Protestant gentry as a class. As well as taking a balanced view of their Old World Anglo-Irish tradition, one also needs to take into account the ways in which their changed circumstances in pre-goldrush Australia influenced the aspirations and behaviour of these Ascendancy Irish. In Australia there was little opportunity or need for these 'establishment' Irish to attempt to recreate what many recognised as a patently unjust and inequitable system in Ireland. At the same time, inspite of their soft gentry origins, many Anglo-Irish were well equipped to take advantage of specific employment and investment opportunities offering in penal-pastoral Australia. Largely because of their Old World tradition and Ascendancy background, the Anglo-Irish were particularly well suited to take on the role of civilising colonists in these remote outposts of Empire.

Published in *Familia: Ulster Genealogical Review*, no. 8, 1992.

Notes

1 Charles Griffith, Diary, 1840–41, 8 December, 1840, La Trobe Library, State Library of Victoria. This brief journal by one of Port Phillip's Irish cousinage and a younger son of Richard Griffiths MP provides an Ascendancy view of early Melbourne Society.

2 Ibid., 1 February, 1841.

3 L.P. Curtis, Jnr. 'The Anglo-Irish Predicament', *Twentieth Century Studies*, Nov. 1970, p. 37.

4 Jonah Barrington, 'Personal Sketches' in *The Ireland of Sir Jonah Barrington: Selections from his 'Personal Sketches'*, ed. H.B. Staples, Peter Owen, London, 1968, p. 6.

5 Arthur Young, *A Tour of Ireland in the Years 1776, 1777 and 1778*, Vol. 1, London, p. 2.

6 For a detailed account of the Bryan case see G.J. Forth, Chapter 3 'The Brothers Bryan: Irish Origins and colonial careers' in *Winters on the Wannon*, Australia Felix Series, Deakin University Press, Warmambool, 1991.

7 Thomas Murphy to Samuel Pratt Winter, 31 October 1848 in Winter Cooke Papers, La Trobe Library.

8 Phillip Guedalla, *The Duke,* Hodder and Stoughton, London, 1921, p. 3.

9 Arthur Young, op. cit., p. 303.

10 Ibid., p. 26.

11 M. Rutledge, 'William Rutledge – pioneer', *Victorian Historical Magazine*, no. 36, 1965.

12 Jonah Barrington, op. cit., p. 303.

13 Superintendent Charles La Trobe to Colonial Secretary, 3 Apr. 1840. Further correspondence relating to the incident is contained in Governor Gipps dispatches 1841–2, Mitchell Library, Sydney.

14 Elizabeth Bowen, *Bowen's Court and the Seven Winters: Memories of a Dublin Childhood,* Virago, London, 1984 (first published 1942) p. 218.

15 Constantia Maxwell, *Country and Town in Ireland Under the Georges,* Tempest, Dundalk, 1949, p. 27.

16 Ibid, p. 21.

17 Arthur Young, op. cit., p. 71.

18 L.P. Curtis Jnr., op. cit., p. 40.

19 Edith Somerville and Ross, Martin, *Irish Memories,* Longmans, Green, London, 1918, p. 71.

20 L.J. Curtis Jnr., op. cit., p. 40.

21 T.R. Henn, *The Lonely Tower,* second edition, London, 1956, p. 3.

22 Ibid., p. 5.

23 E. Bowen, op. cit., p. 248.

24 Ibid., p. 248.

25 Michael McConville, *From Ascendancy to Oblivion: The Story of the Anglo-Irish*, Quartet, London, 1986, p. 154.

26 Nora Robertson, *Crowned Harp: Memories of the Last Years of the Crown in Ireland,* Allen, Figis, Dublin, 1960, p. 99.

27 J.C. Beckett, *The Anglo-Irish Tradition, 1600–1921*, Faber, London, 1976, p. 73.

28 T.J. Kiernan, *The Irish Exiles in Australia*, Burns & Oats, Melbourne, 1954, p. 46.
29 Ibid.
30 J.C. Beckett, op. cit., p. 73.
31 Cited in J.C. Beckett, op. cit., p. 73.
32 Maria Edgeworth, *Castle Rackrent*, first published 1810, G. Watson ed., London, 1964, p. xxi.
33 J. Newcomber, *Maria Edgeworth. The Novelist*, Texas, 1967, p. 155.
34 Maria Edgeworth, op. cit., p. ii.
35 Michael McConville, op cit., and Mark Bence-Jones, *Twilight of the Ascendancy*, Constable, London, 1987.
36 Covernote M. McConville, ibid.
37 As well as *Irish Memories*, see Edith Somerville's novel *The Big Houses of Inver*, Longmans, Green, London, 1925.
38 Elizabeth Bowen, op. cit., p. 126.
39 E. Somerville and M. Ross, op. cit., p. 26.
40 Brian Inglis, *West Britain*, London, 1962, p. 15.
41 C. Maxwell, op. cit., p. 183.
42 J.C. Beckett, op. cit., p. 92.
43 Nora Robertson, op. cit., p. 101.

5
'Prospects of this New Colony': Letters of Ulster Emigrants to New Zealand 1840–1900

Trevor Parkhill

'By one of the Botany Bay ships we learn that Omai is dead and also two of his companions, the New Zealand youths Taiverharroa and Kokoa ...'. This small item was reported in the *Belfast News Letter* of 10 June 1789 and brought to the Ulster public's notice the prospect of communication with the indigenous peoples of New Zealand. It was not for another 50 years, however, that a letter dated 1 October 1840 records one of the earliest cases of migration from Ulster to New Zealand. Ann McCleland had clearly run away from home to New Zealand, via Liverpool, some time before the letter from her mother caught up with her in her new world:

> I suffered after you went away, grieving night and day about you. I hoped you would perhaps rued and changed your mind when you would go to Liverpool, but alas to my sorrow you went on leaving me ... As soon as possible write to me everything about you, both by sea and land, how you are fixed and if you met with friends since you left me ... Sister Nancy longs greatly to hear from you. She intends to go to you if you give her the least encouragement. She would have went with the bearer of this letter, but she wished to wait for a letter from you as she did not know whether you got over safe or not, or where she might find you, but if this comes to hand she expects you will delay no time in writing full and truely all you think and believe about the place as sister Nancy, brothers Samuel, Dilley [?] and Thomas Flack would be disposed to go if it was thought to be answerable ... the Rev. Mr Campbell was grieved that he did know when you went ... it is reported that the place is a wicked place and

little or no clergy or public worship. Please tell us some of the particulars of the treatment of the voyage, and how you came on since, what you are doing and where you worship on Sunday. Also the customs and manners of the people, the climate, produce, trade, lands and prospects of this new colony ... .[1]

This is an exceptional letter in every sense but it demonstrates the general value of correspondence to and from emigrants in its relation of some of the circumstances of the migration. And it is emigrants' letters that are among the most significant sources for a study of migration from Ulster to New Zealand. The McCleland letter is an example of what E. R. R. Green terms a 'reverse emigrant letter' – one written from Ireland to the emigrant in his or her new home and which has somehow been preserved in Ireland.[2] Generally, however, it is letters written in and sent from New Zealand that have survived in Ulster homes and have been deposited in the Public Record Office of Northern Ireland.

Both Green and Kerby Miller,[3] in the case of emigration to America, have adverted to the role emigrants' letters had in perpetuating the migration and it is widely evident in the letters of Ulster settlers in, for example, Pennsylvania in the eighteenth and nineteenth centuries. Their value as sources for a study of migration from Ireland to Australia has been well described by Patrick O'Farrell.[4] In effect, the success of one emigrant in his new environment acted as a spur to the other young people, especially men, at home. Just as crucial was the role of the person who had already emigrated in arranging accommodation and even employment for friends and acquaintances who joined him as soon as they arrived.

The value of emigrants' letters in fuelling the trends towards emigration from Ulster to New Zealand is apparent in a number of collections but none more so than in the correspondence sent back by first, John, and then Andrew (his brother) Gilmore, from Tauranga in 1876. Andrew writing to his brother Robert in Greyabbey, Co. Down in 1881 advises him:

> If you can come with your Mrs and family to Auckland you do not require to be afraid of getting along better than ever you will where you are. With the family you have got and coming [t]o a new land you need not expect to make a fortune but the family would get more

civilised and, I believe, better connected ... I would guarantee you a job for 6 or 12 months at ordinary wages. I also think we might go in together as partners.[5]

The effect the receipt of this letter might have had in reinforcing any thoughts Robert had on the prospect of emigration cannot be discounted. It is not, in fact, clear from subsequent correspondence whether Robert did take up Andrew's offer to be his brother's keeper, at least until he got himself established on arrival. A case can nonetheless be made from these albeit scattered examples for saying that the mechanics of chain migration are as evident in emigrants' letters from New Zealand as in those from Australia or America, although on a much reduced scale.

Emigrants' letters did not have to relate success in a triumphant manner to be effective in communicating the message that a move of such magnitude could work out well. James Moreland McClure's letter from Royal Bush, Invercargill of 17 September 1865 relates in a candid way the possibilities of both progress and setbacks for any new arrival. The overall tone, however, describes a society where an Ulsterman might, on reading it in his home, fancy his chances of modest gains and, if he was inclined to gamble for bigger stakes, head for the gold strikes:

> We are getting on slowly but *steadily* thank God. The changes in this colony are very sudden. Men one year apparently realising fortunes and the next losing everything. This has been the case with many whom we know and with the greater number, nearly all of the people in business in the town, the fluctuations in Colonial affairs being great and sudden. One friend refused to sell some land two years ago at £4 per acre and now offers it at 25/-shillings and cannot get it. Houses in town rented at £100 per annum now let at £25 or so less or merely to be kept in repair and 8 out of every 10 vacant. Yet in a year or two all will be bright again.
>
> We thank goodness through all have continued to hold our own and advance as well, not so fast as we should wish, but still improve. Our house is comfortable and is the best in the neighbourhood ... There has been a great discovery of gold on the west coast: Gordon will soon start for ['them'] diggins; he is right. My wife is all I could wish but do not run away with the idea that she is a humdrum

commonplace woman; she is a gentle woman in every sense of the world and respected and esteemed by all who know her; she is very handsome and only now 29.[6]

The prospects of work, independence, income, house and marriage as represented in McClure's letter must have appeared as a very attractive 'package' to his male kinsfolk and friends in Belfast who got to hear of the letter, or read it for themselves.

The general attractiveness of New Zealand was sharpened by the lure of gold which appeared in letters received in Ulster both from Australia and from New Zealand. Some of the earliest references to Ulstermen in New Zealand arise in fact in correspondence sent back from Australia, principally from young tradesmen who did not find their pot of gold in the diggings in Victoria which attracted them to the Antipodes in the first place, and who then graduated to New Zealand either in renewed search for gold or in an altogether different role. A case in point is Hugh Maguire who emigrated to Victoria in the early 1850s and in December 1853 wrote back to his brother in Strabane, Co. Tyrone:

> I was fourteen months upon the diggings and although I spent no money that I could avoid, and stuck constantly to the work, yet I have been able only to come to Melbourne with about sixty-five pounds sterling.

And, although he says 'I do not mean to give the diggings up, however, as I hope by perseverance to outhector Fortune', his letters by the late 1850s contain references to 'business is quick here at the moment, sales having fallen as low as £700 or £800 p.a.'[7]

He appears to be working for a clothing company, having been apprenticed to a tailor in Strabane before emigrating. By the mid-1860s his letters contain references to New Zealand:

> The war in New Zealand still remains in the position it did six months ago. The English troops, although some 2,000 strong, being afraid to attack the Maoris in their stronghold and in fact can only act on the defensive and in fact unless they are strongly reinforced I question very much if they will be able to maintain their position.

These references are informed enough to suggest that by then his commercial travelling for his company took him to New Zealand on a regular basis. Later still be mentions: 'I am about to sail by first steamer for New Zealand and expect to be absent about 4 months, as McCallum, Neville & Co. do business with the principal houses in nearly every sea port there ...'.[8] And the final letter in the Maguire collection is from J. D. Ranker, Hugh's former boss, in 1882, giving details of his firm's progress which suggests it was by then exclusively a New Zealand business. Maguire himself had, by then (1882), returned home from New Zealand to Strabane, Co. Tyrone, and had married.

A more determined assault in the Otago gold mines is the intent in the letters of Oliver McSparron. Writing from Tuapeka, Otago, to his father in Feeny, Co. Londonderry, in a letter of May 1869 he announces that he has postponed his journey home and is employed at the gold diggings: 'I have always had a great wish to try luck at the gold digging and I am determined to try my luck at last ...'.[9]

In addition to the increasing reputation of gold pickings in the colony, a more realistic prospect of New Zealand as a land of opportunity for those prepared to apply themselves, which was created by the letters of individual emigrants to their families in Ulster, was confirmed and reinforced by the appearance in the *Belfast News Letter* of 11 March 1875 of a letter from George Vesey Stewart. It announced the establishment of his colony of settlers at Kaitkati, perhaps the best known episode in the story of emigration from Ulster to New Zealand.

> To the editor of the *Belfast News Letter*:
>
> Sir, I send you the *Southern Cross*, Auckland newspapers dated 8th and 9th January last, in which you will see our special settlement at Kati-Kati is referred to in flattering terms. I have also received several private letters by the last mail announcing the pleasant intelligence that reefs of gold have been discovered in the vicinity of our block, and that shortly after our arrival we may expect an influx of population consequent on opening up a new gold district. My correspondence informs me that wages continue as high, if not higher, than what were current during my visit to the colony and that the demand for female servants was far in excess of the supply ... the prospects of the farmers were most encouraging. I have applied to the

governing to extend the area of our block ... our numbers at present consists of forty-seven families, including our Episcopalian and Presbyterian clergymen and doctor.

The appearance of Stewart's letter coincided with a series of advertisements which appeared in the Ulster newspapers at this time. Of particular interest are the notices directed specifically at young female adults. Although Andrew Gilmore's opinion about the prospects for female labour, contained in his letters from Tauranga, is that 'there is no outdoor work for girls here' and that 'they are very hard to keep',[10] there were opportunities for female labour as much as there were for males. One of the advertisements announced that 'A lady who proposes leaving this country for New Zealand in March next is desirous of taking out some single girls in the same ship with her. Free passages. Wages from £20 to £40 a year'.[11] In the 1840s the government of New South Wales and the Colonial Office, in association with the Poor Law Commissioners in Ireland, introduced a scheme to take out to Australia female orphans from the workhouses of Ireland as a means of restoring a better balance among the population. New Zealand had something of the same need, in its early years, for suitable females. Indeed, as D.H. Akenson says 'the 1870s and 1880s witnessed a major government immigration scheme, with most of the immigrants' expenses being paid by the colonial government'.[12]

Akenson also adverts to another characteristic of the emigrant trail from Ulster to New Zealand – the better quality of controlled conditions on board ship during the long voyage 'on ships that were more closely inspected with nutritional and medical matters more closely monitored'. Several of the emigrants' letters provide descriptions of the voyage and, in a journal kept by William Clarke of Beltany, Co. Tyrone during his passage in 1879, he provides a description of the rules to be observed on board ship by passengers. Clarke avers that, as a result of the strictness with which the rules were observed, 'a person won't get speaking to the closest female without being apprehended'.[13]

There is a variety of documentation relating to the continuing military role in which Ulstermen found themselves performing in New Zealand, either as British colonial forces or in the New Zealand Expeditionary Force in the First World War.[14] Perhaps the most remarkable letter from a soldier is that from J. N. Armstrong, an officer writing from Bell Block Blockade to his sister in Dublin, 3 December 1861. He describes accompanying Bishop Selwyn on a visit among sections of the indigenous peoples where there had been outbreaks of sectarian violence:

> ... he was I believe tolerably well received though the Taranakis endeavoured to prevent him passing through their country but without any violence towards him ... He explained to them the principles of the new system of government which Sir G. Grey proposes carrying out and they seem pleased with it and anxious to have Europeans settled among them.

Armstrong reports with disapproval that

> Let bygones be bygones in what the Bishop says and it is generally feared that that will be the principle upon which the government will act towards those rebels; if so, the prospects for Taranaki will not be cheering ... among a number of settlers there are sure to be some who on the very first opportunity would take the law into their own hands and then where would the friendship between the races be?

His own solution to the racial tension between Maoris and settlers reflects the colonising tenor of the mid-nineteen century:

> The more I think on the subject the more I am convinced that the perfect subjection of the Maori race to our rule is the only means humanly speaking of effecting permanent peace with them; let them find out the uselessness of prolonging the struggle with us and they will be more careful in future in taking up arms against us and more anxious to our terms of peace'.[15]

A feature of emigrants' letters from America and Australia is that a considerable proportion of them are long runs of correspondence between various members of a family, who usually emigrated over a period of time. This is not, however, reflected in the letters of emigrants to New Zealand partly because of the distance involved and the fact that there is a shorter time span between the arrival of emigrants to New Zealand and the introduction of more sophisticated means of keeping in contact with family in Ireland. Of the sources referred to here, only the McCleland, Gilmore and McClure letters form part of a collection. In addition, however, there are smaller groups of letters which, because enough is known about the value of emigrants' correspondence from elsewhere, may also be regarded as broadly representative of the experience of Ulster immigrants in New Zealand. In general terms, they relate to a story of modest achievement of Ulster emigrants making a new life in a country which, in climate, land and temperament of older settlers, was closer than America or Australia to their place of origin. That more than anything else may account for the steady stream of emigrants from Ulster (and from Munster) to New Zealand from the early 1860s.

Published in *Familia: Ulster Genealogical Review*, no. 5, 1989.

Notes

1. PRONI D3034/1–18. Ann McCleland married John Veldt, a German cabinet maker at Scotch Church, Wellington, 7 July 1843. They subsequently went to Valparaiso in Chile, visited Moneymore, Co. Londonderry, and finally returned to New Zealand.
2. E. R. R. Green in *Essays in Scotch-Irish History*, Ulster Historical Foundation, Belfast 1969.
3. *Emigrants and Exiles: Ireland and the Irish Exodus to North America*, Kerby A. Miller, O.U.P., 1985.
4. *Letters from Irish Australia 1825–1929,* Patrick O'Farrell. Published by New South Wales University Press and the Ulster Historical Foundation, 1984.
5. PRONI T1611/5.
6. PRONI D1745/5/2.
7. PRONI D1420/1/118.
8. PRONI D1420/1/122.
9. PRONI T2743/2/3.
10. PRONI T1611/5.
11. *Belfast News Letter,* 6 Mar. 1875, and subsequent issues.
12. Trevor McClaughlin, 'Barefoot and Pregnant', *Familia: Ulster Genealogical Review*, Vol. 2, No. 3 (1987). D.H. Akenson, 'The Irish in New Zealand', *Familia: Ulster Genealogical Review*, Vol. 2, No. 5 (1989).

[13] PRONI T2727.
[14] See particularly Trevor Parkhill, 'Sources for the Study of Emigration from Ulster to New Zealand 1840–1940' in Genealogical Research Institute of New Zealand *Yearbook* (1988) which discusses the papers of Sergeant R.J. Ross, born in Belfast and who fought in the New Zealand Expeditionary forces in Egypt and in Europe, with distinction, throughout the First World War.
[15] PRONI T1978/2.

6

Green Threads of Kinship!
Aspects of Irish Chain-Migration to New South Wales

Richard Reid

Growing up in Ireland the image of America loomed large for me as THE Irish emigrant destination. Australia was a distant echo in a solitary family letter from somewhere called Toowoomba in 1866. Written by my great, great uncle to his brother at Reskatirriff, County Tyrone, it spoke of exotic fauna, farm prices and the sorrow of family tragedy experienced in exile: 'I got your long looked for letters. I shut myself up in my room and read them a dozen times, but sorrowful news did they bring to me, your poor little namesake met with a sad end, such a fine bright boy as he was. I cannot restrain the tears from running down my cheeks when I think of it. My letter to you could not convey the tenth part of my suffering'.[1]

Years later in a NSW Municipal Cemetery I encountered again this nineteenth-century immigrant sense of exile. Carved on the gravestones were words and phrases revealing an enduring Irish identity with home: 'A native of Astrah, County Tyrone', 'Native of Tubbercurry, County Sligo', 'Born at West Meath', 'Native of Banagher, King's County'. Occasionally there is a precise definition of origin and identity as in 'Native of Annaghmore, County Tyrone'[2] for Annaghmore is a 'townland'. These small divisions of Irish parishes have been described by historical geographer, William Nolan, as 'possessing intimacy and association with homeplace … our most meaningful micro-regions of the mind'.[3] Within the nineteenth-century townland lived, in the words of Professor Estyn Evans, 'communities of related families bound together in 'friendship' – the word 'friend' means a blood relation in Ireland'.[4] To those critical of nineteenth-century Irish immigration to New South Wales, such as the Reverend John Dunmore Lang, it seemed that the worst effect of this immigration was the creation of closed Irish communities – 'townlands' in the bush as it were. An infamous example of this tendency was to be found at Boorowa, near Yass. Here, in Lang's words, was 'the headquarters and paradise of the Ryans, and might be supposed to be a veritable slice of the County of Tipperary'.[5]

No friend of Irish Roman Catholic immigration, Lang's attitude to it is neatly summarized in the title of his polemic against it 'The Fatal Mistake or how New South Wales has lost Caste in the World through misgovernment in the matter of immigration'.[6] Nevertheless he well understood the process that had produced an accumulation of Tipperary Ryans at Boorowa – chain-migration whereby a pioneer immigrant encourages out another family member, who encourages out a friend, who encourages out her uncles, aunts, cousins, and so on. Many contemporaries commented on this Irish commitment to family and friends. Giving evidence to the N.S.W. Legislative Assembly's Select Committee on Irish Female Immigrants in 1858 Sydney bookseller, Jeremiah Moore, cited as typical the case of an Irish orphan girl who had remitted home all her meagre savings to bring out her family. Moore recalled her employer, an Englishman, coming to him in great distress when news of the wreck of the 'Dunbar' off the Sydney heads first reached Sydney: '… I never saw any man in greater trouble'. He said 'I have a little Irish orphan girl … who has sent home all her savings to bring out her family, and if I cannot return home with good news of them, poor girl, I think she will break her heart!'[7]

However, anecdotal evidence of individual behaviour, while it points to the existence of chain-migration, goes nowhere near describing its extent, complexity of importance in the overall movement of approximately 90,000 free emigrants from Ireland to New South Wales in the fifty years between 1836 and 1886. An ideal period for a study of this process are the mid-century decades of the great Australian gold rushes, the 1850's and 1860's. Two factors account for this. Firstly, by the mid-1840's New South Wales had an Irish community of recently arrived government assisted immigrants and more established convicts and emancipists, both capable of exerting an influence on the choice of emigrant destination of family and friends at home. Secondly, throughout the 1850's and 1860's,

New South Wales continued to offer assisted passages to bring from Britain and Ireland that much needed class of labourers and domestic servants who could not afford the fare. As is well known the Irish were almost totally dependent upon state assistance to reach New South Wales at a time when the fare to Sydney was three to four times that to New York or Boston.[8] From the records created by the colonial Immigration Department to administer state assistance it is possible to draw out not only a general statistical picture of assisted immigration but also to observe patterns of individual, family and group behaviour. In short, using these records one can break down and describe the process of Irish immigration to New South Wales more precisely than for other major nineteenth-century Irish emigrant destination.[9]

When an assisted immigrant ship arrived in Sydney in the 1850's all on board were interviewed by the colonial Immigration Board and personal particulars recorded. This information included name, age, occupation, religion, place of origin, parent's names and brief address, and some details about relations already in New South Wales. Given the small space provided on the form for recording information concerning relatives what is recorded there is often but a signpost to a much wider network of colonial relatives and friends. One girl stated simply that she had a large number of cousins in the colony. In addition to these Board's Immigrant Lists as they are known, extensive records were being kept by the Immigration Department on the administration of the Remittance Regulations. This was a system of providing free passages, first introduced in 1848, whereby residents of New South Wales could pay a proportion of an immigrant's passage money in the colony and have their nominated friends and relatives brought out at government expense. The colonial nominator filled in a form giving basic particulars about the nominees – name, age, occupation, address and names of referees. In Sydney this information was then transcribed into ledgers.

Initial statistical analysis of these records hints at the existence of chain-migration. Approximately 44,960 assisted Irish arrived at ports within the present boundary of the state of New South Wales between 1848 and 1870.[10] They came from every county in Ireland but certain definite regional concentrations are evident. These were situated in the south west centred round Tipperary, Clare, Limerick, Cork and Galway, in the midlands round Offaly and Kilkenny, and in west Ulster in the counties of Tyrone, Fermanagh, Donegal, Armagh and Cavan. The range from the lowest to the highest county reveals the density of these concentrations. Louth on the east coast sent 141, Tipperary in the south west 7,240. Ever more revealing is the fact that if you met a recent arrival from Ireland in the streets of Sydney in the 1850s your chances of hearing a Clare or Tipperary accent were almost one in three. Compare the county figures for these years with those from the earlier years of assistance for which statistics are available – 1841/1845 – and with the final years of assisted passages – 1875/1886 – and the existence of these emigrant chains seems clear.[11] Virtually from the outset these same regional concentrations are evident and, with minor variations, persist for the fifty years which gave New South Wales its free Irish immigrant population.

If these statistics point to an enduring relationship between emigrant regions over time the ships' lists reveal the existence of similar relationships between individuals in all their variety and complexity. The *Emma Eugenia* arrived in Sydney in 9 June, 1849. On board was Thomas Lennane from Drumherst, County Clare with a cousin, Pat Donough, in West Maitland, Robert McDougall from Coleraine, County Derry with a brother in Maitland, Eliza Quinn from Ballymena, County Antrim with an aunt, Mary Maguire in Sydney, Sarah Newell from Bailieborough, County Cavan with four brothers and one sister in Maitland, and so on.[12] Presumably these relatives had all arrived in earlier years and quite possibly exerted some influence on those at home to follow them out.

With the implementation of the Remittance Regulations in the 1850's we can move beyond this assumption of influence to a recorded causal link between emigrant in Ireland and nominator in New South Wales. Fifty-eight per cent of all Irish assisted between 1848 and 1870 were so sponsored; indeed by the late 1850s virtually all Irish assisted were arriving under the Remittance Regulations. By bringing together the information on the ships' lists with that in the nomination records we can examine not just the total web of emigrant relationship between Ireland and New South Wales but unravel individual threads of that web linking individuals back to a Galway parish, even townland. What kinds of patterns can we see within the web?

Firstly there are the one to one relationships – one immigrant bringing out one member of the family. Bridget Davies of Scariff,

County Clare came to Sydney in February 1850 on the 'Thomas Arbuthnot' under the British government's orphan emigration scheme from Irish workhouses during the Great Famine.[13] Bridget's willingness to put herself forward for selection for New South Wales may have had something to do with the fact that she had an uncle in the colony. However, on arrival she made no mention of him. In November 1853 a Patrick Davies arrived from Scariff and declared Bridget Davies to be his sister. From family letters we know Patrick induced her to sponsor him. Writing from the townland of Gortaveha, parish of Feakle, County Clare on the 7th of August, 1852 Bridget's uncle, Matthew Kennedy, conveyed to her Pat's anxiety to join her in New South Wales: '... your brother Pat is in anxiety to go to you when he read your letter he cried as you did not send for him do not delay as he will repay you accordingly as he will earn it'.[14] From then on Pat and Bridget disappear from the records and do not appear to have sponsored any further family and friends. Which is not to say that letters they may have written home did not entice out others from Scariff.

A second pattern visible in the records reveals a complex chain through inter-related families stretching often over many decades back to specific parishes within those areas of emigrant concentration already described. Bridget and Pat after all were but part of a larger movement of people from Scariff to Sydney. Tipperary, however, is a good county from which to elicit one of these complex chains; it was Tipperary, that Reverend Lang encountered at Boorowa. It was also Boorowa, and its Tipperary characteristics which produced the old story that if you asked a Boorowa man 'Have you been to Ireland?' he would reply. 'No, but I've been to Boorowa'.[15] Virtually every parish in Tipperary was represented on the shipping lists in Sydney but one which developed a close connection with Boorowa was Clonoulty, situated roughly six kilometres north west of the Rock of Cashel. Between 1848 and 1870 346 assisted Irish gave their place of origin as Clonoulty, about 4.5 per cent of the Tipperary total and 8 per cent of the parish's 1851 population.[16] 173, 50 per cent of these Clonoulty emigrants, were sponsored. Here was a whole complex of kin and friendship relationships between Quinlans, Ryans, Dwyers, Butlers, Gleesons and many others.

One of these kinship/friendship groups involved the Corcoransm Dwyers, Ryans and Stapletons. On 11 March 1858 James Ryan nominated Thomas, Mary and Ellen Corcoran and a family of Dwyers all from Clonoulty.[17] According to the Board's List when Thomas arrived James Ryan was his brother-in-law and lived at Boorowa. Thomas settled there and in May 1864 nominated Stephen Stapleton of Clonoulty.[18] When Stephen arrived he said he already had a brother in the colony living at Boorowa.[19] This brother, Patrick, arrived in 1861 having been sponsored by a Malachi Dwyer who had arrived in 1855 with his family from Clonoulty saying he had a brother-in-law called Ryan in the colony.[20] And finally in 1865 a James Dwyer of Boorowa sponsored Stephen Stapleton's family from Clonoulty who duly arrived on the *Africana* in 1866.[21] Clearly there was a relationship between these Corcorans, Dwyers, Ryans and Stapletons; in fact it was a link stretching back to 1817 when two cousins, Ned Ryan and Roger Corcoran, were transported from Clonoulty. By the mid 1820s they were depasturing stock in the region beyond Yass round Boorowa.[22] This is only one small thread of the Tipperary – New South Wales connection; similar threads could have been unravelled through the records for a dozen other parishes such as Quin in County Clare, Ballynakill in Galway, Shanagolden in Limerick, Muckalee in Kilkenny or Dromore in Tyrone.

A third pattern is one to be expected – the regrouping of whole families in the colony. Typical in this respect were the McQuades of Ballyshannon, County Donegal. Hugh and Margaret McQuade appear to have had eight children; they appeared on immigrant ships arriving in Sydney in the following order, Margaret and Mary in 1859, Thomas and Celia in 1861, Catherine and Bridget in early 1863, Hugh in late 1863 and finally Anne with Hugh and Margaret themselves in 1867.[23] Margaret who arrived in 1859 appears as the sponsor for the other members of the family. So it would seem that all the McQuades came to New South Wales over eight years. Or did they? A similar emigration pattern is visible in the Miskelly family from Glenarm in County Antrim. Mary Miskelly, a widow, and her eight children all emigrated to the Goulburn area between 1859 and 1863. Irish records however, show that one of Mary's sons remained in Ireland on a small farm in Glenarm.

These patterns described so far all revolve around clear kin relationships. A fourth pattern revolved round a colonial middleman nominating either on behalf of others in the colony or even, as seems likely, on behalf of prospective emigrants in Ireland who would send him or her the required sponsorship money. Naturally the records are silent on the incidence of these remittances in reverse as it were. In January 1862 Nixon Fife of Goulburn sponsored a Sarah Logan of Ballinamallard, County Fermanagh in addition to his two brothers.[24] He was induced to do this by his father, William Fife of Drumcullion, Ballinamallard. William wrote to Nixon of how a neighbour, Sarah Logan, was urging him to send a cheque for three pounds to Nixon, this being the sum required in the colony to nominate a single female.[25]

James Madden is a more dramatic example of middleman activity. He arrived in Sydney from O'Briesbridge, County Clare in 1851. Between 1862 and 1865 he nominated no less than 86 people from that same region of Clare.[26] A check on 14 of these nominees who arrived on two ships in 1863, the *Peerless* and the *Severn*, reveals no family relationship with their sponsor and indeed only two of them had any relatives in the colony.[27]

Finally there is a spectacular example of what could be called a generalised sense of kinship on the part of the Irish community in New South Wales with those at home who possessed no means of escaping to greater opportunities overseas. On July 8, 1858, acting on behalf of the 'Donegal Relief Committee' of Sydney, Dean McEncroe deposited enough money with the Immigration Agent to bring out 225 people from Donegal.[28] This was to be the first of a series of deposits which brought out approximately 1,200 emigrants from Donegal to Sydney between 1859 and 1864. The vast majority of them came from the remote Gweedore/Cloghaneely region of the north-west coast, an area described by their parish priests in 1858 as, 'the bleakest and most mountainous in Ireland ... broken up by huge, abrupt and irregular hills of granite, covered with a texture of stunted health, while the space between is but a shaking and splongey marsh'.[29] These lines come from an appeal published by these same priests in January 1858 on behalf of the people of Gweedore and Cloghaneely, who they described as in need of rescue 'from death and starvation'.[30] The response of Sydney's Celtic Association was the formation of the 'Donegal Relief Committee' to raise money among the Irish of New South Wales, to whom, in the words of an open letter to the Committee, belonged 'the duty of bringing those victims of tyrannous exaction and evil laws to a land of freedom where they may by honest toil earn a future livelihood'.[31] Englishmen were not excluded from contributing and Anglican cleric, H.N. Woolfrey, asked the Committee to 'accept the mite of a poor Saxon priest'.[32]

Having collected sufficient funds the Committee approached the Colonial Secretary for permission to appoint an agent in Ireland to nominate locally those from Donegal willing to accept a passage to Sydney. The first ship carrying Relief Committee immigrants, the *Sapphire*, arrived on 24 May 1859. Virtually all on board were from Gweedore and Cloghaneely and the complexity of the possible relationships between them emerges from the *Sapphire*'s list which recorded no less than 33 Gallaghers.[33] Within two years the names Gallagher and Cloghaneely began appearing in the nomination records.

Such a group might be thought to be an ideal target for those who, in New South Wales, opposed Irish immigration; they were extremely poor, largely unskilled, Gaelic speaking and Roman Catholic. An official at the Birkenhead Emigrant Depot in England, through which the Donegal people passed on their way to Sydney, was not impressed with them:

> The difficulty in dealing with these people is that they do not speak English and of making them understand the requirements of the Board as to clothing. What has sufficed them at home they consider sufficient on board ship ... Their filthy habits render them very undesirable emigrants, but of course the Commissioners are not responsible for their selection.[34]

That champion of Protestantism in New South Wales, John Dunmore Lang, was silent. He saw the Donegal people as victims of a greater enemy than the Pope – those Anglo-Irish landlords who he saw as living off the tenantry of Gweedore and Cloghaneely and doing little to alleviate their distress. He contributed £1 to the Relief Committee.[35]

These emigrant chains, visible in the records of the Remittance Regulations, had the obvious effect of ensuring the persistence over time of regional concentration of emigration to New South Wales. At times, as in the case of the Corcorans of Boorowa, they point back to the very origin of the movement in the convict past. With the

Donegal immigrants the whole process begins anew and extends into the 1870s and 1880s. Indeed the extension of family ties over time revealed in these records, alerts us to the dangers of drawing conclusions about the nature of the whole process of Irish emigration to New South Wales from any limited period of ten years. Ulster Protestant emigration to Kiama, for example, from distinct parishes in Tyrone and Fermanagh begins with the Osborne brothers of Dromore, Tyrone in the 1820s and extends through to the 1880s when emigrants from those same regions were being sponsored out by kith and kin in Kiama. What was being created in New South Wales throughout the nineteenth century was not just an amorphous Irish community but one derived from distinctive sub-regions of Ireland. However the effect of having the majority of the colony's Irish Roman Catholic population largely from south and west Ulster is another problem, as is the whole question of the social composition of these immigrants.

However these New South Wales immigration records can be manipulated to show the complexity of immigrant behaviour, they convey little of the emotional experience and effects of the process. One distinct region of Protestant emigration in Ulster was an area north of Enniskillen in Fermanagh stretching round the shores of Lough Erne to Pettigo in the west and north into Tyrone as far as the town of Omagh. A small thread of this movement involved the five children of William Fife of Drumcullion, parish of Magheracross, by his first wife, Bessie Nixon. All of them left for New South Wales as nominated emigrants between 1859 and 1865. Generally our understanding of the effect of emigration on individuals comes from the diaries and letters of the emigrants themselves; in the case of the Fifes, who lived on at Drumcullion till 1881, to his children in New South Wales. The post-Famine Irish farmer has recently been depicted as a calculating 'Economic man', the world to send home remittances to keep the family farm intact.[36] William might have fitted this picture as from two marriages he produced 13 children, most of whom emigrated and who may well have sent home money to support him.

But this is not the William Fife of his letters to his scattered children in New South Wales between 1860 and 1879. Farm prices, local disasters, curiosity about his son Nixon's life as a bullock driver and advice on health and behaviour – this is the small talk of his correspondence. At a deeper level is the trauma of emigration, its unsettling effect on the community, the parent at home yet in exile from the family 12,000 miles away. In his *Letters From Irish Australia 1825–1929* Professor O'Farrell talks of an Ireland exploding, literally disintegrating under the impact of the mass exodus of the post-Famine period.[37] William Fife was caught up in that disintegration. Sarah Logan, who had approached him for sponsorship, had been affected by, in William's words, 'the news of the Australian letters [running] through the country like wildfire'.[38] William was no exponent of emigration feeling it to 'be a very serious thing to advise anyone to go there'.[39] America too was exerting its influence: 'the emigration to America is beyond description there cannot be ships got to take them, three thousand has left Derry this spring'.[40]

Leave taking, one of the emotional high points of the emigrant experience, was a common event in Drumcullion. In December 1865 William watched two of his children, James and Eliza, depart for Sydney:

> I hope I will never witness such a parting as that was, every one bewailing their own, but no, that farewell brought to mind all the former ones with me, Thomas Heaslip is with Eliza and James, and two of the Croziers from Ballinamallard and many others from below Irvinestown ...[41]

Here indeed was a small Irish community exploding outwards over the earth.

The former leave taking brought to mind for William, the first he had experienced which touched his own children, was that of Nixon and Faithey's departure from Derry in 1859. His letter describing it conveys an emotional intensity beyond transcription: 'Both of yous mentioned that you saw me on the quay at Derry when the Boat was going out, that was the second or third time that I stole down as it were from I parted with yous, I kept a distance thinking I might see yous in the crowd among the people I did not wish that either of yous would see me as I did not wish to have a second parting, the thoughts of parting with yous so preyed upon me that I wished the moment to arrive that I might have it past. My dear children you might think this strange of your father although I parted with you in body my heart and the affections of a father went with yous, I thought I would have stopped in Foyle Street until the boat would have gone away, but when I saw her going away I hurried down close to the side of the water thinking I might have got one sight of Faithey's Black Bonnet or your jacket ... I then came to the side of the wall where I bid yous farewell and I stood until I could not discern the Liverpool boat from the Glasgow one, the cry of my heart at that moment was Farewell, Farewell, Farewell my children ... I often wish I could forget the moment I took my last look at yous both, But it is not so recollection is ever at hand with me and when I think and think again am I never to see either of yous in this Life this is what wounds my heart the thoughts of this seems to haunt me like a spirit ...'[42] In this letter William journeys with Nixon and Faithey to Sydney in spirit, feels the danger and alarm of the storm at sea, shares with them the elation of arrival and their sense of being strangers in a strange land.

Now the whole importance of the colonial sponsor, but a name in the Remittance Regulations, is revealed. The Fifes were nominated by Mary Keenan of Goulburn, who had left Ballinamallard in the mid 1850s. William realises what it must have meant to Nixon and Faithey to have waiting for them at Goulburn a familiar face 12,000 miles from Drumcullion: 'I was sorry when I saw the expense that attended yous to Goulburn, it was well you had your never to be forgotten friend Mary Keenan Before you ...'.[43]

There is one entry in the ledgers however, which conceals a remarkable story, exemplifying this disintegration of Irish society and the reassembling of some of its fragments on the far side of the earth. In 1853 a John Tighe sponsored a Margaret and Mary Tighe, a John and Honora McDonough and a Patrick McDonough.[44] None of them arrived as assisted immigrants and, but for a letter in the correspondence of the Immigration Department, this family's experiences would have remained hidden from history.

The letter was written by Edward Feeny, parish priest of Riverstown, County Sligo to John Tighe of Wollongong on 18th August 1848 during the Great Famine. From documentation accompanying this letter Tighe is shown to have been a convict transported from Sligo in 1833. One can only assume John's reaction to the information Feeny now gives him:

> On receipt of your letter I sent for your wife as I was well acquainted with all your friends and family since I came to this parish, this is five

years ago. Your two daughters are also alive – the eldest, Honora was married by me about three years ago to a young man, John McDonogh of Drimshonagh – they have one child, a son, about two years old – the second girl, Mary, has been living with her uncle Pat McDonogh of Annaghcarty for the last three years. She is a very good, dutiful and industrious young girl – your wife has been living in Annaghcarty as also Honora and her husband in a house belonging to Patt McDonogh, her brother, during the last year, as the landlord of Heapstown, Mr McTernan, obliged all the small cottiers to leave his land – your brother Hugh Tighe, left this country about twelve weeks ago for America – I read a letter from New York which came on yesterday to another parishioner of mine in which it stated that Hugh Tighe landed there the day before that letter had been written. Hugh often told me during the past year that he would strive to travel as far as you to Sydney if the Lord should please to spare his life. Your mother died about last April twelvemonth, your sister Nancy and her husband are still living at Heapstown but in poor circumstances.[45]

There were at least five recorded attempts to bring John's family from Ireland. On the expiry of his sentence in 1841 he applied, as an emancipist of good record, to have them brought to the colony at the expense of the British government.[46] He made a similar application to the Convict Department in 1848 and he sponsored them again under the Remittance Regulations in 1853.[47] Also in 1847 Caroline Chisholm twice offered the family a free passage but Feeny's letter reveals why they were unable to avail of her offer:

> I recollect the time Mrs Chisholm's letters arrived here for her to go as far as London and to get a free passage for them. But it so happened that your poor wife, and all the family, were then in the fever, some of them recovering slowly, and others only in the commencement.[48]

At some point in the 1850's the Tighes and McDonaghs certainly reached Wollongong. John Tighe, Margaret Tighe, Honora McDonagh and John McDonagh be buried side by side in Wollongong General Cemetery testifying to the eventual success which crowned one convict's determination to reassemble his fragment of the townland of Heapstown in New South Wales.

Chain-migration functioned as a social mechanism, easing the immigrant's inevitable sense of exile and loss by making it possible to surround themselves with some familiar faces. Using the Remittance Regulations they could fulfil kinship obligations and try to recreate, however partially and fleetingly, something of the atmosphere of the townlands of their past. On their gravestones their colonial born children, knowing nothing beyond parental memories of Reskatirriff, Scariff, Clonoulty, Ballyshannon, Drumcullion or Heapstown, testified to the enduring hold of these places on their parent's minds by having inscriptions cut in stone such as this one in Queanbeyan Cemetery: 'Margaret Grady, A Native of Mother Ireland'.

Published in *Familia: Ulster Genealogical Review*, no. 3, 1987.

Notes

1. James Reid to Thomas Reid, 4 Apr. 1866, in possession of R. Reid, Canberra.
2. Gravestone inscriptions, Roman Catholic section, Riverside Cemetery, Queanbeyan, NSW.
3. William Nolan, *Tracing the Past: Sources for Local Studies in the Republic of Ireland*, Dublin, 1982, p. 21.
4. E. Estyn Evans, *Irish Heritage*, Dundalk, 1943, p. 48.
5. Reverend D.D. Lang, *Notes of a Trip to the Westward and Southward*, Sydney, 1862, p. 27.
6. Reverend D.D. Lang, *The Fatal Mistake, Sydney*, 1875. See especially p. 29 for Lang's views on the baleful effect of Irish Roman Catholic immigration on NSW.
7. Evidence of Jeremiah Moore, *Report From the Select Committee on Irish Female Immigrants*, Sydney, 1859, p. 27.
8. R.B. Madwig, *Immigration into Eastern Australia, 1788–1851*, Sydney, 1969, p. 60.
9. Records relating to assisted immigration held by Archives Office of N.S.W. are described in *Guide to Shipping and Free Passenger Records, Concise Guide to the State Archives of New South Wales* and various quarterly *Supplements* to the *Concise Guide*, all published by A.O. of NSW.
10. Statistics compiled by author using NSW Immigration Board's shipping lists, 1848–70.

[11] NSW Immigration Agent's Reports, 1840–86, *Votes and Proceedings if the Legislative Council*, Sydney, 1840–86.
[12] Board's List, 'Emma Eugenia', Archives Office of NSW (hereafter AONSW) 4/4908.
[13] Board's List, 'Thomas Arbuthnot', AONSW, 4/4914.
[14] Letter, Matthew Kennedy to Bridget Davies, 7/8/1852, in possession of Mr Col Graham, Sydney.
[15] 'Reminiscences of Marguerite Dale', quoted in James Waldersee, *Catholic Society in New South Wales, 1788–1860*, Sydney, 1974, p. 156.
[16] Board's Lists, various ships, 1848–1870, AONSW; *Census of Ireland*, 1851.
[17] Immigration Deposit's Journal, December 1857–1858, AONSW, 4/4579.
[18] Ibid. AONSW, 4/4586.
[19] Board's List, 'Himalaya', 3 Mar. 1865, AONSW, 4/4989.
[20] Agent's List, 'British Trident', 7 Jan. 1861, AONSW, 4/4796; Board's List, 'Matoaka', 17 May, 1855, AONSW, 4/4952.
[21] Board's List, 'Africana', 15 March, 1855, AONSW, 4/4991.
[22] Waldersee, *Catholic Society*, p. 150.
[23] Board's Lists, various ships, 1859–1867, AONSW.
[24] Immigration Deposits Journal, January 1862, AONSW, 4/4583.
[25] Letter, William Fife to Nixon Fife, 11 Nov. 1860, in possession of Fife family, Wagga Wagga, NSW.
[26] Board's Lists, various ships, 1862–5, AONSW.
[27] Board's Lists, 'Peerless', 23 Sep. 1863, AONSW, 4/4984; 'Severn', 10 Oct. 1863, AONSW, 4/4985.
[28] Immigration Deposits Journal, December 1857–8, AONSW 4/4579.
[29] 'Appeal' by Roman Catholic clergy, N.W. Donegal, *Freeman's Journal*, Sydney, 12 May 1858.
[30] Ibid.
[31] *Freeman's Journal*, Sydney, 12 May 1858.
[32] *Freeman's Journal*, 22 May 1858.
[33] Board's List, 'Sapphire', 24 May 1859, AONSW, 4/4980.
[34] Letter, James Chant, Birkenhead Depot to S. Walcott, Land and Emigration Commissioners, 15 Dec. 1863, Ship's Papers, 'Montrose', 27 Mar. 1864, AONSW, 9/6284.
[35] Letter, Reverend John Dunmore Lang, *Freeman's Journal*, Sydney, 5 June 1858.
[36] See David Fitzpatrick, *Irish Emigration, 1801–1921*, Dublin, 1984, pp 29–30.
[37] Patrick O'Farrell, *Letters from Irish Australia 1825–1929*, Belfast/Sydney, 1984, p. 6.

38 Letter, William Fife to Nixon Fife, 11 Nov. 1861, Fife family, Wagga Wagga, NSW.
39 Letter, William Fife to Faithey Fife, 11 Nov. 1860.
40 Letter, William Fife to Nixon Fife, 12 May 1864.
41 Letter, William Fife to Nixon Fife, 10 Dec.1865.
42 Letter, William Fife to Nixon Fife, 18 Jan. 1860.
43 Ibid.
44 Immigration Deposit's Journal, 1853/1854, AONSW, 4/4/576.
45 Letter, Father E. Feeny to John Tighe, 18 Aug. 1848, Immigration Correspondence, AONSW, 9/6191.
46 Applications for free passage for wives and families of convicts, 1835–42, AONSW, 4/2550.
47 Returns of convicts, applications for wives and families to be brought to NSW at the Government's expense, 1847–50, AONSW, 4/4533.
48 Feeny to Tighe, loc. cit.

7

Lives moved to New South Wales Free Passage for Convicts' Families

Perry McIntyre

Abstract

Between 1788 and 1840, 80,000 mainly English and Irish convicts were transported to New South Wales. A considerable number of studies of convicts have appeared in the last twenty years but detailed studies of free emigration to colonial Australia prior to 1840 are surprisingly few and assumptions remain that any examination of the people in the early colony would simply address convict populations. Convicts have been regarded as a people without choice but for one group of approved and well-behaved convicts the British and colonial governments facilitated colonisation through family reunion. Over 2,000 married convicts applied under a formal scheme for their families to have a free passage to the colony. This paper looks at the 237 Ulstermen who took up the scheme available to reformed convicts and applied for their families. It provides a glimpse of their experiences and cuts across historical assumptions about convicts, transportation, emigration and the colony of New South Wales, making connections that are otherwise obscured. Historical understanding is informed by detailed studies such as this which show how personal and family life impinged on the broader economical and political events in Ulster and the colonies.

Under Governor Lachlan Macquarie, who arrived in New South Wales in 1810, huge changes were made to the colony which had been established as a place to dispose of the convict population of Great Britain and Ireland twenty-one years earlier with the arrival of the first convicts from England. Macquarie's vision was to transform this penal colony into a productive settlement. He erected substantial buildings and innovated road work schemes. As well as these physical changes, he implemented new policies, many of which, naturally enough related to convict management and reform. These innovations included the beginnings of an immigration scheme whereby the families of reformed transported married men who had demonstrated good behaviour in the colony and a willingness to embrace the values of colonial life, could have their families brought to the colony free of charge. This article focuses on what was the first immigration scheme to Australia, linking transportation and free immigration. It was formally gazetted under Governor Macquarie in 1817 but had existed in an *ad hoc* manner from the very beginning of transportation to New South Wales in 1788.

Some men transported on the second fleet in the early 1790s and following the 1798 rebellion in Ireland had their wives or *de facto* wives accompany them. Of the approximately 1,000 men transported from Ireland between 1800 and 1806 on six ships, at least 500 are identified as political prisoners.[1] Many of these men differed from other convicts because they were educated and 'articulate, as well as politically trained and (often) militarily experienced'[2] which explained the paranoia associated with their arrival in the colony.[3] Rev. Henry Fulton, John Brennan and Edward Tully, all transported from Ireland on the *Friendship* in 1800 for political crimes, were accompanied by their families.[4] Andrew Doyle, having escaped the death sentence for forgery, was accompanied on the *Rolla* transport in 1803 by his wife and three children who travelled as cabin passengers. This separation from his homeland was far from a distressing voyage of banishment. Doyle described the month they spent in Rio de Janeiro on the way as 'the happiest days we ever spent in our lives.'[5] Hugh Byrne and Michael Dwyer transported on the *Tellicherry* in 1806 were two Wicklow state prisoners accompanied by their families.[6] The permission for these Irish men to have their families was perhaps a means of ensuring they remained in the colony and that their insurgent activities and influences would have little impact in Ireland.

By 1804 the British government accepted Arthur Phillips' argument that established families would contribute to the development of the colony. By the time it was gazetted in 1817, the process was very organised and regimented. A detailed application form had to be completed by any convict who indicated a keenness to be a respectable settler by requesting his family be sent out. By allowing ready-made families a free passage, the colonial and British governments believed they would contribute to the stability and growth in the colonies. The pleas of the women and children left behind fell on deaf ears unless the husband in the colony formally applied. While the early cited examples illustrate the formation of the scheme, it is well worth examining the Ulstermen who took advantage of this first scheme of assisted emigration to Australia.

Over 2,000 male convicts formally applied for their wives and children to come to New South Wales of whom 237 were natives of Ulster. A handful was tried away from their native countries but most were sentenced in courts in or near their home townland. What this analysis further indicates is that those who successfully achieved the aim to reunite their families contributed significantly to the gene pool of free people in the colony during this initial period of free settlement. While 237 men from the nine countries of Ulster applied for their families only 108 (46 per cent have been confirmed as being successfully reunited in the colony of New South Wales. However, the successful applicants contributed 404 free women and children to the settlement (see Table I below).

There is nothing uniform about the applicants other than that they formally expressed a desire to help their wives and children obtain a free passage. A large number had been transported for forgery, perjury, passing forged notes or making unlawful oaths: over 30 had stolen livestock in the form of sheep, horses, cattle, pigs and poultry; one man was a convicted rapist; 15 were transported for murder or manslaughter, one for aggravated assault, one was arsonist and Charles MacClean, a Belfast man, was transported on the *Minerva* in 1800 for political crimes. A number had been caught robbing houses, committing highway robbery, and two stole yarn. Lesser offences (depending on what they actually stole of course) were perhaps the pick-pockets, those who stole leather, furniture, or cloth from the bleaching greens throughout Ulster. Others made off with harness, a kettle, timber, vegetables from a garden and a quantity of oats. For these crimes only six received a sentence of ten years and 38 were transported for 14 years. The shortest sentence of seven years was given to 92 Ulstermen and an almost equal number, 96, were transported for life.

TABLE I
Ulster convicts in NSW who applied for family left in Ireland

Native place in Ulster	Male convict applicants	No. of families arrived	Individual family members
Cavan	46	18	58
Antrim	40	18	60
Tyrone	34	14	40
Down	31	14	61
Armagh	23	17	78
Derry	21	8	33
Monaghan	16	7	15
Donegal	14	8	38
Fermanagh	12	5	21
TOTAL	237	109 (*c.* 46%)	404

What is also of interest here is to look briefly at how many convicts from Ulster were transported to New South Wales. Due to the work of Peter Mayberry in Canberra it is now possible to search electronically for Irish convicts transported to New South Wales, not only by their names but by any of the fields on the convict indents.[7] Thus a search for each country as a trial place and native place was undertaken and appears in Table II. Additionally, by searching a combination of 'native place' and 'marital status' a figure for the number from each country who were married was obtained. No search for widower or variation was undertaken as this would have complicated this simple search, although there were a few widowers who applied for a free passage for their children, particularly after remarrying in the colony. Similarly a search in the marital status field under father, mother, brother, sister, aunt, uncle, son, daughter etc would have revealed other colonial relationships. I simply wanted an overview figure from each county to compare with the numbers who formally applied for family members under the wives and families of convicts scheme.

Each table was sorted showing the largest number from each county as the first line. So from Table I it is straightforward to see that 46 convict men from Co. Cavan applied for their families and 18 were successful in obtaining a free passage for an eventual total of 58 family members. Table 2 shows that 520 convicts born in Co. Cavan were transported to NSW, 102 of who were married. Thus 46 of the 102 (45%) married convicts from Cavan applied for family members under the wives and families of convicts scheme. This analysis, although very simplistic and open to errors on many levels does open an area for further research. Other factors would need to be analysed in greater depth. For example, native places and marital status was not recorded on quite a number of the indents, particularly before 1826. Even the recording of Londonderry or Derry has given a variation in this analysis indicated but these raw figures alone are of historical interest and thanks goes to Peter Mayberry for painstakingly going through all the convict ships to New South Wales and extracting those from Ireland. His database will be a brilliant tool of convict analysis in Ireland and the diaspora. The rest of this moves from the basic statistics to the individual experiences of the convicts and their families.

In early 1822, political prisoner Charles MacClean wrote a letter to his daughter, Elizabeth, living at 39 Brown Street, Belfast, to let her know he had permission to bring her to the colony.[8] He had applied for Elizabeth and her sister Mary Ann. No arrival was located but Colonial Secretary's correspondence the previous year shows that Charles was working as a constable and, with his wife and another unnamed daughter, was supplied with food from the government stores. By the time of his application for two other daughters in 1822 he had an assigned convict servant and two years later applied to lease land in Sydney.[9] He was obviously the kind of settler envisioned by the instigators of this emigration scheme. After twenty years in the colony he had proved himself reformed and was accepted as a respectable citizen capable of supporting his family and worthy to have them join him at government expense.

TABLE II

County [combined with native place]	Native Place	Trial Place	Married
Antrim	1139	938	159
Down	661	603	120
Armagh	510	509	107
Cavan	520	447	102
Tyrone	563	435	123
Monaghan	445	397	99
Londonderry/Derry	250/453	320/329	48/102
Fermanagh	298	254	73
Donegal	288	211	58
TOTAL	4674/4877	4114/4123	889/943

The life stories of men some men like MacClean who arrived in the colony in 1800 are often difficult to reconstruct while others are much easier to piece together. Connor Quinlan, variously Cullen, from Killinkere near Bailieborough, Co. Cavan, was forty years of age when tried for house robbery in the Cavan assizes in 1820. A ploughman, he received a life sentence, arriving in Sydney per *Isabella* on 9 March 1822. He left behind seven children, ranging in age from Bartholomew aged 17 to Connor aged 4 and a wife, whom he had married in 1807. These details are all gleaned from convict records or correspondence to the Colonial Secretary in New South Wales. At the time of his application for his family in April 1823, Connor Quinlan worked for Phillip Ward, a settler at Bunbury Curran near Campbelltown within the environs of the modern Greater Sydney sprawl. Exactly three years later his wife, Mary and children arrived on the *Thames*. She immediately applied for her husband to be assigned to her, stating that she could not provide for the children without the 'joint exertion' of her husband. The petition was supported by the Catholic priest Rev. John Joseph Therry and three justices of the peace. Her plea was granted.[10]

In Cork the previous year Mary Quinlan was received into the Penitentiary House at Cork with her family and 83 other free women and children assembled there, waiting to be shipped to the colony.[11]

They were not prisoners but were given refuge while they awaited a suitable vessel to take them to the Antipodes. Dr Edward Trevor, in charge of organising the despatch from Cork, provided a list of the names and ages of all these free women and children with their dates of arrival in Cork. The Quinlans had left Cavan and made their way to Cork arriving at the Penitentiary House on 2 July 1825 where they remained until the *Thames* finally got away early in 1826. Similarly Edward Murray, a 33-year-old agricultural worker from Tyrone, arrived in New South Wales in July 1824 with a life sentence, and applied for his wife and children in 1826. His wife and youngest son Michael aged 4 arrived on the *City of Edinburgh*, the other four children arrived within a month on the *Sir Joseph Banks*.

Their life stories are not always simple, linear narratives of unrest, crime, transportation, reform and life happy ever after in an Utopian part of the British empire. There is evidence that some families survived despite the conduct of their convict relatives. Jacob Whitfield was a ploughman transported in 1822 from Tyrone. The convict indent records his age as 62 with a wife and six children. Sixteen months after his arrival he applied for a passage for his wife which was granted but she died on the way to the colony; however, three daughters and a son did arrive with a free passage. Whitfield was then assigned to one of his daughters but failed to take advantage of family support and by 1828 was in a chain gang.[12]

Despite his misbehaviour, his children survived and prospered in the colony. Within two years of their arrival, all three daughters had married ex-convict men and his youngest child, a son, was supported by one of his married sisters.[13] By 1832 Jacob Whitfield sought a new wife and twice applied to banns to remarry two different women, both very much his junior. His first application was to marry Jean Connell or Cornel, a convict per *Lord Liverpool* in 1831.[14] The other application was to marry Anne Lindsay who had been transported in 1832 on the *Southworth*.[15] The correspondence which resulted from these applications to marry sheds considerable light not only on the process of application to marry and the circumstances in individual cases but also and perhaps, more importantly in this example, the attitude of the two major government officials concerned – Fredeick Hely, the Principal Superintendent of Convicts, and Richard Bourke, the Governor.

Richard Hill, the Church of England minister to whom Whitfield applied in January 1832, refused the application because neither prisoner held the 'indulgence' of a ticket of leave.[16] The Governor asked that an enquiry be made into the case stating that he was 'very obverse to the prohibition of marriage.'[17] Hely was concerned about the forty year difference in ages between the bride and groom but conceded that Whitfeld was only nominally assigned to his daughter was 'virtually free', therefore not bound by rules as a convict. Hely had little doubt that this marriage was 'one of those disgusting matches of convenience which I am sorry to say are but too common in the Colony.' Despite his personal abhorrence, Hely could see 'no sufficient reason for refusing' to allow the marriage to proceed.[18]

The marriage to Jean Cornel took place in 1832 but she died the same year and Jacob again applied to marry the much younger Anne Lindsay.[19] This time his application was refused by the Presbyterian minister, Rev. John Dunmore Lang, following a report from the senior clerk to the Principal Superintendent of Convicts which stated the intending groom was 'not capable of maintaining a wife'. The report confirmed the first marriage had taken place ten months previously and that the wife had died shortly afterwards in hospital.[20] There is no indication or suggestion of foul play by Whitfield in the death of his young wife but perhaps the colonial authorities thought that Anne Lindsay could find a more suitable man than Jacob, who was aged in his early seventies by 1832. Despite the consent of both masters, Rev. Lang obviously agreed with Hely who noted that Whitfield was 'a very old and infirm man and certainly is not capable of maintaining a wife' and his second application to find a wife in the colony was refused.[21]

The extent to which these few case studies illustrate the diversity of convict material available in the colony highlights the sad loss of much of the convict records in Ireland. Some of these case studies have also been enhanced by Chief Secretary's Registered Papers in the National Archives in Dublin and a more extensive comparison needs to be made of Ulster men in general and the support system that may have existed in Ulster for the families abandoned when their primary breadwinner was transported. Those who behaved and successfully applied for free passages for their families had the chance to reform long standing relationships and benefit from colonial land grants and work together to pursue opportunities which must have appeared well beyond their hopes only a few years earlier when circumstances, crime and transportation had torn their families apart.

This paper is developed from the author's PhD which has been published as *Free Passage: The Reunion of Irish Convicts and their Families in Australia, 1788–1852* by Irish Academic Press.

Published in *Familia: Ulster Genealogical Review*, no. 26, 2010.

Notes

1. The six ships (in order of arrival) were the *Minerva, Friendship, Anne, Hercules, Atlas I, Atlas II*. Two others, the *Rolla* and *Tellicherry* arrived in 1806.
2. Michael Dwyer, Martin Burke, Hugh Byrne, Arthur Devlin and Samuel McAlister were a few known to possess military knowledge. Whitaker, Anne-Maree, *Unfinished Revolution: United Irishmen in New South Wales 1800–1810* (Darlinghurst: Crossing Press, 1994).
3. For more discussion on 1798 rebellion and those subsequently transported, see several works by Anne-Maree Whitaker, Ruan O'Donnell and Kevin Whelan. For example Ruan O'Donnell, 'General Joseph Holt and the Historians' in Bob Reece (ed.), *Irish Convicts: The Origins of Convicts Transported to Australia* (University College Dublin: Department of Modern History, 1989), pp 25–47. Kevin Whelan, *A Bibliography of the 1798 Rebellion* (Dublin: Keough-Notre Dame Centre and Four Courts Press, 2003) cites numerous works on the 1798 rebellion. Also see An tAthair Micheál Ó Súillebháin) *Sydney 1798 Memorial: Tomb of a man who fought an empire* (6/55 Gladstone Street, Kogarath NSW 2217: self-published, 2003), pp 7–9. Chris Lawlor, *In Search of Michael Dwyer* (Naas, Co. Kildare: Leinster Leader, 2003).
4. Whitaker, *Unfinished Revolution*, p. 201. *1814 Muster*, entry 4872, p. 110. Pamela Jeanne Fulton (ed.), *The Minerva Journal of John Washington Price, A Voyage from Cork, Ireland to Sydney, New South Wales, 1798–1800* (Carlton: Miegunyah Press, 2000), p. 60.
5. *HRA*, 1, IV, pp 573–7. Andrew Doyle letter, British Library MSS 35644, p. 295 in Whitaker, *Unfinished Business*, pp 81 & 168.

6 State prisoners were those who were suspected of being United Irishmen. In this case from Co. Wicklow, Ireland, an area which had a large concentration of political activity during 1798. Whitaker, *Unfinished Revolution*, p. 202. King to Camden, 22 Feb. 1806, *HRA*, 1, V, p. 636.

7 See http://members.pcug.org.au/~ppmay/convicts.htm

8 Miscellaneous Correspondence 1822, CO 201/111, p. 456.

9 Colonial Secretary correspondence, 8 Sep. 1821, SRNSW 4/5781, p.62; received an assigned convict, 20 Feb. 1822, SRNSW 4/4570D p.5 & application to lease land in Sydney, 25 Mar. 1824, SRNSW 4/3510, pp 580–81.

10 Mary Cullen petition received 4 May 1826, SRNSW 4/1637, 26/2538, p. 237; SRNSW 4/2079, 31/708.

11 NAI CSORP 1825/11913, Dublin, 4 Aug. 1824.

12 J. Whitfield per *Isabella*, Iron Gang No. 3, *1828 Census*.

13 Husband Jacob Whitfield per *Isabella* assigned to daughter who came per *Thames*, SRNSW 4/2097, 31/708; 1828 *Census* shows Mary aged 20, wife of Daniel Sweeney convict per *Daphne* 1819, Catherine aged 18, wife of William Aaron per *Prince Regent* 1821 and Judith wife of Edward Doyle per *Daphne* 1819 and William aged 12 living with the Sweeney family; also list of passengers on the ship *Thames,* compiled by Sidney Sheedy with notes, ML MSS 703, CY 3281.

14 He was aged 72 and she was 32; marriage Banns 1832, St James, Sydney, 10 Jan. 1832, SRNSW 4/2150.1.

15 He was aged 73 and she aged 22; marriage Banns, Scots Church, Sydney, 12 Dec. 1832, SRNSW 4/2150.5.

16 Annotation by Rev. Richard Hill, 24 Jan. 1832, Jacob Whitfield's petition to marry Jean Cornel, SRNSW 4/2134, 32/1216.

17 Gov. Richard Bourke, petition by Jacob Whitfield to marry Jean Cornel, SRNSW 4/2134, 32/1216.

18 F.A. Hely, petition by Jacob Whitfield to marry Jean Cornel, 7 Mar. 1832, SRNSW 4/2134, 32/1216.

19 Death of Jean Whitfield, aged 33, NSW Death 1832 65/102; marriage of Jacob Whitfield to Jean Connell, NSW marriage 1832 1038/16.

20 Annotations by Rev. J.D. Land 22 Dec. 1832 and Thomas Ryan, clerk to Hely, Dec 1832, SRNSW 4/2150.1, marriage banns, Scots Church, Sydney.

21 Marriage banns, Scots Church, 22 Dec. 1832, Rev, Dr Lang, SRNSW 4/2150.1

8

Barefoot and Pregnant? Female Orphans who Emigrated from Irish Workhouses to Australia, 1848–50

Trevor McClaughlin

One of the subjects neglected by family historians and historians of emigration is the role played by Irish women who went to settle in Australia in the nineteenth and twentieth centuries. Part of the problem is that so many sources were written by and concerned with men rather than women: it requires a real act of historical imagination to view things from the vantage point of the females themselves and to understand them on their own terms. How many readers, for example, know of Earl Grey's scheme whereby over 4,000 young adult women were sent from Irish workhouses to Australia, at the end of the Great Famine? The author is at present preparing a detailed monographic study of the emigration and settlement of these female orphans but is happy to share with the reader the results of some of his research to date.[1]

Most of the female orphans can be identified very precisely by means of shipping records in Australian archives. Shipping records in Sydney provide very full details of individual orphans, her name, age, birthplace, occupation, parents' names, address if still alive, religion, health, level of literacy and whether or not she had any complaints about the voyage and whether she had any relatives in the colony. Thus, for example, on the *Digby* which arrived in Sydney harbour, in April 1849, after a voyage of 109 days, from Plymouth, was Catherine Harrigan, a sixteen-year-old Roman Catholic girl who could neither read nor write but was in good health, could be employed as a domestic servant, was born in Ballintemple, County Cavan, the daughter of Barney and Ann, both of whom were dead, and who complains that 'the

Master struck her and beat her head against the bed and then blackened the eye of Ellen McF... who came to take her part'. Slightly less informative are the shipping lists in Melbourne: on board the *Pemberton* which arrived in Port Philip in May 1849, was Bridget McCartney a seventeen-year-old Roman Catholic housemaid from Mallow in County Cork who could read. Least informative of all are the shipping records in South Australia where the most that is available is simply an incomplete list of names, sometimes only reproduced in an Adelaide newspaper column on 'shipping arrivals'. It would be an extremely difficult and uncertain task to reconstruct the lives of 606 orphans who went to South Australia. Many, if not most, of them are lost to us.

In addition, the names of the vessels carrying the orphans and the dates of their departure from Plymouth and arrival in Adelaide, Sydney or Melbourne are also known. The departure date is important because about seven or ten days before this date, the young women would have been discharged from their workhouse, and taken to their port of embarkation in England. This knowledge helps identify individual orphans in workhouse registers where these have survived, as it happens, mostly in Northern Irish unions.

Before going any further it should be made clear that the female orphans were not children for they were all ostensibly fourteen years and over; the charge for their passage to Australia would be that of an adult. Remember, too, that the Australian colonist was paying the cost of their passage. In a few cases the young women even had both of their parents still alive. Rather more of them, about 25%, had one parent still alive. The important thing was that the parents were unable to look after their daughter. Perhaps they had deserted her, were in gaol, in the Poor House itself, in a lunatic asylum or incapacitated in some other way. In effect, the orphans of Earl Grey's female emigration scheme had to have come from an Irish workhouse and to have travelled to Australia in one of the following vessels. The date of departure and arrival of each vessel is provided to assist readers who may wish to do research for themselves.

TO SYDNEY went the *Earl Grey* (3/6/1848–4/10/1848), *Inchinnan* (4/11/48–13/2/49), *Digby* (16/12/48–4/4/49), *Lady Peel* (14/3/49–3/7/49), *William & Mary* (25/7/49–21/11/49), *Lismoyne* (22/8/49–29/11/49), *Panama* (6/10/49–1/1/50), *Thomas Arbuthnot, John Knox*

(6/12/49–29/4/50), *Maria* (7/3/50–29/6/50)
and *Tippoo Saib* (8/4/50–30/7/50).

TO ADELAIDE, the *Roman Emperor* (27/7/48–23/10/48), *Ramillies* (10/12/48–April(?) 1849), *Inconstant* (15/2/49–8/6/49) and *Elgin* (31/5/49–11/9/49).

TO MELBOURNE, the *Lady Kennaway* (11/9/48–6/12/48), *New Liverpool* (25/4/49–9/8/49), *Pemberton* (29/1/49–14/5/49), *Diadem* (13/10/49–1/50), *Derwent* (9/11/49–26/2/50) and *Eliza Caroline* (31/12/49–31/3/50).

To date many orphans have been identified in workhouse registers in the Public Record Office of Northern Ireland and the Public Record Office of Ireland. As an example those on the Earl Grey are given below.[2] In some instances, more information than their admission and discharge, on the occasion immediately before their leaving for Australia, is given; a demonstration of how useful workhouse registers can be in reconstructing family histories.

The female orphan immigration scheme was designed to help solve a labour problem in the Australian colonies, redress the balance of the sexes which stood at two males to one female in the cities and eight males to one female 'beyond the boundaries' and apply a woman's civilizing influence as well. Despite the controversy and prejudice which brought the scheme so quickly to an end, it seems to have succeeded admirably in the eyes of its Victorian social engineers. What other results it had, from the point of view of the women themselves, yet remain to be seen.

Published in *Familia: Ulster Genealogical Review*, no. 3, 1987.

Notes

[1] The author extends his warmest gratitude to Macquarie University and the Australian Research Grants Scheme for their financial support and to Roisin Lundy, Evelyn McKittrick and the staff of the Public Record Office of Northern Ireland for all their help.

[2] The complete list of those identified will be printed in the UHF *Interest List* for 1987.

FEMALY ORPHANS WHO EMIGRATED FROM IRISH WORKHOUSES, 1848–50

Name	Age	Religion	Origin/Occupation/Condition on Entry	PRONI Ref./No. in Book	Date of Entry/Discharge
ANTRIM PLU					
Best, Ann Jane	15	EC	Craigarogan/Dirty	BG1/GA/1 (3943)	06/01/1848–26/05/1848
Beste, Margret	17	EC	Craigarogan/Dirty	BG1/GA/1 (3942)	06/01/1848–26/05/1848
Burt, Sarah	16	EC	Crumlin/Dirty	BG1/GA/1 (4276)	23/03/1848–26/05/1848
Magee, Cathy	21	RC	Crumlin/Servant/Dirty	BG1/GA/1 (4317)	06/04/1848–26/05/1848
McCann, Mary	14	P	Antrim/Servant/Dirty	BG1/GA/1 (1343)	12/11/1846–26/05/1848
McClusky, Mary	16	RC	Antrim	BG1/GA/1 (3756)	01/12/1847–26/05/1848
McCracken, Eliza	21	EC	Antrim PLU/Servant/Dirty	BG1/GA/1 (3750)	02/11/1848–26/05/1848
McCrudden, Jane	24	EC	Antrim/Dirty	BG1/GA/1 (3755)	09/12/1847–26/05/1848
McDermot, Eliza	16	RC	Antrim/Servant/Dirty	BG1/GA/1 (3939)	06/01/1848–26/05/1848
O'Neill, Margret	19	EC	Randalstown/Dirty	BG1/GA/1 (3736)	02/12/1847–26/05/1848
ARMAGH PLU					
Carroll, Mary	18	RC	Armagh/Servant/Thinly clothed, Destitute	BG2/G/2 (3090)	28/12/1847–24/05/1848
Carson, Isabella	15	EC	Armagh/Thinly clothed, Destitute	BG2/G/2 (2755)	23/11/1847–24/05/1848
Chambers, Sophia	16	EC	Barrack Street, Armagh/Comfortable	BG2/G/2 (4131)	04/04/1848–28/04/1848
Chambers, Sophia	18	EC	Barrack Street, Armagh/Comfortable, Clothed	BG2/G/2 (4567)	23/05/1848–24/04/1848
Conn, Eliza	16	EC	Ballinahone	BG2/G/2 (2309)	22/10/1847–29/10/1847
Conway, Cathy	15	RC	Markethill/ Thinly clothed, Hungry	BG2/G/1 (4316)	28/02/1846–26/06/1846
Conway, Cathy	15	RC	Markethill/Servant/ Tolerably well clothed	BG2/G/1 (6626)	12/12/1846–29/12/1846
Conway, Cathy	15	RC	Markethill/Servant/In a starving condition	BG2/G/1 (7333)	09/02/1847–24/05/1848

Name	Age	Religion	Origin/Occupation/Condition on Entry	PRONI Ref./No. in Book	Date of Entry/Discharge
ARMAGH PLU (continued)					
Curry, Elizabeth	16	RC		BG/2/G1 (7895)	page of details missing
Devlin, Rose, widow	39	RC	Crossmore/ Healthy (3 children 609–11) Margret 9, Patrick 6, Bernard 4	BG2/G/1 (608)	19/04/1842–11/08/1842
Devlin, Rose, widow	37	RC	Healthy (4 children 1325–8) Anne 12, Margret 10, Patrick 7, Bernard 5	BG2/G/1 (1324)	17/11/1842–06/03/1843
Devlin, Rose, widow	40	RC	Crossmore/ Thinly clothed, Hungry (4 children) Sarah Anne 12, Margret 10, Patrick 8, Bernard 6	BG2/G/1 (2396)	05/03/1844–30/04/1844
Devlin, Rose, widow	41	RC	Keady/Thinly clothed, Hungry (3 children) Margret 11, Pat 9, Bernard 7	BG2/G/1 (3700)	14/08/1848–15/09/1845
Devlin, Rose, widow	44	RC	Keady/Thinly clothed, Hungry Sarah Ann 14 (left 30/3/47), Margret 12 (left 29/7/47), Pat 10, Chas 10	BG2/G/1 (5660)	14/11/1846–14/01/1847
Devlin, Sarah Ann	15	RC	Keady/Thinly clothed, Hungry	BG2/G/2 (300)	29/04/1847–29/07/1847
Devlin, Rose, widow	40	RC	Crossmore/Thinly clothed, Hungry Patrick 9 (left 21/7/48), Margret 13 (left 24/5/48), Bernard 9 (left 21/7/48)	BG2/G/2 (1507)	16/08/1847–06/09/1847

FEMALY ORPHANS WHO EMIGRATED FROM IRISH WORKHOUSES, 1848–50

Name	Age	Religion	Origin/Occupation/Condition on Entry	PRONI Ref./No. in Book	Date of Entry/Discharge
ARMAGH PLU (continued)					
Devlin, Rose, widow	40	RC	Crossmore/Thinly clothed, Destitute. Children in workhouse	BG2/G/2 (1927)	25/09/1847–11/10/1847
Devlin, Sarah Ann	15	RC	Racarby/Thinly clothed, Hungry	BG2/G/2 (2606)	16/11/1847–24/05/1848
Devlin, Rose, widow	40	RC	Crossmore/Comfortably clothed. Children in workhouse	BG2/G/2 (4309)	25/04/1848–15/05/1848
Dowey, Ellen	17	EC	Armagh PLU/Thinly clothed	BG2/G/2 (2598)	16/11/1847–24/05/1848
Fox, Cathy	15	RC	Union at Large/No employment, Thinly clothed, Hungry	BG2/G/2 (1203)	10/07/1847–24/05/1848
Goudy, Hannah	16	EC	Chapel Lane, Armagh/Comfortable appearance	BG2/G/2 (4082)	30/03/1848–04/10/1849
Gowdie, Hannah	15	EC	Union at Large/Thinly clothed, Hungry	BG2/G/2 (1431)	07/08/1847–27/08/1847
Gray, Mary J.	14	EC	Armagh/Left service/Orphan	BG2/G/1 (3696)	10/08/1845–24/05/1848
Hunter, Jane	19	EC	Union at Large/Thinly clothed, Destitute	BG2/G/1 (3827)	29/02/1848–24/05/1848
Hunter, Anne	16	EC	Union at Large/Thinly clothed, Destitute	BG2/G/1 (3983)	21/03/1848–24/05/1848
Hunter, Jane	19	EC	Union at Large/Thinly clothed, Destitute	BG2/G/2 (3827)	29/02/1848–24/05/1848
Hunter, Anne	16	EC	Union at Large/Thinly clothed, Destitute	BG2/G/2 (3828)	29/02/1848–17/03/1848
Hunter, Anne	16	EC	Union at Large/Thinly clothed, Destitute	BG2/G/2 (3983)	21/03/1848–25/05/1848

Name	Age	Religion	Origin/Occupation/Condition on Entry	PRONI Ref./No. in Book	Date of Entry/Discharge
ARMAGH PLU (continued)					
Just, Elizabeth	16	EC	Annaghmore/No occupation/Thinly clothed, Starving	BG2/G/2 (87)	10/04/1847–06/09/1847
Just, Elizabeth	16	EC	Annaghmore/No occupation, Thinly clothed, Hungry	BG2/G/2 (2503)	09/11/1847–24/05/1848
Kelly, Mary Anne	19	RC	Middleton/ Thinly clothed, Destitute	BG/2/G1 (3119)	28/12/1847–24/05/1848
Kelly, Mary Anne	19	EC	Middletown/Thinly clothed, Hungry	BG2/G/2 (439)	30/04/1847–06/05/1847
Rose, Mother,	40		Patrick 12, Michael 10, Rose 15		
Kelly Mary Anne	19	RC	Middletown/Thinly clothed, Hungry, Fever	BG2/G/2 (1417)	08/08/1847–08/11/1847
Rose	15				
Kelly, Rose	15	RC	Middletown/Recovering from fever	BG2/G/2 (1418)	07/08/1847–13/09/1847
Kelly, Rose	15	RC	Middletown/Thinly clothed, Hungry	BG2/G/2 (1819)	14/09/1847–24/05/1848
Patrick	12		Michael 10. Both left 26/9/49. All fatherless		
Kelly, Mary Anne	19	RC	Middletown/Thinly clothed, Destitute	BG2/G/2 (3119)	28/12/1847–24/05/1848
Littlewood, Mary, widow	54	EC	Union at Large/Thinly clothed, Destitute	BG2/G/2 (1469)	14/08/1847–06/09/1847
			John 11, Ann Eliza 9, Thomas		
Littlewood, Mary widow	15	EC	Richhill/Thinly clothed, Destitute	BG2/G/2 (2076)	05/10/1847–24/05/1848
			Mary 52, Thomas 13, John 11, Ann Eliza 9. Mary died 10/3/48, Thomas absconded 11/7/48, John left 10/9/50, Anne 18/7/51		

FEMALY ORPHANS WHO EMIGRATED FROM IRISH WORKHOUSES, 1848–50

Name	Age	Religion	Origin/Occupation/Condition on Entry	PRONI Ref./No. in Book	Date of Entry/Discharge
ARMAGH PLU (continued)					
Littlewood, Mary	15	P	Richhill/Thinly clothed, Hungry Mary (married) 54, Thos. William 13, John, Ann Eliza. Husband's name Samuel, Ragged and dirty	BG2/G/2 (5441)	02/11/1846–28/12/1846
Littlewood, Mary	15	P	Richhill Mary (married) 54, Thos. William 13, John, Samuel 57. Samuel dies 25/2/47, Mary, John, Ann left 14/8. Father a Weaver	BG2/G/2 (7532)	00/00/1846–10/08/1847
McAlister, Jane	16	EC	Charlemont/Thinly clothed, Destitute	BG2/G/2 (868)	27/05/1847–04/10/1847
McLaughlin, Mary	16	RC	Grange/Servant/Thinly clothed, Hungry	BG2/G/1 (7523)	16/02/1847–24/05/1848
Moore, Martha	16	EC	Crossmore/Thinly clothed, Hungry	BG2/G/2 (1428)	07/08/1847–24/05/1848
Tamoney, Cathy	16	RC	Armagh	BG2/G/1 (456)	01/02/1842–15/08/1842
Mother Ellen	59			BG2/G/1	01/02/1842–14/10/1842
Tamoney, Cathy	16	RC	Armagh	BG2/G/1 (1166)	01/09/1842–14/10/1842
Tamoney, Cathy	16	RC	Armagh 1474 Mother Ellen, age 60, widow, RC, Delicate. Mother left 10/04/1843	BG2/G/1 (1475)	12/01/1843–08/04/1844
Tamoney, Eleanor widow	62	RC	Armagh/Tolerably well	BG2/G/1 (3899)	29/11/1845–16/03/1846

Name	Age	Religion	Origin/Occupation/ Condition on Entry	PRONI Ref./No. in Book		Date of Entry/ Discharge
ARMAGH PLU (continued)						
Tamoney, Cathy	19	RC	Armagh/Thinly clothed, Hungry	BG2/G/1	(3967)	13/12/1845–16/03/1846
Tamoney, Cathy	19	RC	Armagh/Thinly clothed, Hungry	BG2/G/1	(4356)	07/03/1846–24/05/1848
Toner, Mary Anne	20	RC	Keady Crosdenea/Thinly clothed, Destitute	BG2/G/2	(2217)	14/10/1847–24/05/1848
Bridget	18		Lame, Left her behind			
Williamson, Margret	15	RC	Union at Large/Thinly clothed, Destitute	BG2/G/2	(2568)	18/11/1847–24/05/1848
Wilson, Margaret	17	P	Crossmore	BG2/G/2	(2654)	16/11/1847–24/05/1848
Wilson, (Susan)	13	EC	Broolally/Thinly clothed, Destitute, Bastard	BG2/G/2	(3080)	21/12/1847–24/05/1848
BALLYMENA PLU						
Blair, Margaret	14	P	Union at Large	BG/G/2	(49)	11/08/1847–22/05/1848
Booth, Nancy	20	RC	Ballymena	BG4/G/2	(2202)	10/04/1848–24/05/1848
Hogan, Jane	16	RC	Ballymena	BG4/G/1	(4884)	23/07/1847–24/05/1848
Kyle, Matry	20	P	Union at Large	BG4/G/2	(1859)	28/02/1848–24/05/1848
McFee, Isabella	19	RC	Galgorm	BG4/G/1	(4169)	17/05/1847–24/05/1848
Mary A., Widow	40		Eliza 14, Jane 17, Margaret 7, Joseph 4			
O'Hara, Margaret	16	RC	Ballymena	BG4/G/1	(3590)	04/03/1847–22/07/1847
O'Hara, Margaret	17	RC	Ballymena	BG4/G/2	(1996)	16/03/1848–24/05/1848

FEMALY ORPHANS WHO EMIGRATED FROM IRISH WORKHOUSES, 1848–50

Name	Age	Religion	Origin/Occupation/Condition on Entry	PRONI Ref./No. in Book		Date of Entry/Discharge
DOWNPATRICK PLU						
Hannah, Margret	18	RC	Castlewellan/From Hospital	BG12/G/1	(5847)	05/04/1848–25/05/1848
McCreedy, Eliza	18	RC	Union at Large/Servant/2nd admission, Houseless	BG12/G/1	(2803)	04/10/1846–22/09/1847
McCreedy, Eliza	18	P	Downpatrick/3rd admission	BG12/G/1	(5703)	13/06/1847–25/05/1848
McMullen, Eliza	17	RC	Downpatrick/3rd admission	BG12/G/1	(2729)	22/09/1846–12/01/1847
McMullen, Eliza	18	RC	Downpatrick/Service	BG12/G/1	(4371)	24/04/1848–25/05/1848
Price, Mary	17	EC	Downpatrick/Houseless	BG12/G/1	(5603)	01/01/1848–25/05/1848
Quinn, Margaret	18	P	Seaford/Service	BG12/G/1	(18)	00/02/1847–25/05/1848
ENNISKILLEN PLU						
Brown, Sara	20	RC	Enniskillen	BG14/G/4	(1556)	26/10/1847–24/05/1848

9

Horesman, Pass By ...
Irish-Australian Gravestones

Trevor McClaughlin

Today, Australia deals with death like most other western countries, in a deodorized and distant manner. Perhaps the tragic images from Ethiopia and Somalia which have appeared on our television screens have helped de-sensitize us and prevent us from making any deep public display of our grief. Occasionally, we trespass upon the private grief of individuals by reading death notices in newspapers or about the funerals of the rich and famous. In private, of course, things are very different and, in practice, Australia has a rich variety of ethnic groups each of which celebrate death in their own distinctive fashion. But superficially and in the main we seem to be heading in the direction of an American way of death as represented by their funeral parlour slogan, 'You die and we do the rest'.[1]

Such a state of affairs has not always been the case. There is indeed scope for a study of changing Australian attitudes to death, over time, from the Dreamtime to the present. Merely talking to some of the elderly members of our community brings to light some of the changes which have occurred in the last forty or fifty years. Old folks lament that the breeze, the 'outwalkers' flanking the hearse, is a thing of the past. The cortege now speeds by on its way to the cemetery or crematorium unwilling to hold up the traffic. No one stops to remove their hat or pay their respects. Visits to the cemetery are no longer a frequent occurrence made at some discomfort to the mourner. At best they happen two or three times a year, on Mother's Day or Father's Day and at Christmas.

However impressionistic all this is, it is nonetheless a useful starting point. Recollections such as these, oral history in other words, will be an important source in any study of Australian attitudes to death over time. The interested student will also want to consult G.M. Griffin and D. Tobin, *In the Midst of Life ... The Australian Response to Death,* Melbourne University Press, 1982, probably the first book of its kind in Australia. From the vantage point of its authors, one a Uniting minister the other a funeral director, it provides a fascinating survey of European burial practices and mourning customs. The subject obviously has wide appeal and should attract interest and discussion in academic and other circles in the years to come.

This essay, however, has more modest aims. It merely wants to pass on to the reader some of the author's impressions of changing Irish-Australian attitudes to death and to inform acolyte family historians of the very precise information sometimes contained on Australian headstones. It was sparked off by a report in a Sydney newspaper of a woman who had been mugged. Having had her handbag snatched, she appealed for its return: it contained the cremated remains of her husband. She had been carrying his remains in her handbag for the past two years, in readiness for the day when she might take them back to Ireland. Assuming the story was not a hoax, here we were in the late twentieth century being confronted by an age-old belief from peasant Ireland that one should be buried in Ireland, a belief held by many an Irish emigrant to the Antipodes during the nineteenth century and yet one which could be so rarely acted upon. The questions almost posed themselves: what attitudes and customs relating to death had the Irish brought with them to Australia? Had many, or any, of them survived? Like Irish settlement in Australia generally, which concentrated neither on the frontier nor in urban ghettoes, Irish attitudes to death were gradually and easily assimilated into an Australian way of dying. In the long run, they became noted for their ordinariness rather than being distinctive or aberrant.

Recently, for example, it has become fashionable to describe Ireland as having a funerary culture or as having a preoccupation with death which stretches from the megalithic tombs of New Grange to the politics of the late twentieth century.[2] However accurate this claim may be, little evidence exists for such a preoccupation on the part of the Australian-Irish. Indeed, the laconic, down-to-earth Australian character would eschew such a romanticized adulation of death. Australian circumstances were very different from Irish ones. Loneliness, isolation, the tyranny of distance militated against the development of that kind of culture, the sentimentality of balladeers notwithstanding. Isolation and the vastness of Australia were the very things which the balladeers extolled in their description of 'the dying stockman' or 'the stockman's last bed',

> His whip is silent, his dogs they do mourn
> His steed looks in vain for his master's return,
> No friend to bemoan him unheeded he dies,
> Save Australia's dark sons no one knows where he lies.[3]

How could the old customs and old ways of celebrating death have survived in such a new and totally different environment? Different political realities, the demands of land and economy, the harshness of the landscape and the urgency of the living stopped Irish Australians from developing a fixation with death. But some survivals there were. The word 'wake' passed into Australian currency although what it signifies nowadays is a pale shadow of its former Irish self. So too, many an Irish Australian used gravestones to record and identify where exactly in Ireland they came from. Their headstones display a well developed and acute Irish sense of place.[4]

Fragments of evidence exist to show that the Irish brought their wake customs with them to Australia. In October 1794 Deputy Judge Advocate David Collins recorded in his *Account of the English Colony of New South Wales,* the burial of the murdered Simon Burn:

> This poor man was buried by his widow (an Irish woman) in a corner of his own farm, attended by several settlers of that and the neighbouring districts, who celebrated the funeral rites in the manner and with orgies suitable to the disposition and habits of the deceased, the widow and themselves.[5]

Evidently the traditions of peasant Ireland were alive and well in early New South Wales. As in Ireland clerical opposition would in time lead to the disappearance of such 'orgies'. Moreover, the new Australian environment could never offer enough support for traditional peasant Irish culture. What did survive was the meaning of the wake as a mourning, sometimes as a death watch, when friends and relatives sit with the corpse between death and burial, sometimes as an occasion when food and even alcohol (though this is rare) is consumed and the dead is farewelled with tales retold and memories recalled of the dead person's life and the mourner's bond with him or her.[6] Today mourners will 'bring a plate' to a 'wake' but there is no sign of dancing or games or the old peasant customs.

On the other hand, a specific Irish sense of place did survive. This sense of place is particularly evident in Australian cemeteries. Acutely aware of their displacement, of not belonging either to here or there, a number of Irish Australians seem to have striven to preserve their identity in their final resting place. As with others, their gravestone appeals to the passer-by to remember death:

> Good people all as you pass by
> As you are now so once was I
> As I am now you soon will be
> Prepare yourselves to follow me

but it also appeals to the passer-by to remember and commemorate a particular individual whose identity merged with and depended upon a precise place of origin: Patrick Bourke, native of Bourisleigh, Co. Tipperary, Ireland, or Winifred Kennedy native of Wicklow, parish of Hollywood, Ireland. Of the migrants to Australia in the last century, the Irish seem to have felt this need most of all. More than others, they felt the need to carve into their headstone the exact place where they were born, the place they grew up in, 'place' meaning not just a physical place but the people and the memories and the community who identified them. Was the same need felt by Irish migrants in other places? Whatever the reason for the survival of this record of their sense of place, it is a great boon to family historians who today are searching to discover their own roots and to clarify their own identity.

Accompanying this essay are illustrations of this Irish sense of place extracted from my own collection of photographs and graveyard jottings from a variety of cemeteries in Australia. The list takes examples from every county in Ireland and shows how very specific birthplaces were recorded on gravestones. Some examples were easier to find than others. The counties which sent the most migrants to Australia, Tipperary, Cork, Clare, Galway and Fermanagh, for example, were the easiest to find. They were also easiest to find in areas of relatively high Irish settlement, in cemeteries in Telerah and East Maitland in the Hunter Valley in New South Wales, at Kiama,

Gerringong and Jamberoo in the Illawarra, south of Sydney where Ulster Irish were to be found in abundance, and at Kilmore, Kyneton and Gordon in Victoria.

In passing, it is worth noting that many of the earliest burial places for white settlers are lost to us. The majority of those which have survived are general cemeteries with separate sections set aside and marked for different religious denominations, Anglican, Presbyterian, Uniting Church, Roman Catholic, Greek Orthodox, Jews or whatever. They were first established as public cemeteries and administered cemeteries and were as much concerned about public health as anything else. Cemeteries thus tended to be located at least one or two miles from town beyond the rivers or creeks which were the source of a town's water supply. One can only imagine, perhaps with the help of some of the engravings of S.T. Gill, the funeral cortege of bullock drays, horses and walkers making their slow way along a dusty road to the dead person's grave some distance from town.

Among the more interesting cemeteries is the New Cemetery at Gordon, just a few miles east of Ballarat, in Victoria. Local historian and one of the restorers and unofficial caretakers of the cemetery, Roy Higgins, has told the author that the New Cemetery consists of ten acres and was allocated when the town was surveyed in 1863–4. Unfortunately no record exists of the burials made in an earlier two-acre Pioneer cemetery at the west end of town and no manuscript record for burials in the New Cemetery before 1878. But what the New Cemetery has is an impressive collection of Irish-Australian gravestones. The area between Gordon and Ballarat was an intensive potato farming area and many of the inhabitants of the region are of Irish descent. Some of these same potato farmers must also have hit paydirt on the goldfields and been prepared to use it on funeral monuments. The work at Gordon displays the familiar symbols of Irishness, celtic cross, shamrock, round tower and harp as well as an acutely developed Irish sense of place. Performed chiefly by stonemasons S. Jaegers and sons, F.W. Commons and McDonalds, and Thorntons, it reaches a standard even higher than that by the same stonemasons at Ballarat or Melbourne. Gordon is an exceptionally well preserved, and cared for, example of memorials to the Irish.

Family historians and perhaps schoolchildren in Ireland and

Australia engaged in a joint local history project or the study of migration and settlement will be attracted by the very precise information which such headstones contain. Transcriptions of the information on headstones in a number of Australian cemeteries have already been made by enthusiastic genealogists and local historians. Some have been published or are available in typescript form. May I suggest that in the first instance interested parties write to the Hon. Secretaries of major genealogical societies such as

> The Society of Australian Genealogists,
> The Genealogical Society of Victoria
> The Genealogical Society of Queensland,
> The Royal Australian Historical Society

They will then be certain of being guided in the right direction. Perhaps it is not amiss to suggest that they too may be interested in the other aspects of this story, an Irish sense of place, the disappearance of funeral customs, and changing attitudes to death, all of which cry out for further research and examination.

Irish-Australian Gravestones

BIRTHPLACE   BURIAL
Antrim   *Waverley*
Erected to the memory of John McAllister late of West Australia Died 10th Feby 1905 aged 63 years RIP Eldest son of the late James McAllister of Tavnachoney Cushendall Co Antrim Ireland

Armagh   *Waverley*
In loving memory of Rachel Willis born 23rd Sept. 1865 at Derrycorr Co Armagh Ireland Died at Bondi 14th May 1910 Erected by her sister Elizabeth

Belfast   *West Geelong*
Mary in fond remembrance of her beloved husband James Lyle native of Belfast Ireland who died 6th April 1887 Aged 64 years

Carlow   Bald Hillis
Hardy Eustace[7] son of Hardy and Bridget Annie (née Brown) Eustace of Newtown Co Carlow, died 3 March 1895 aged 52 years

Cavan   Kiama
In memory of Captain O.M. Stevenson VD E Kiama Co. 2nd A.I. Reg. Born Cavan County Cavan Ireland January 25th 1860 died February 11th 1909

Cork   Gordon
Erected by Margaret Burke to the memory of her beloved husband Edmund Burke who departed this life 9th April 1889 Aged 46 years Native of Clenworth County Cork Ireland also his beloved daughter Margaret who died 18th April 1884 aged 3 years, 8 months. May their souls rest in peace Amen Also his wife Margaret died 29th July 1924 aged 78 years

Clare   Yass
In memory of John and Bridget Conroy who departed this life 17th March 1868 aged 65 and 60 years natives of Killaloe Co Clare Ireland Erected by their children

Clare   Wallan
Erected by her children to the memory of Margaret Moroney Native of Tulla, Co. Clare, Ireland who died 16th May 1875 aged 66 years RIP

Clare   Ballarat
Erected by John Torpy native of the parish of Kilfenora, Co Clare, Ireland; in loving remembrance of his beloved wife Bridget died 11th Jany 1887 aged 54 years, their beloved children John, Michael, James and Michael Henry who died in infancy, Andrew Died 16th Augt 1890 aged 26 years, Also the above John Torpy died 12th July 1907, aged 80 years. May their souls rest in peace Amen

Derry   Muswellbrook
Of your charity pray for the repose of the soul of Patrick Rogers of Kilrea, Co. Derry, Ireland. Who died 31st May 1884 aged 22 years

Donegal   Waverley
In loving memory of Edward Charles son of the late John Loughrey Binion Clonmany Co Donegal, Ireland and Grand-son of John

Hogan (The Irish Sculptor) who died in the Hospice, Darlinghurst, Sydney 25th July 1911 RIP "To be resigned is to place God between one's self and suffering" This cross is lovingly erected by his sorrowing mother, sisters and brothers.

Down   Kiama
In loving memory of Mary Ann Bruce of Knock Co Down Ireland died 1st August 1905 Aged 64 years Also Alexander Bruce of Knock Co Down Ireland died 25th January 1920 aged 76 years

Dublin   Field of Mars
Robert beloved husband of Bridget (Delia) Cruikshank born Dublin, Ireland 1851 Died 29th May 1908 Aged 58 years Sweet Jesus have mercy on his soul ... Also Delia beloved wife of Robert Cruikshank born Dublin, Ireland, 1850 Died 15th May 1931

Fermanagh   Bungendore
Dedicated to the memory of Daniel Gallagher (1789–1871) Native of Ederny County Fermanagh, Ireland Buried Bungendore according to the rites of the Roman Catholic Church ... Erected by the descendants of Daniel and Ellen (nee McCaffery 1809–1860) to commemorate the 150th anniversary of the family's arrival in Australia

Galway   Uralla
Gloria in Excelsis Deo In loving memory of Delia Beloved wife of Luke Riley who died at Wollun Aug. 17th 1901 Native of Lismakage Co Galway Ireland Aged 41 years Requiescat in pace Erected to her memory by her loving husband

Kerry   Sandgate
Thomas Aloysius Bourke Born Tralee Co. Kerry Ireland Nov. 10th 1837 Died at Newcastle, Sept 14th 1907 ... Also Bridget Ethel Bourke wife of Thomas Aloysius Bourke Born Clashmore, Co. Waterford, Ireland 17 March 1849, Died Strathfield Sydney 6 Nov, 1929

Kerry   Gundagai
Gloria in Excelsis Deo Sacred to the memory of John J. Quiler A native of Ballyreehan Co. Kerry Ireland who died at Cobarralong July 29th 1875 aged 78 years Also of his son Thomas William who died at Cobarralong Dec 25th 1865 aged 10 years On whose souls sweet Jesus have mercy

Kildare   Telerah
In loving memory of Michael Donnolley Born in Rose Town, Parish of New Bridge County Kildare, Ireland 29th Sept 1799 Died 28th August 1875 ...

Kilkenny   Gordon
In loving memory of Thomas Murphy native of Smithstown, Co. Kilkenny, Ireland Died 29th April 1874 aged 66 years and of his wife Margaret Died 4th June 1883, aged 86 years. Also of their daughter Bridget the dearly beloved wife of James Cody Died 31st July 1919, aged 89 years Thomas Cody beloved husband of Ellen Cody Died 26th April 1918, aged 42 years, RIP

Kings (Laois)   Queanbeyan
Pray for the soul of John Darmody Native of Banagher King's Co Ireland died at Queanbeyan 20 Feb 1877 Aged 60 years Requieca in pace. Also his beloved wife Mary Darmody who departed this life July 13 1887 Aged 72 years Requiescat in pace

Leitrim   Field of Mars
Mary Ann beloved wife of Francis O'Rourke Native of Ardlougher, Co. Leitrim died 17th March 1911 aged 57 years RIP

Limerick   Melbourne General
In loving memory of James O'Connell of Richmond who died 21st July 1904 aged 68 years Native of Shanagolden Co. Limerick Ireland

Limerick   Gore Hill
In loving memory of Patrick Leahy Mayor of Mosman 1905–1909 Born at Foynes Co. Limerick 17th March 1855 Died at Mosman 20th January 1909 Requiescat

Longford   Waverley
In memory of Anne Farrell Born Longford Eire Died 20th March 1911 Aged 40 years Mary Elizabeth Fitzgerald Died 3rd June 1946 RIP

Louth   Field of Mars
In loving memory of our dear son and brother John Joseph McRae who died in the snow on Mt. Bogong Aug. 1943 aged 27 years Also Margaret McRae Born Cullon Co Louth Ireland Died 25th June 1956, Aged 67 years Also Alexander N. McRae Born Greenock, Scotland Died 17th Jan. 1972 Aged 86 years RIP

Mayo   *Melbourne General*
Erected by Ann Joyce to the memory of her beloved husband Thomas Joyce native of Clarenorris Co Mayo, Ireland who died 15th February 1889 aged 48 years

Meath   *Waverley*
Sacred to the memory of my dear husband Michael Norris Native of Kells Co. Meath, Ireland who departed this life, 8th May 1910 Aged 57 years ...

Monaghan   *Stanthorpe*
Charles McKenna b. Truagh Monaghan bur 7 Sep 1911 Stranthorpe

Queen's (Offaly)   *Parramatta*
Sacred to the memory of John Dunphy late of Queen's County Ireland who departed this life 23rd April 1856 aged 71 years also Catherine beloved wife of John Dunphy who departed this life 24th Oct. 1859 aged 55 years May their souls rest in peace Amen

Roscommon   *Waverley*
Ireland who died 2 December 1891 Aged 46 years

Sligo   *Stanthorpe*
Ferdinand Trumble McDonagh b. Carrowkeel, Sligo, bur 7 Jul 1933 Stanthorpe

Tipperary   *Kyneton*
To the memory of Patrick Kelly Native of Kilrowan, Co Tipperary Ireland Died 6th November 1905 age 75 years Also James Kelly Died 8th May 1915 age 79 years Also his beloved wife, Mary Kelly Died 22nd May 1919 age 72 years RIP

Tipperary   *Branxton*
Of your charity pray for the repost of the soul of Matthew B. Hayes, Native of Pallasmore Co Tipperary Ireland Died 18th June 1904 Aged 70 years

Tipperary   *Wangaratta*
Michael Cusack 1808–1865 Wangaratta Pioneer Native of Nenagh, Tipperary RIP Erected by his great-grandson L.M. Harris OBE 1981

Tyrone   Queanbeyan
Erected by Francis Devlin to the memory of his beloved wife Catherine native of Anaghmore County Tyrone Ireland who departed this life at Micalgo1st Nov 1880 in her 65th year of her age Aeternam illi requiem precare viator

Waterford   Waverley
Gloria in Excelsius Deo In loving memory of Patrick O'Brien[8] Native of Strancally Castle County Wexford, Ireland who died 5th July 1898 Aged 83 years

Westmeath   Kilmore
James Allen native of Feakle, County Clare Ireland beloved husband of Theresa Allen who died on 22nd August 1906 aged 75 Also Theresa beloved wife of the above born at Castleost Richford Bridge Westmeath Ireland 15th April 1838 Died on the 25th November 1912 Aged 74

Wexford   Kurrajong
In memory of Charles Lary who died August 28 1854 Aged 70 years Charles Lary is my name Ireland is my nation Wexford is my native place And Christ is my salvation Good people all as you pass by As you are now so once was I As I am now you soon will be Prepare yourselves to follow me May he rest in peace Amen

Wicklow   Muswellbrook
Of your charity Pray for the repose of the soul of Winifred Kennedy Native of Wicklow, Parish of Hollywood Ireland Aged 84 years [broken headstone]

Published in *Familia: Ulster Genealogical Review*, no. 9, 1993.

Notes

[1] 'Chauna, Lebrun, Vovelle: The New History of Death', E. LeRoy Ladurie, *The Territory of the Historian,* Sussex, 1973, p. 275.

[2] See, for example, N. Witoszek, 'Ireland: A Funerary Culture?', *Studia*, lxxvi, 1987, pp 206–15.

3 'The Stockman's last bed', Anon., *Old Bush Songs and Rhymes of Colonial Times*, enlarged and revised from the collection of A.B. Patterson, Douglas Stewart and Nancy Keesing eds., Hong Kong, 1981, p. 144.

4 On this sense of place, see Patrick Sheerin, 'Genius Faulae: the Irish Sense of Place', *Irish University Review*, xviii no. 2, 1988, pp 191–206; 'The Sense of Place', Seamus Heaney, *Preoccupations*, Selected Prose 1968–78, London 1980, pp 131–49, and Patrick O'Farrell, 'Defining Place and Home: Are the Irish Prisoners of Place?', *Home or Away? Immigrants in Colonial Australia Visible Immigrants: Three*, David Fitzpatrick ed., ANU, Canberra, 1992, pp 1–18.

5 David Collins, *An Account of the English Colony in New South Wales*, 2 vols., Brian Fletcher ed., Sydney, 1975, I, pp 328–9; see also Roger Therry on the wake of Abel Death in his *Reminiscences of Thirty Year's Residence in New South Wales and Victoria*, London 1863, Facsimile edition, Sydney, 1974, pp 321–3.

6 In much the same manner as Maurice O'Sullivan described the wake of old Kate Liam in his *Twenty Years A-Growing*, M.L. Davies and G. Thomson trans., New York, 1933.

7 *Memorials to the Irish in Queensland*, Daithu UaLorcain ed., Brisbane, 1988 p. 45.

8 Op. cit. p. 58.

10

Ulster and the Bay of Plenty
The Katikati Special Settlement in North Island

N.C. Mitchel

The late 1860s were years of economic depression in many parts of New Zealand as wool prices fell and gold production declined. Public works expenditure had virtually ceased. In the North Island there was the added disruption of the Maori wars. The year 1870 saw a reassessment of the needs of the young nation with the advent of Julius Vogel as Colonial Treasurer. Vogel's aim was to speed up the settlement and development of the colony by means of large-scale immigration and extensive public works. This involved the borrowing of considerable sums of money overseas and reviving the idea of special settlements. During the 1850s and 1860s a number of these special settlements had been established in the North Island; the Nova Scotians at Waipiu is the earliest example. They were now to be followed by the Scandinavians at Dannevirke and Norsewood and Ulster settlements at Katikati and Te Puke on the shores of the Bay of Plenty, an area aptly named by Captain Cook a century before.

The special settlements were highly favoured for a time. It was thought that small groups of settlers possessing specific national characteristics had a better chance of overcoming pioneering challenges than 'free' immigrants. Usually these settlements stemmed from the inspiration and leadership of an individual who contracted with the government (Vogel had appointed an Agent-General to administer the new immigration programme in London) to provide a specific number of settlers by a certain date, settlers with some capital who, in return for title to Crown Land, would transform the bush into farms. From the Government's point of view such group settlements had advantages over 'free' immigration as their members were unlikely to become burdens on the colonial treasury if things went wrong. The government's sole liability was to assist with passage money and to survey the land. The Ulster special settlements were the last to attempt the establishment of a national group in New Zealand.[1]

The Bay of Plenty with its favourable climate and soils was a terrain much prized and fought over by Maori tribes in the days before the pakehas arrived. The strong Maori presence meant that there were few European settlers there before 1860. Except for the Church Missionary Society's block of land at Te Papa, little land had been acquired. In 1864 land south of Tauranga was confiscated from the Ngaiterangi after the battle of Gate Pa and Te Ranga. This land was given to military settlers as part of the government's plan to subdue the area. For a variety of reasons military settlement at Tauranga was not very successful. Soldiers did not necessarily make good pioneer farmers, especially when their capital was inadequate, and their fifty-acre holdings were too small to be economic; lack of communications and Maori hostility were additional disadvantages. Many drifted away. In 1870 only some 257 Europeans were settled in the district.

The government now sent an Immigration Officer, a Mr Halcombe, to look at the area's possibilities for group settlement. He reported to the Minister that the Katikati block, to the west of Tauranga, offered the best field for experimental immigration on an extensive scale. He stated in his report: 'The Katikati block is of so good a character that I think an effort might be made, with a fair chance of success, to induce a body of capitalists from England, or elsewhere, to take up the whole in from 200 to 640 acre blocks, on condition of actual occupation and improvement, and paying say £1 per acre for the fee simple of 'the land'.[2] 'The Katikati block', he continues, 'offers a very fine field for special settlement of a superior class of men'. The circumstances for group settlement were now favourable. All that was needed to translate recommendations into action was somebody to organise such a settlement. In the case of Katikati that person was George Vesey Stewart.

Born in 1832, Stewart was the son of Captain Mervyn Stewart of Martray Manor near Ballygawley in Co. Tyrone, and a grandson of Sir John Stewart, MP for the county. The family came of Ulster planter stock and Stewart, in effect, became the New Zealand equivalent of a seventeenth-century Ulster plantation undertaker. After a distinguished career at Trinity College, Dublin, he settled down to farm in Tyrone and dabble in commercial ventures which included sinking large sums of money in the linen industry. But although he had a capacity to make money, he had an incapacity to keep it. This brought him to the verge of bankruptcy so that when, in his fortieth year, his attention was drawn to the possibilities for group settlement in New Zealand, he seized the opportunity to make a fresh start. He was always a highly controversial person and quickly antagonised Dr Featherson, the Agent-General in London, who actively disliked him. But Stewart, with characteristic tenacity, set out for New Zealand in 1873 to select land. After much searching throughout the colony, he returned to Ulster with a grant of 10,000 acres in the Katikati block. A fierce press controversy accompanied him with New Zealand papers maintaining that 'it was monstrous to give away lands worth £3 and £4 and acre when old colonists and their sons could not even buy land'.[3] The better situated Te Puke block, east of Tauranga, to which Stewart was to send settlers in the 1880s, was not available for settlement at this time. So for good or ill the more physically difficult Katikati block was chosen for the first Ulster settlement.

The 40,000 acre Katikati block had been purchased by the New Zealand government from the Maoris in 1871. It stretched for eleven miles along the shores of Tauranga harbour from Athenree in the west to the Aognatete river in the east. It consisted largely of lowlands hemmed in by highly dissected hill country to the south and west. Stewart tells us that he selected these lowlands in preference to land in the South Island and near Wellington because they fulfilled his three main requirements – land of first class quality that could be easily cleared, proximity to a town (Tauranga), and access to gold fields (Waihi) to the north, which would provide a market for local produce. The lowlands were covered with fern (bracken) and scrub (manuka mostly) and there was a fringe of swamp with mangroves and flax along the shores. Soils were mostly derived from volcanic ash showers and in consequence were light except near the harbour where they became peaty and sandy. Tauranga, then a small port town founded by mission enterprise, was about fifteen miles away to the east. Access to it was easier by the almost land-locked waters of Tauranga harbour than by land. Only Maori trails led to the interior while in the west the heavily forested ranges came near the coast at Athenree restricting access to the Waihi goldfields to the narrow Athenree gorge.

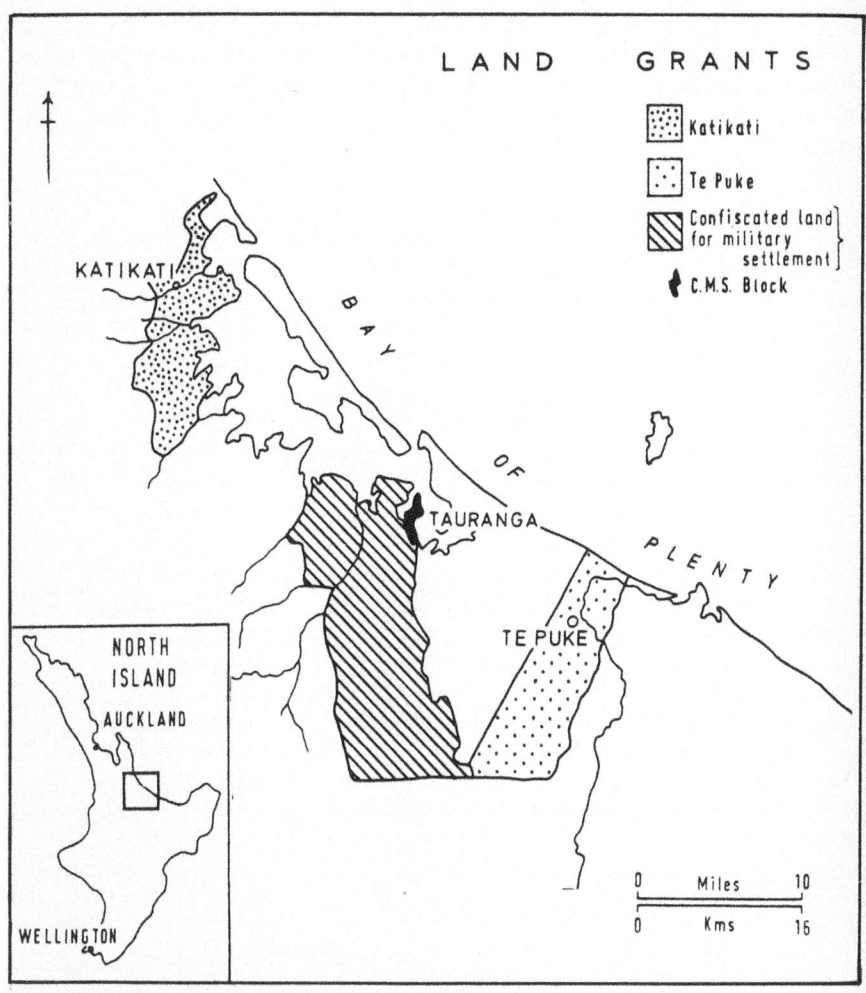

Figure 1

Taken as a whole the Bay of Plenty lowlands were extremely favourable terrain for Maori settlement. Their fortified earthen *pas* on commanding hills and promontories were common. Fish and shellfish were plentiful and clearance of lowland bush for patches of cultivation presented no problems. It is highly likely that the fern and scrub cover, which the Europeans welcomed, was Maori-induced through burning. There is evidence of once more extensive forest cover, including the majestic kauri. Competition for this land became acute as population increased. The peace the military settlers helped bring by their presence after the Maori wars with the pakehas at least meant that the Ulster settlers who followed in their wake were spared one of the troubles of frontier life and, unlike the Scotch-Irish in the New World, could afford to be magnanimous to the indigenous inhabitants whose population had dwindled to less than 1,500 by 1870. 'They vanish like moths before the blaze of civilisation', records Stewart.[4] Maori numbers were even fewer when the first Ulster settlers arrived and near Katikati probably not more than 100 lived in five small reserves. These Maoris welcomed the new arrivals and helped them to adapt to the strange surroundings. Stewart tells us that the Maoris considered the Irish also to be hau haus or rebels. He thought it 'unwise to tell them that there was a difference between northern and southern Irishmen'.[5]

To recruit members for his first Katikati settlement, Stewart gave public lectures, made newspaper appeals, sent circulars to Orange lodges, and canvassed among his tenants in Tyrone. For him, the venture was a mixture of business – he received 1,000 acres – which had most chance of success when made by a group of people from the same district, and an opportunity to live like a patriarch in a new land. In June 1875, the *Carisbrooke Castle*, a sailing ship of 1,400 tons, sailed from Belfast with 238 settlers aboard who prided themselves on the fact that they were special settlers which they considered meant something more than the ordinary run of emigrants. Their departure caused a stir in Belfast for this was the first time a party of Ulster people had been organised to emigrate to New Zealand. The settlers were welcomed in Auckland with much enthusiasm, which involved a street parade and a public banquet before departing for Tauranga. The first sight of their new home must have come as a shock. Bush was anything up to twelve feet high and household belongings had to be dragged in across tidal mud. Lots were drawn for holdings which were mostly between 200 and 300 acres each. But just over a year later the *Daily Southern Cross* of 12 December 1876, was able to comment on 'the remarkable strides made by the settlement, thanks to the industry and energy of the special settlers backed by a fair modicum of capital'. By 1877, 1,000 areas were under cultivation and Stewart was sufficiently encouraged to ask the government for an additional 10,000 acres which had been half-promised some years before.

Katikati No. 2 settlement came into existence only after prolonged negotiations and acrimonious correspondence between Stewart in Ballygawley and Vogel, now the Agent-General in London.[6] Vogel had changed his mind about Stewart and had adopted an obstructive attitude. But Stewart went ahead despite all difficulties. Always a prolific writer, the first of his seven comprehensive pamphlets appeared extolling the advantages of life in New Zealand and including glowing reports of high crop yields from members of the No. 1 settlement. It was soon followed by a sequel, also published in Omagh. In it Sandy Turner, always one of Stewart's staunchest supporters, writes: 'Tell them, sir, at home that they will be coming to the finest climate in the world ... to till ground they could plough for a month without meeting a stone ... that it would be more easy to labour 5 acres of it rather than one in Ireland'.[7] Of the large number of newspapers, both in Ulster and in Britain, that reported developments in Katikati, the *Belfast News Letter* was the only one to antagonise the settlers. Stewart in his second pamphlet is at pains to refute, not very convincingly, the paper's argument that it was not good for Ulster to lose tenant farmers with capital.

Stewart's first three pamphlets relate solely to Katikati; the remainder are to do with Te Puke. Although his enthusiasm and eagerness to compete with the greater attractions of Canada as a field of emigration for Ulster people – 'a country where it is too cold to bury the dead' – at times cause accuracy to be sacrificed and difficulties to be glossed over, these pamphlets provide a rare insight into pioneer settlement. As part of his persuasive powers, they quickly helped him to attract support for his No. 2 settlement. The *Lady Jocelyn*, over 2,000 tons and then one of the finest sailing ships afloat, was engaged to carry his party to New Zealand. She left Carrick Roads in Belfast Lough on 20 May 1878 with 378 passengers, all but 93 Irish. Whereas the No. 1 settlement was composed entirely of tenant farmers, this second party included country gentlemen with considerable capital. Among the passengers were Stewart's parents, his brother Hugh and wife Adele, two retired generals, a canon and a doctor. Social graces were to be added as well as capital to a degree unusual in pioneering settlements. Arthur Gray in his pioneering book on the settlement, *An Ulster Plantation*, contends that the gentlemen and the tenant farmers merged successfully without snobbishness. However, the terms that Stewart eventually had to accept for this settlement were very much less favourable than for his first party. He had to buy the land at £1 an acre, carry out his own survey, produce a minimum of 122 adult immigrants who were to stay on their holdings until 1 January 1833 and by that time have at least one-fifth under cultivation. No person was to receive more than 500 acres and no family member more than 1,000 acres. Stewart was liable to forfeit £5,000 if the conditions were not fulfilled. He fixed a price of £2 an acre for the sale of the land to the settlers: 10/- to be paid on application and the balance at any time within five years. He was soon over-subscribed to the extent of 4,000 acres.

The major part of the land allotted to the second party lay directly behind the No. 1 settlement (Fig. 1), extending from the Tuapiro river to the Te Aroha track. Much of it was swamp and upland and inferior to the land of the first settlement. The government was as much to blame as Stewart for this state of affairs. In all the negotiations its attitude had been evasive for land was becoming more and more valuable and half-promises made to Stewart years previously were now an embarrassment. Some of the new settlers made vociferous complaints about what they regarded as Stewart's misrepresentations but he had the capacity to handle opposition 'with the easy assurance of a test-match cricketer playing havoc with an up-country eleven'.[8] Such was the progress made that by 1879 the visiting Crown land ranger was able to report that the No. 2 settlement had made a good beginning.[9] Borrie, in his authoritative study of immigration to New Zealand, contends that the success of the Katikati settlements was due not only to the enterprise of its leader but to 'the clan spirit which gave it unity of interest and outlook, a powerful factor in easing the shocks and hardships in the first years'.[10] Hardships there certainly were. The economic depression that hit New Zealand in the 1880s was particularly difficult for a struggling settlement still in the process of breaking in farms and without any marketable product. Land, especially if soil was poor, reverted quickly to bush, and many discouraged settlers simply walked off their holdings. In 1881 the population of the block was 526; ten years later it had fallen to 198.[11] Stewart's judgement in including gentlemen of means was now proved sound for the richer settlers were able to help those less well off through these difficult times. Mr Shaw of Woodlands, for example, employed twenty-six men, certainly at no profit to himself.[12] It was worth noting that relief measures were not needed at Katikati. Many of those who stayed tried new ventures; there was even an ostrich farm owned by the Rev. Katterns, the vicar, who found his stipend inadequate.

How did the Katikati settlers adapt to their new environment? Unlike the Scotch-Irish they were coming to a peaceful frontier; they had capital and relatively easy access to supplies brought in from overseas. There was less need to live off the country. Surprisingly enough, timber was in short supply locally, for the forested backblocks were almost inaccessible. It was customary for grooved timber, window frames and doors, bricks and corrugated iron sheets to be bought in Tauranga or Auckland. The settlers quickly adapted the colonial style of architecture. Houses were of weatherboard, usually

Plate 1
Abandoned home, old style, Katikati settlement.

had three or four rooms with a verandah in front, a brick chimney and a corrugated iron roof. Plate 1 illustrates an abandoned home in the block which is representative of the old style. The settlers cleared the land by burning; a few matches were all that was needed. Once cleared, the land was sown in English grasses and crops of wheat, maize, potatoes and turnips. The first season's yields usually exceeded all expectations as the settlers, following the Maori practice, sowed seeds in the potash-rich ashes left from the firing of the fern. In subsequent years yields diminished as the soil became exhausted. This was a process imperfectly understood by the settlers just as was the bush sickness which affected livestock on the Te Puke block. Not until fertilisers were used more scientifically and, in the 1930s, bush sickness related to cobalt deficiency was the environment brought under more effective control. The settlers also cleared swamp land where possible, drained it and brought it under grass. These wetter soils, mostly in the No. 1 settlement, provided some of the best soils and sustained yields. Probably because soils tended to be light elsewhere, Stewart makes the interesting comment that he is against lazy bed cultivation except in swampy ground. The Maoris gave the settlers gifts of fruit and vegetables and taught them to cultivate the kumara and to thatch their temporary dwellings with *raupo* (a type of bullrush). The settlers in their turn produced a bewildering variety of new plants and animals.

Most settlers had an orchard and garden planted soon after arrival. A nursery at Tauranga supplied shelter trees – cypress, beech, radiata, oak, elm and chestnut – all newcomers. Gorse and blackberries and sweet briar were introduced early on and soon became a pest. Used as hedging plants they were usually associated with the ditch-and-bank fence. This type of fence is not to be explained in terms of available material but in the previous experience of the immigrant farmers. Undoubtedly popular with the first Ulster settlers, especially in swampy ground where it aided drainage, the ditch-and-bank fence, usually of three sods, proved less satisfactory in areas of light soils. Stewart says that of several kinds of fence he prefers 'the old fashioned ditch-and-bank and quickset white thorn hedge'. It is more permanent, offers shelter and gives a prettier and more homely landscape.[13] But it appears that thorn quicks were susceptible to a fungus disease in this new environment and few traces of thorn hedges

THE KATIKATI SPECIAL SETTLEMENT IN NORTH ISLAND

Plate 2
Mount Stewart, G.V. Stewart's former residence

remain.[14] Other types of live fences tended to run riot in these conditions and soon the settlers began to replace them with wire fences with puriri, totara or kauri posts. Fencing of all types protected both plants and animals, preventing the latter from eating the poisonous tutu and from wandering into creeks and swamps where they often drowned. The settlers also introduced game birds – pheasant and quail – and Stewart suggested that each of them take out a pair of songbirds – thrushes, blackbirds or bullfinches.[15] He tells us that he was thinking of introducing hares and beagles but there is no evidence to suggest that he did so. The depredations of the rabbit were well known at this time, so it is unlikely that the settlers would have introduced any. Its absence from Katikati was held to be one of its advantages. Besides a few cows, for domestic milk supply, and perhaps some sheep and pigs, most settlers also kept one or two horses for transport. Buggies, drays and four wheeled waggons were widely used once the settlements became established but for some time many settlers only had sledges, akin to Ulster slipes, or *konekes*, a form of transport with a skid in front and small diameter wheels, sometimes made of wood. Sledges came to be restricted more to hilly country while the *konekes* were used on the lowlands.[16]

What remains of the past in the present landscape? The most striking relics are the old homes of the leading Katikati founder

Plate 3
Athenree as it was in 1948

Plate 4
G.V. Stewart's grave, Katikati. He died in 1920, aged 88

families who were renowned for their hospitality. The best known are *Mount Stewart* – George Vesey Stewart's residence – *Athenree* – the once lovely home of Hugh and Adele Stewart and the social focus of the settlement – *Martray, Castle Grace, Woodlands, Larkspur* and *Claremont.* Unfortunately most of them are now in ruins. The generation which built them was unaware of the damage that insect borers could do in certain types of immature timber which was used in addition to kauri. In the Bay of Plenty's subtropical conditions timber houses deteriorate quickly if left vacant and uncared for. *Mount Stewart,* with its fine site commanding extensive views over Bowentown Heads, is now beyond repair (Plate 2). There is little trace of its ballroom and billiard room where the cadets brought out by Stewart to learn farming for a fee of 150 guineas a year once sported themselves. *Athenree* was better preserved until more recent years but it too has fallen into disrepair. Built in the old colonial style and with a galleried dining room, it must have been an elegant and attractive residence (Plate 3). It is sited near the entrance to the Athenree gorge and has excellent views over sea and hills. It comes alive in Adele Stewart's much admired book, *My Simple Life in New Zealand,* in which she relates how in 1884 Te Kooti, once the most feared Maori rebel chief in North Island but later amnestied, descended from the hills with a hundred armed warriors, camped on the lawn and was given tea.[17] The Stewarts left it in 1906. It is now used as a farm outbuilding.

In Tyrone the original Martray still overlooks a small lake near the main Dungannon-Ballygawley road, its elegant Georgian front hiding an older court-yard arrangement of dwelling and outbuildings. The date of the original home may well be seventeenth century. Carved in the kitchen door in the older part are the names of Hugh Stewart, 1855 and G.V. Stewart 1846. Not far away, near the roundabout which acts as a gateway to the Clogher Valley to the west and Omagh to the north, is another fine Georgian farmstead which Stewart lived in after he married. Such links remind us that not enough is known about Stewart's other settlers. Usually shipping lists give details of passengers' occupations and residences but both in New Zealand and Britain these appear to be missing for voyages with special settlers. New Zealand newspapers at least give names of arriving passengers. A letter to the *Belfast News-Letter* complaining about its attitude to the

Katikati settlement and signed by twenty-three of the settlers at least gives some clue to Ulster origins. Seven came from the Ballygawley-Dungannon area but bearing in mind Stewart's widespread recruiting activities it is not surprising to find others from the Ballymena area, from Fermanagh and even from the south of Ireland. Much work remains to be done on this aspect of migration which is poorly documented in comparison with the Katikati settlements.

In many ways Stewart was ahead of his time. It took 30 years and more for his predictions to come true. His vision was quite breathtaking in its scope and perspective. But he made enemies too easily and he lacked, in Arthur Gray's estimation, 'the supreme quality of leadership, the capacity to win devotion'.[18] So near in time to the present are his pioneer settlements that when I first visited them in 1966 there was one surviving member, a Mr Hingston, a 93-old Englishman who had come to Te Puke as a small boy. Arthur Gray himself a descendant of one of the original Katikati families, also talked to me from first-hand knowledge of this much praised and derided man whom he compares with the better known coloniser Edward Gibbon Wakefield. He was often accused of profiteering from the settlements but Gray in his classic account of them considers that his reward was anything but excessive. Stewart made mistakes when he failed to select enough experienced settlers in the second party and he certainly misjudged the quality of the Katikati soils. But it was widely agreed that he got more money for the Bay of Plenty than did all its parliamentary representatives put together. In all he sent 4,000 settlers to the Bay of Plenty, a record not equalled by any of his contemporaries. It is not possible to say exactly how many of these settlers came from Ulster but a reasonable estimate would be something between one quarter and one third. The great majority were Protestant. However, we know that the centre of social life in the small township of Katikati – which began life as Waterford[19] – was the Talisman Tavern run by Barney McDonnell, a Roman Catholic and man of great character.[20]

Katikati retained its Ulster identity longer than Te Puke which, because of its rapid success, was swamped by newcomers before 1900. Gray says that twenty of the pioneer Katikati families were still represented in that community as late as 1950. Today only a handful are left. But many of Stewart's predictions have come true. The

Tauranga lowlands, including Katikati, have become an extremely prosperous farming area with an impressive record of agricultural development and cooperation. It is first class dairying country and its superb climate permits a wide range of fruits to be grown. In recent years dairying has lost ground to the extensive orcharding of kiwi fruit. The landscape changes brought about by this development have been quite remarkable since 1975. For Katikati this prosperity came only after the belated gold-mining boom in Waihi in 1886, the advent of refrigeration, the introduction of new grasses, the scientific use of artificial fertilisers, the establishment of the dairy factory in 1902 (which is now closed), and some 50 years after Stewart first considered it, the railway from Waihi in 1928. These developments were all needed to fulfil Stewart's hopes. He died in 1920 and lies buried in Katikati, the place he loved the most. As an instrument of colonisation both his Katikati and Te Puke settlements must be regarded as important elements in the story of New Zealand. Their history is not widely known, except in New Zealand, perhaps because their record is one of quiet achievement rather than of spectacular accomplishment.

From the viewpoint of European settlement, a century is a long time in New Zealand's history. As a consequence its cities and towns celebrate their first centenary with great determination. Small towns are just as anxious as the large centres to 'do it well'. In 1975 the New Zealand press was unanimous in praising Katikati for providing one of the best centenary celebrations ever to be held in a small town in the North Island. As one of a small number of Ulster people able to accept an invitation to attend, I can only add that the press could well be right for the range of activities on offer over a period of four days seemed quite remarkable. Everything was carried out with great enthusiasm whether the participants be pakeha or Maori. The attention to detail of Katikati's past was delightful. Imagine finding table mats at the Centenary Dinner depicting the *Lady Jocelyn*, the noble ship which left Belfast in 1878 with its Ulster settlers!

The highlight of the Centenary 'week' was a re-enactment of the original landing of the Ulster party on the banks of the Uretara river. They were preceded by a superbly carved Maori war canoe paddled by a crew of some twenty chanting 'warriors'. These Maoris landed in time to greet the settlers who, dressed rather too grandly in period costume, now came into sight on the river in a fleet of small boats. To the

Plate 6
G.V. Stewart

uninitiated, Maori greetings can appear to be more of a threat than a welcome but eventually the pakehas were accepted as coming in peace and were allowed ashore. Some 4,000 people, more than double the town's population, attended this particular function. Other activities included the Centenary Dinner already mentioned which was to have been attended by the Prime Minister, the Centenary Ball, a Maori Concert Party, a rugby match some All Blacks included, a Centennial Parade – which produced some farm implements brought out by the original settlers – and a fly-past by the New Zealand Air Force.

For visitors there was an excellent programme of tours in the local area to look at historic homes or working farms. The organisers of the Centenary programme also made sure that some very good publications were on sale including a reprint of Arthur Gray's An Ulster Plantation and The Katikati Story published by the Tauranga Historical Society. There was also an inter-denominational service with a collection for Corrymeela in Co. Antrim. The Governor-General attended the ceremony to open the George Vesey Stewart Centennial Park and drew lots for new holdings just as the original settlers had done a century before. George Vesey Stewart would have approved!

Published in *Familia: Ulster Genealogical Review*, no. 5, 1989.

Notes

1. Ulster immigrants to New Zealand came as individuals and families prior to the group settlements. Under the terms of the New Zealand Government Act of 1846, the name 'New Ulster' was given to a large part of the North Island. But it is not clear whether this choice of name implied the presence of Ulster settlers or, more likely than not, the whim of somebody in authority. In the 1860s European immigrants came in increasing numbers but it is not possible to separate those from Ulster from immigrants listed as 'Irish' in official records. However, many present-day families with Ulster connections trace their origins to this period. On this rather unsatisfactory evidence, Ulster immigrants appear to have ranged widely from Auckland, Tuakau on the Waikato and Taranaki in the North Island to Canterbury and Otago in the South Island. Two New Zealand premiers were Ulster-born, John Ballance from near Glenavy and William Massey from Limavady.
2. Stokes, E., 'The Settlements of the Ulstermen in *The Katikati Story* (Centennial Souvenir Issue, Tauranga Historical Society, 1975), pp 8–9.
3. Gray, A., *An Ulster Plantation* (2nd edn., Wellington, 1950), p. 5.
4. Stewart, G.V., *Notes on the Origins and Prospects of the Stewart Special Settlement, Kaitkati and Notes on New Zealand as a Field for Emigration* (Omagh, 1877), p. 82.
5. Ibid. p. 80.
6. *The Katikati Special Settlement (Correspondence in the Matter of its Further Extension)*. Immigration File D./3, 1878, National Archives, Wellington. Examples are: *Enclosure No. 2 in No. 25:* letter from the Agent-General to Mr G.V. Stewart, 7 January, 1878. 'I think, as I have said, the delay in forwarding the agreement is much to be regretted, but not because of any loss you have sustained. My reason for regretting the delay is that it has occasioned me a very troublesome correspondence, one in which you will permit me to say you have not shown yourself unmindful of the difficulty in which I was placed'. *Enclosure 3 in No. 25,* Mr G.V. Stewart, Martray House, Ballygawley to the Agent-General, 14 January, 1878. 'You complain about the troublesome correspondence that you have suffered at my hands, but with all due respect to your opinions I think you have no person to blame but yourself. I consider I have as much reason to complain of the position which you as Agent-General have taken in the matter'. *No. 30,* the Hon J. MacAndrew, the Minister of Immigration to the Agent-General, 17 April, 1878. 'The class of emigrants selected by Mr Stewart has always been a very superior one, and judging from the past, I think we may fully confide in his future selections'.

7 Stewart, G.V., *Sequel to Notes on the Origins and Prospects of the Stewart Special Settlement, Katikati, New Zealand* (Omagh, 1878), p. 2.
8 Gray, A., op. cit., p. 59.
9 Ibid., p. 23.
10 Borrie, W.D., 'Immigration to New Zealand since 1854' (PhD thesis, University of Canterbury, Christchurch, 1938), pp 272–3.
11 Gray, A., op. cit., p. 73.
12 Stewart, G.V., *Notes on the Stewart Special Settlement No. 3 at Te Puke, Bay of Plenty* (London, 1880), p. 37.
13 Stewart, G.V., *Notes on the Origins and Prospects*, loc. cit., p. 63.
14 Appropriately enough one of the few places where thorn hedges still flourish is at Mount Stewart, Stewart's old home.
15 Stewart, G.V., *Sequel to Notes on the Origins and Prospects*, loc. cit., p. 6.
16 The *koneke* appears to have been adopted by the Ulster settlers. I do not know its origin. It is still used in some parts of the North Island, for example on the Hauraki plains. Sledges were more likely to have had their origins in Ulster.
17 Stewart, A.B., *My Simple Life in New Zealand* (London, 1880), p. 34.
18 Gray, A., op. cit., p. 7.
19 The name was changed to the Maori 'Katikati' when Stewart realised that there was confusion with the Irish 'Waterford' and that cablegrams were costing him 10s. 0d. extra to have New Zealand inserted. On the letter Te Puke block the first planned township was called Stewartstown but it too gave way to the Maori place name. Katikati township is now a thriving small market and service centre with a population over 2,000.
20 When a scrupulous member of the Orange Lodge protested against the iniquity of buying liquor for the annual celebrations from a Roman Catholic, Barney promptly sent the Lodge half a dozen bottles of whiskey as a present. There were no further complaints.

11

The Goldrush to Lamplough, near Avoca in Victoria, Australia during 1859–60

Denis Strangman

Introduction

In 1986 a woman who was undertaking family history research in England came across the name 'Lamplough', Victoria, Australia, on an ancestor's birth certificate. Hoping to obtain some further information about this place she sent a letter addressed to the 'Postmaster, Lamplough'. Her letter was not delivered to the Postmaster because the Lamplough Post Office had closed its doors about fifty years ago and all that remains of it today are a few wooden stumps in the ground. Fortunately, her letter found its way to officials of the Avoca and District Historical Society (ADHS) and they were able to send her some background information about Lamplough.

What a contrast with the Lamplough of 1860 when anxious gold miners, most of whom had come to Australia from Europe with the great tide of gold seekers in the early 1850's, jostled and fought for their letters from England and elsewhere at a small window of the Post Office. In that year 91,296 letters and 21,203 newspapers passed through the Lamplough Post Office.[1]

The Lamplough gold rush has somehow escaped the history books. In his comprehensive study of the period of the history of Victoria Geoffrey Serle acknowledges that 'the later alluvial rushes to the western fields have never received their due' and identifies the rush to

Lamplough in late 1859 as merely one of the 'chief minor rushes on which ten thousand or more took part', compared with the 'stampedes' to Fiery Creek, Dunolly, Ararat, Pleasant Creek (Stawell) and Back Creek (Talbot) which attracted 'as many as fifty thousand perhaps'.[2]

This essay is an attempt to redress the balance and is based on a wider local history research project in which the course of the rush has been recreated from contemporary sources. This research has led to the construction of a database of the names of more than 3,000 people who had some contact, however fleeting, with Lamplough in the gold rush days and complements an impressive card index system of at least 20,000 names relevant to the early history of the Avoca district, which is maintained by the ADHS.[3]

In recreating the details of the rush it has been possible to draw on the contemporary reports of the correspondents for the various provincial newspapers, including the principal newspaper for the district, the *Maryborough and Dunolly Advertiser* (*MADA*), the *Ballarat Star* (*BS*), the *Ballarat Times* (*BT*), the *Mount Ararat Advertiser* (*MAA*), and the *North Western Chronicle* (*NWC*). As well, there were references to the progress of mining at Lamplough in thirty-two consecutive editions of the weekly 'Mining Report' in the *Melbourne Age* newspaper, covering the period from 8 December 1859 until 26 July 1860, and further frequent references until 13 December 1860. Similarly, references to Lamplough featured in the weekly 'Mining Intelligence' column in the *Melbourne Argus* newspaper almost continuously from 7 December 1859 until 27 December 1860 when it was displaced by the reports from a new rush in the Avoca district at Mountain Creek (Moonambel).[4] Unfortunately, there are no known surviving copies in Australia public libraries of the nearest local newspaper existing at the time, the *Amherst and Back Creek Advertiser* (*BCA*), whose correspondents were among the first to report the rush. However, their reporting was so good that the reports were often reproduced in other newspapers which, fortuitously, have survived.

The Gold Rush

The rush to Lamplough commenced during the weekend of 26–7 November 1859 and followed the discovery of payable ground by two

Welsh brothers, John and Daniel Owens, who had been prospecting 'for some time past' in various parts of a flat leading from the Avoca township which was about three miles to the north. Their find was officially reported on Saturday, 26 November 1859.[5] The Avoca area had been the scene of an earlier large rush in September 1853, initially to an area with the curious name of 'Donkeywoman's Gully' which was in the direction of Lamplough. Indeed, even earlier in 1849, Tommy Chapman, who was a shepherd on the nearby Glenmona property had found some gold in the district but declined to reveal the exact location. Chapman's find was among the first discoveries of gold in Victoria.[6]

Around the time that the Owens brothers were securing their prospecting claim, William Stanley Jevons, who was later to achieve fame as a logician and the economist who expounded the marginal utility theory of value, was telling an audience of the Literary and Philosophical Society of Manchester that based on his observations of the gold fields in Australia, he said:

> ... Not much, perhaps, is to be hoped from the future discovery of alluvial gold. The chief diggings of Victoria have, during the past eight years, been so vigorously undermined and turned up small parties of miners that scarcely a square yard of untouched auriferous ground is left'.[7]

As if to prove Jevons completely wrong, in the same month (November) that gold was discovered at Lamplough there were also major discoveries at (New) Inglewood in Victoria and at Kiandra (Snowy River) in New South Wales. The Lamplough area had already been subjected to the scrutiny mentioned by Jevons but the various prospectors had missed any evidence of a lead and even though some had sunk holes two or three years previously to a depth of 70 and 75 feet, water had come in and swamped them out. But the gold was there, waiting for the Owens brothers and their colleagues.[8]

In some early reports the diggings were identified as the 'Clare Castle diggings', after a hotel of that name run by a George Cartwright which was located on the main road between Avoca and Burn Bank (Lexton), eleven miles to the south. Burn Bank was one of the earliest provisioning centres to be established in the district. It was suggested that the owner of the 'Clare Castle' had backed the prospectors. This was quite likely – gold attracted miners who had a mighty thirst after a hard day's digging and a large gold mining population was good for business. The 'Clare Castle' hotel at this time was an unpretentious structure of about 24 feet by 10 feet, with slab walls 6 feet in height, and a canvas roof.[9]

Prior to the discovery of gold Lamplough virtually consisted of Cartwright's Hotel and nothing more except perhaps for some miners in tents on nearby Rutherford's Creek, a tributary of the Avoca river. This creek had been named after Andrew Rutherford who was the occupant of the Lamplough property during 1851–3. However, he was not the original owner, for the property had been established in 1840–41, just four years after the explorer Major Thomas Mitchell had opened up this territory to the white man. At the time of the rush the nominal owner was John Matheson but he was absent in England during 1860 and the property was managed by William Macoboy Wise.

On the Sunday following the discovery there were 500 diggers at Lamplough. The news must have raced around the district because on the following day, Monday 28 November 1859, there was an estimated 3,000 people on the field. They had come during the night, wending their way through the bush from nearby diggings at Back Creek (Talbot), Kangaroo, Mountain Hut, Amphitheatre, and other places.[10]

By Wednesday every road leading to the district was '... thronged with parties eager to reach the scene of action'. According to one correspondent:

> ... People are not entering, they are literally pouring in. Every conceivable avenue leading to the flat swarms with people. Tents are going up as if by magic. You gaze on a clear spot one moment, turn your attention for a short half-hour to another, then twist round and look at the spot, and find where there was no sound save the neighing of horses or the response of cattle, a small canvas town stands, erected in the short space of time before mentioned. Along the roads leading to our El Dorado, streams of wagons, drays, equestrians, and pedestrians, travel along in one continuous line ...[11]

In the reports of the early days of the rush there are two common features commented on by all the correspondents: the grog and the dust. This was the middle of the Australian summer. There were scorching hot winds and many people preferred to travel at night when 'the tread of men, the clinking of tin bullys, and the rumbling of drays' denoted the great numbers on the outlying roads. But when they reached Lamplough there was dust everywhere:

> ... such a place for dust is not to be described. For minutes after the passing of a wagon or a horse, you cannot see a yard beyond you, and every puff of wind – as I said before is not to be described – is horrible beyond words; and in the midst of this plague bread and meat is openly exposed, not an effort of any kind made to secure either from an increase of their weight by the adhesion of this horror, and to lay the account that would be a task heavier than any laid on the Israelites by the Egyptians.[12]

In one of the few non-journalistic accounts, written thirty-three years later by a former carrier, John Chandler, who had taken supplies from Melbourne to Lamplough and other rushes in the 'fifties', the three things that remained in his memory about Lamplough after all those years were the dust, the grog, and the wickedness. The dust was half way to the axle of his cart, he could only buy a glass of sour beer which cost a shilling and, '... every man was a law unto himself, and the weakest had to go to the wall ... this was a very hell for every sort of wickedness and vice ...', he wrote. Chandler's recollections is confirmed, to some extent, by a contemporary letter written to a friend at nearby St. Arnaud by one of the people on the rush who referred to the 'violence, drunken brawling, crime and debauchery' at Lamplough.[13]

The town appears to have settled down when the Superintendent of the Detective Police in Melbourne sent Detective Thomas Evans of Back Creek on a reconnaissance to Lamplough. In the written report of his visit made during 5–8 December, which was included among some documents only recently catalogued at the Victorian Public Records Office, Detective Evans wrote:

> There is about 300 of the Criminal Class. 250 men and 50 Women on the above diggins. There is a great number of stores and immense number of Grog Shantys. One Theatre in course of erection and 7 dancing Rooms and one Sparring Booth ... the Criminal Class are walking about and they seem very dissatisfied with the diggins. When the Theatre and Dancing Rooms are finished they begin to work ...[14]

Detective Evans was correct about the immense number of grog shanties. One newspaper correspondent referred to a street '... more than half a mile long, the structures of either side being shanties, and there is nothing but grog!'. Another correspondent said Lamplough had been christened the 'Shanty Rush':

> The great trade of the place is in grog, and the principal supporters of the liquor vendors appear to be the visitors who, finding themselves in a strange place, roam about from shanty to shanty in search of acquaintances'.[15]

Still they came: from Ampitheatre, Mountain Hut, Back Creek, Pleasant Creek, Ararat, Dunolly, Epsom, Forest Creek, Amherst, Maryborough, Inkerman, Bendigo, Ballarat, and Castlemaine. Special coaches were put on to transport the miners. Even Cobb & Co. organised special services. The largest initial influx of people appears to have come from Back Creek (later named Talbot) only 10–11 miles away. The road from Back Creek was lined 'by a grand motley caravan'. John Bennett, J.P., one of the magistrates at Back Creek and later the proprietor of the Lamplough Theatre Royal, seized on a novel way of promoting the population flow between the two towns: at the Back Creek Police Court on 3 December he released Margaret Westcott, who was charged with habitual drunkenness, on her promise to go to the new rush.[16]

Ararat was another town to be affected by the Lamplough discoveries, even though it was forty miles distant. A four-horse coach undertook the journey between the two towns and the fare was twenty shillings but many of the miners probably walked the distance. The effect on Ararat trade was illustrated two months later when William Watt, a coffee dealer at Ararat, became insolvent. One of the causes he cited was that all his Ararat customers had gone to Lamplough. Other more enterprising Ararat shopkeepers either followed their customers and transferred to Lamplough or opened branch establishments there.[17]

On 3 December 1859 the Inspector of Police at nearby Avoca, Hugh Ross Barclay, had estimated the population of Lamplough at between 10–12,000 people. In mid-December the District Surveyor, Richard English, estimated a figure of 12,000 but added a qualifying comment that not more than 5,000 were bona fide miners. Already there were suggestions that the area was 'over-rushed'.[18]

The original diggings, which had been relatively shallow at between 6 to 14 feet, had been concentrated on an area near the Owens's prospecting claim, but on Saturday, 17 December – a day when it was 110 degrees in the afternoon shade – a party had bottomed a shaft at 33 feet, about three-quarters of a mile from the old diggings, on the Amphitheatre road. This prompted a second rush and the estimated population on 31 December had grown to 16,000. The population of Victoria at the time was 529,933 which included a total gold-fields population of 201,422 people. Lamplough, with 16,000 people, had by far the greater number of people of any of the 214 gold fields listed in the Registrar-General's return. During the Christmas and New Year of 1859–60 it was the place to be for the Victorian gold seekers and the opportunistic storekeepers who followed the rushes.[19]

The town itself was changing: the main street, Commercial Street, was quickly assuming a settled appearance, the National Bank had opened an office, the dust nuisance had been reduced by the spreading of gravel, there was a better feeling in business and more confidence among the tradesmen. 'The rush, indeed, is losing the shifty and unsettled character that earned for it the sobriquet of the 'shanty rush", one correspondent wrote.[20] For the moment there was cause for cautious optimism. Charles Lawrence, originally from Coleraine, wrote to his sister in Ireland on 27 December advising her of his transfer to this new location and stating that the Lamplough field was a new field 'not yet fairly tried'.[21]

Following the discovery of the new ground, the miners were in exuberant spirits during the Christmas and New Year holiday period. On Monday 2 January 1860 'Christmas Sports' were held on the ground behind the Clare Castle Hotel. According to one correspondent:

> There were platforms erected for the dancers of various classes, six detachments of musicians; and everything calculated to make the assembled miners feel 'glorious o'er all the ills of life victorious.' The pig was there as usual, and our cousins from Cornwall tumbled one another much to our amusement. There were at least four thousand miners on the ground, and the sports were to be continued this day (Tuesday 3 January) and tomorrow.

Another correspondent added that there were wrestling, racing, dancing, and shooting prizes. The pig referred to above was part of the fun, to be chased by the crowd but evidently a large dog, and not a 'biped pork-chaser', caught it.[22] The 'cousins from Cornwall' were the Cornish miners who had found their way to the Avoca district, via South Australia, where they had worked in the copper mines at Burra Burra.

At Lamplough came into the New Year it could boast of a police camp, a Warden's office, surveyed streets, a Post Office, and even its own newspaper, the *Lamplough Advertiser* (*LA*). The *LA* was more of an advertising sheet than a proper newspaper. As with the *BCA*, no copies appear to have survived or to have found their way into any public library in Australia. However, in that year Victorians posted 552,853 copies of newspapers to Great Britain and other foreign parts. Who knows? Individual copies of the *BCA*, *LA*, and other missing Australian newspapers might very well be hidden away in family and library collections in the UK and elsewhere. The *LA* was established by the firm of Nuthill and Gearing who specialised in sending one or other of the partners to a new rush to launch an 'advertising sheet' which usually contained lists of unclaimed Post Office letters and other useful information and was distributed gratis. The manager was Robert Clark, a Scotsman who had once set type for Charles Gavan Duffy on *The Freeman* in Dublin. The journalist was probably Edward Bateman who, at the end of 1860, purchased the *North Western Chronicle* (*NWC*), which was published at Back Creek, from J.H. Gearing (Nuthall had died in Brisbane in October).[23]

In those days journalistic by-lines were rare and while the dispatches from the various newspaper correspondents at Lamplough are an invaluable source in recreating the events of 1859 and 1860, the authors are mostly unknown. It is almost certain, however, that the author of the eighty-five reports from Lamplough which appeared in the *BS* between 3 January 1860 and 19 December 1860 was George Humphreys who had come with the miners from Back Creek in the first few weeks and after the Lamplough rush had been supplanted by a new rush to Mountain Creek (Moonambel) in December 1860, and again accompanied the miners to their new location from where he also sent reports to the *BS*. Humphreys trailed his coat sufficiently so as to be identifiable more than a century later. The authors of other correspondents' reports might have been Godfrey Morgan (who had been associated with the *Mount Ararat Advertiser*), his business partner Henry J. Cope who later went to Inglewood, and another journalist known to be at Lamplough at the time, Thomas McHugh, who was later the sole proprietor and editor of the *Avoca Free Press* newspaper.[24]

Entertainment

The correspondents, not unlike their modern counterparts, appear to have been given free admission tickets to the various public entertainments and so they have left us with useful descriptions of these events. Initially there were two major theatres, the Theatre Royal and the Garrick Theatre. The Theatre Royal, which was a building of 150 by 50 feet, opened on Saturday, 10 December, 1859, and performances were staged by Henry Neil Warner and the Back Creek Company whose previous venue at Back Creek had closed down as a consequence of the Lamplough rush. Competition between the two theatres was fierce and by the first week of February the Garrick had closed and its proprietor, James Rich Bunn, was insolvent.[25]

The performer who probably decided the issue in favour of the Theatre Royal was the American-born actress, Miss Avonia Jones, who appeared between 9–21 January 1860. Her first performance in 'Medea' on 9 January attracted

> ... by far the largest audience that has been seen in Lamplough. Every part of the house was densely packed with people, and all appeared highly pleased. It was very gratifying to witness dignified talent overawing the vulgar whistlers and brawlers who ever attended a theatre, and are popularly known as the Gods. During every speech delivered by Miss Jones, the most illiterate seemed to hold their breath ... .

On the following night the audience also held its breath when the Theatre '... was filled to suffocation and the audience was immeasurably delighted'. An audience estimated at 1,800 attended when she played 'Lucretia Borgia'.[26]

Miss Jones was followed a week later at the Theatre Royal by her future husband, the famous tragedian Gustavus Vaughan Brooke.

Brooke had been touring the provincial theatre circuit and at some venues was either very noticeably under the influence of drink or simply failed to turn up for the performance, but his visit to Lamplough was a resounding success. At Lamplough Brooke played the role of O'Callaghan in 'His Last Legs', Matthew Elsmore in 'Love's Sacrifce', and Iago in 'Othello'. For Brooke's Iago there were 1,200 people crammed into the theatre and they were even perched on the cross pieces holding the sides of the building together.[27]

Henry Burton's Circus was the next major attraction. Two miners who had prior knowledge of Burton's proposed site proceeded to sink a shaft near two essential pegs for the circus tent. The Warden suggested they shift, which they did – to another crucial spot, which they only left after a satisfactory pecuniary arrangement had been made.[28] Other performers at Lamplough were Mr and Mrs Robert Heir (née Fanny Cathcart), Warner, Miss Glyndon, Mr Burton, Mr Furrian, Miss Melville, Miss Evadne Evans, and Mr and Mrs R.B. Dale. The plays performed at Lamplough included 'The Hunchback', 'Honeymoon', 'Fraud and Its Victims', 'Stranger', 'The Marble Heart', 'The Lady of Lyons', 'My Precious Betsy', 'The Cricket on the Hearth', and 'The Iron Chest', most of which would now be familiar only to a student of nineteenth-century theatre.

In April the Theatre Royal was transferred from Royal Street, near the Police Camp, to Commercial Street, two doors from the 'Clare Castle' Hotel. The first performer in the new premises was John Drew, the 'delineator of Irish character' whose 'Hibernian eccentricities' at the Parthenon Theatre in Melbourne during March had been described as '… racy to the last degree and a perfect antidote to ennui'. At Lamplough he performed in 'Handy Andy', the 'Irish Attorney', and the 'Irish Immigrant'. Drew left Australia several months later for England and Ireland where it is believed he made a favourable impression.[29] Another theatrical visitor was the comical singer Charles Thatcher who was very popular with the miners. He made a return visit in September.

The theatrical scene was rather quiet during winter. The first major amusement in spring was the Klaer Brothers and their performing dogs and monkeys which drew a crowd of 1,000. The brothers were Jean, Louis, and Rudolf, described as:

Professors of the Parisian and Turin Verein Schools of the Gymna with their Troupe of Educated Dogs (13) and French Monkey Artistes … This novel and pleasing exhibition is visited by persons of every denomination and shows the mastery of man over the Canine and Simian Races.[30]

In the nineteenth century magicians, hypnotists, and various other entertainers adopted the title of 'Professor'. In September 'Professor' James Eagle demonstrated to his audience the inexhaustible bottle trick in which he was able to fill 100 glasses with drinks of the audience's choice. Prior to coming to Lamplough, 'Professor' Eagle had a run-in at the Inglewood gold fields with a 'Professor' William Montague who stole his apparatus (specially crafted in Birmingham ten years beforehand) and conducted rival shows. The law caught up with 'Professor' Montague and he received a sentence of twelve months imprisonment with hard labour.[31]

In late September 'Worrell and Gardiner's North American (Circus) Company' performed on the ground behind the Shamrock Hotel. William Worrell was a celebrated American clown and his partner at the time, Charles Gardiner, was also from America. There were 'astounding feats' by Herr Christophe. This was the pseudonym of George Christopher, 'one of England's famous tight rope dancers'.[32]

In October 'Professor' L. Bushell's 'Wonder Striking Entertainments in Electro-Biology' (i.e. hypnotism) turned out to be a failure. For some 'inexplicable reason' he was unable to exercise his power. He was advertised as returning soon to California and his dissatisfied audience hastened him on his way.[33] Lamplough was about to be hit by the effects of a new rush and, as if in anticipation, the Theatre Royal wound down its activities.

The Law

Another aspect of the rush which was well chronicled were the proceedings of the Lamplough Police Court, or 'Petty Sessions'. Its first meeting was held on 27 January 1860 in a room provided by John Mylrea, landlord of the 'Lexton Hotel'. It usually met on Monday, Wednesday, and Friday. Between January and December 1860 the highlights of ninety-three sittings were chronicled, at first in the *MADA* and later, when it was established, in the *NWC*. The Avoca

Police Magistrate, Francis Knox Orme, who had been appointed to the area as early as 1 August 1854, sat in the Court on sixty-nine of the ninety-three days reported in the newspapers and the Resident Warden, William Templeton, who had been appointed as a Police Magistrate and Warden at Avoca on 1 July 1855, sat on the Bench on at least twenty-one occasions. Not all defendants had legal representation, but four barristers, Messrs Samuel Boyle, Maurice Travers McDonough, Charles Truwhitt, and Leonard Worsley, undertook most of the Court work during 1860. Serious cases were referred to the Carisbrook General Sessions.

There was always a lengthy Civil List and the impression remains that a number of people waited until they received a summons before giving any thought to paying their bills. One unlucky person who attempted to operate in this way was restaurant keeper James Francis Bentley who had played a key part in the events at Ballarat in 1854 leading to the Eureka Stockdale affair. Originally transported to Australia in 1843 from the Lancashire Assizes for a conviction of forgery he was pardoned and later ran a successful hotel at Ballarat. Following a derisory sentence on a manslaughter charge he was re-tried after agitation by the diggers and received a three year sentence. After obtaining his ticket of leave he came to Lamplough from Ararat.

At Lamplough he ran up various debts, including one of sixteen pounds to a butcher who obtained a summons against him. Bentley skipped Lamplough and went to Melbourne, his personal description and notice of a warrant for his arrest had been published in the *Victorian Police Gazette*. While on his way to the new job one of his children became dangerously ill. Leaving his wife and family camped near their bullock dray he ventured to a nearby town for medicine where he was recognised by a policeman and arrested. He was conveyed the 500 miles back to Lamplough where the butcher reduced the debt from sixteen to eleven pounds. However, Bentley was unable to pay and was sentenced to ten days' imprisonment. The only bright spot was that he did manage to convince his escort to detour past his family so that he could leave the medicine there and tell them what had happened but they were unable to follow him and remained camped beside the bullock dray. It took sixteen days to cover the 500 miles journey.

The episode was publicised in other districts and was no doubt pointed to as an example of the 'long arm of the law'. As a footnote to history, the insertion of the notice in the *Police Gazette* was initiated by Inspector Hussey Malone Chomley, the recently appointed Inspector of Police at Lamplough. Chomley, who went on to become the Chief Commissioner of Police in Victoria, was a nephew of Sir Richard Griffith in Ireland – a name well known to genealogists and historians, by virtue of 'Griffith's Valuation'.[34]

Many of the other, less-newsworthy cases at the Court involved charges of stealing, vagrancy, drunkenness or obscene language. The kind of sentences handed down by the Magistrate were: Drunk and disorderly (40 shillings or 48 hours imprisonment); Insulting and obscene language (3 pounds or 24 hours); Lying in the street (one pound or 48 hours); Vagrancy (3 months); Receiving two stolen blankets (3 months); Sheep stealing (6 months and hard labour); Stealing two loaves of bread worth one shilling (one month, hard labour); No business licence (one pound).[35]

The Assistant Clerk at the Lamplough Police Court during 1860 was Reynell Eveleigh Johns. He kept a daily diary for fifty-five years of his life, including the eleven months he was at Lamplough. His diaries are held in the Australian Manuscripts Collection of the State Library of Victoria and, while they give an interesting insight into the routine of office work and the pastimes of a young and single middle-class civil servant on the Lamplough gold field, he seemed to be careful to avoid direct comment on the proceedings of the Court. For example, even when the Lamplough correspondent of the *BS* alleged that perjury of the 'blackest dye' was indulged in to an 'indescribable extent' at the Lamplough Court, and this allegation was repeated in the Melbourne *Age*, there was not even one passing reference to it in the John's diaries.[36]

Johns was friendly with two of the barristers who appeared in the Court, Samuel Boyle and Leonard Worsley. Boyle was an 'Ararat man' and Johns spent occasional evenings chatting and 'liquoring' with him and Father Richard Fennelly, the Carisbrook-based Catholic priest who ministered at Lamplough. Later, when Worsley came to live at Lamplough. Johns and his younger brother Louis always seemed to be presenting dead or captured possums as a gift to Mrs Worsley, which makes one suspect that either she had a secret passion for the otherwise unpalatable, eucalyptus-flavoured meat of the possum, or skinned them to make possum coats or rugs.[37]

In one of the few personal references in his diary R.E. Johns showed his dislike of another of the Lamplough barristers, M.T. McDonough, by describing him as a 'drunken hound', but McDonough had his supporters. In March 1860 he had given an amateur performance of the part of Dr O'Toole in the 'Irish Tutor' at the Theatre Royal and when he walked on the stage had been greeted by applause which reportedly lasted for three minutes. Reports of a similar performance a few days later appeared in newspapers in Ballarat, Castlemaine (where he had once practised), and Melbourne.[38] McDonough had come from Back Creek to Lamplough to reside but later returned to Back Creek where he died, age thirty-five years, on 5 May 1861, following an attack of delirium tremens. Although he was already a graduate of Trinity College, Dublin, it was claimed in 1853 that he was the first colonial law student to complete the prescribed course of study for admission to the Bar in Victoria, an historical 'first' which has been seemingly overlooked in the two standard texts of his history of the Victorian Bar.[39]

During January 1860 there were several reports in Melbourne newspapers of a population between 20–30,000 at Lamplough, Many (including the criminal element) were quickly attracted to the Inglewood diggings, which by March had an estimated population of between 25–30,000.[40] January and February were characterised in mining affairs by unsuccessful attempts to find a 'main lead' and the absence of a plentiful supply of water for 'washing up' purposes. There were numerous arguments over disputed claims. The 375 disputes adjudicated on by Warden Templeton on the Lamplough diggings in January were the highest number for that month on any gold fields in Victoria, including the longer-established fields of Sandhurst/Bendigo (241) and Ballarat (60).[41]

Armed with their Miner's Rights the diggers on 3 February advanced on William Macoboy Wise's carefully cultivated garden which contained vines and apple trees and turned it upside down in the search for a good patch of gold. Wise was the manager of the Lamplough Station and the adjoining Woodstock Station which often seemed to be conducted as a joint concern. However, the miners did leave standing a willow which had been nurtured from a cutting said to have been taken from a willow overhanging Napolean's grave on St. Helena.[42]

There were hundreds of 'paddocks' of excavated dirt unable to be washed because of a critical lack of water but on 29 February the rain fell in torrents which 'saved us from almost destitution', according to one correspondent.[43] By April a kind a 'lead' had been established and came to be known as the 'Deep Lead' because of the depth of sinking which was, in some instances, as much as 80 feet.

In early May the Chinese diggers arrived. They had been in the Avoca district once before, after the 1853–4 rush. Their method was to rework the old ground. On this occasion there were reports of between 300–500 Chinese miners at Lamplough. They established their own village near the Police Camp but the Warden, William Templeton, encouraged them to move to another site. They must have kept to themselves because there are only a few references to their activities, one exception being a curious court case in October involving the unlawful interception of a consignment of opium addressed to Barrister Boyle. Presumably it was thought that a valuable package of this nature, addressed to a respectable barrister, but intended for the Chinese community, would not attract the attention of potential thieves.[44]

During the Australian winter and spring of 1860 there appears to have been a concentration of mining activity on the Deep Lead and small rushes to other locations within a radius of about six miles of Lamplough, including such places as 'Linger and Die', 'Green Hill Flat', 'Mosquito Gully', 'Fiddler's Hill', 'One Speck Gully', 'Barber's Gully', and 'Woodstock'. The largest of these secondary rushes was to 'Four-Mile Flat', east of Avoca, which attracted 5–6,000 miners. Warden Templeton christened it 'Homebush' and the location was actually surveyed as a town. These unusual but descriptive names caught the attention of English authoress Clara Aspinall who wrote a book entitled *Three Years in Melbourne*, which has been described as 'a vivacious and very feminine account of her visit to Australia'. She visited Avoca and Lamplough in October and informed her readers of the amusing names of the 'Linger and Die' and 'Donkey woman flat' which she had encountered.[45]

Evidence of the restlessness of the digging population was the number attracted in October to the Londonderry rush near Ararat. Doubtless there were also some, including the Chinese, who were attracted to the Kiandra or Snowy River diggings in New South

Wales, but not in the volume forecast by one Lamplough miner who wrote to the *Age* newspaper in June suggesting that if there was good news in Spring, one third of the Victorian miners would leave for the Snowy. The emergency of Four-Mile Flat helped to keep the diggers attracted to the Avoca district.[46]

Daily Life

Life on the diggings was fairly primitive compared to city life but the prices for basic goods were not always as exorbitant as one might expect. The enterprising store keepers who followed the rushes competed with each other and this kept prices down. If washing up was delayed by lack of water or the lead was lost, then business suffered. After the numbers had thinned out the remaining miners at Lamplough obtained sufficient to earn a 'competency' but there were also cases of poverty.[47]

Gold was bought for £3-17-6 an oz., either by the gold-buying storekeepers or one of the three banks with branches at Lamplough, viz the London Chartered, the National, and the Victoria. (In one very lucky case, 108 ozs. were obtained from only five loads of washdirt.) Henderson's the bootmakers advertised that they would make a pair of boots to order for 20 shillings. This was also the price of a seat on the coach between Lamplough and Ararat (a distance of 40 miles). Teeth could be extracted at Avoca for 5 shillings. The 'four pound' loaf of bread cost one shilling but quite often weighed less than four pounds. A letter weighing under half an oz. could be posted anywhere in Victoria for 4d. Boxes at the circus were four shillings and 2/6d in the 'pits'. Beef and mutton fluctuated in price. At nearby Back Creek in October each was 6d per pound and when a price war broke out at Lamplough in the same month the price fell to 2d per pound.[48]

The civil servants had less of a worry about an adequate income but, as R.E. Johns recorded in his diary, they were not often paid on time. Warden Templeton received a salary of £950 per annum. The Police Magistrate, F.K. Orme, received £800. Inspector Barclay received £350 and R.E. Johns, the Assistant Clerk at the Police Court, received £250, which was £50 more than that paid to the Postmaster, Daniel F. O'Connor.[49]

As far as their accommodation was concerned, most of the miners lived in tents or slab huts. If ever a fire broke out the close proximity of the tents and their inflammable nature meant that whole streets or blocks were at risk. Fires were stopped by dismantling those properties in their path. Naptha was burnt for illumination and the 'new light' Kerosene was introduced into Avoca during July and presumably also to Lamplough around the same time.[50]

A seemingly unrelated incident in Melbourne in March provides an insight into what was regarded as neat casual clothes at the time. Three miners from Lamplough visited the Public Library in Melbourne but were asked to leave because they were not suitably attired, being in jumpers (i.e. pullovers, or overshirts). An indignant observer of this incident wrote to the *Argus* newspaper contrasting their appearance with that of another visitor in tattered clothing 'who was in the embraces of Morpheus' and snoring loudly in the 'philological department' of the Library. The 'unsuitably attired' Lamplough miners were dressed in white moleskin trousers, with a crimson silk sash in place of a belt, new fine-woolled grey American jumpers, straw hats and good shoes (one with American knee boots).[51]

Relationships with the pastoralists were two-edged. On the one hand the miners were good customers for supplies of meat. On the other hand, their very numbers interfered with sheep and cattle grazing and the sheep tended to fall down the miners' holes! Also, many of the miners kept dogs as pets and they used to chase sheep and worry them. A group of the miners from Lamplough used to hunt kangaroos with the help of their dogs on a nearby property. The owner objected and laid poisonous baits for the miners' dogs, some of which died. The miners retaliated by facilitating the escape of 160 of the squatter's sheep.[52]

There were two circulating libraries in the town and several of the hotels encouraged custom by providing books and magazines for the use of their customers. Apart from pasting items in his scrap books, the pastimes of R.E. Johns, as recorded in his diary, included walking (50 minutes to reach Avoca), whittling, carving, shooting practice, hunting possums, and playing interminable games of chess and cards – écarte, whist, and piquet – with his friend, R.H. Jenkyns the chemist, who in September also became the Deputy Registrar of Births and Deaths in Lamplough.

In August Mr Joseph Bolderstone had a grand opening of his 'Pleasure Gardens' on the banks of the Bet Bet Creek, about three miles from Lamplough. It was apparently not as bacchanalian as it sounded but consisted of a bowling green ('that can well view in construction with most witnessed in the mother country'), fruit trees, and summer houses. It was described as being near Samuel Scrase's brewery. The area is now known as Lillicur and no evidence of either the brewery or the garden remains.[53]

There were many more men than women on the rushes but there were also some family groups. Sadly there were cases of wife desertion and child neglect. Several of the coronial inquests held during 1860 were on the bodies of very young children who had wandered away from their parents and drowned in waterholes. The Avoca Cemetery Register illustrates the whirlwind nature of the rush. In 1859 there were three entries for interments of Lamplough residents. In 1860 there were 152, and in 1861, only four entries, with an average of less than one a year for the next nine years. The major causes of death were dysentery or diarrhea (39), consumption or infection of the lungs (18), and teething or convulsions (13).[54]

Doctors who practised in the area included the district coroner, Dr F.M. Laidman, Dr Alvara Lofthouse Slater, who in February lost his own daughter aged seven months, Dr Trenery, who specialised in 'diseases of a secret nature' and was charged with malpractice in 1861, and Drs Robert Carr, Richard Close, and Edward Dehane.

The nearest hospital was at Amherst and had been opened in January. There was a larger and longer established hospital at Maryborough, sixteen miles distant, but admission was not guaranteed at either place, however serious the injury or illness. Take the case of Robert Kearney, who had come to Australia from County Down. He was working in the Deep Lead when a drive fell in, breaking his spine and several ribs and dislocating his shoulder. Warden Templeton recommended his admission to the Amherst Hospital. He was taken the eight miles in a springless cart but was refused admission because Templeton was not a subscriber. So, back they went to Lamplough and travelled an additional sixteen miles to Maryborough where he died an hour and a half after admission. Similarly, Charles Winch, a restaurant keeper who had been burnt in an explosion, was transported to Maryborough but was refused admission because the hospital was full. He was conveyed back to Lamplough, arriving at 3 a.m. after an eight-hour trip, and died that night. Owen Owens, a brother of the prospectors, was another victim of a cave-in when fifteen tons of earth fell on him and a mining companion George Juby. Juby died instantly but Owens with a fractured spine and several broken ribs and internal injuries, lingered for another fourteen hours.[55]

Religion

The only surviving evidence of any religious activities at the rush in the very early days is an item in the published diary of an itinerant preacher, the Rev. J.J. Westwood, who visited Lamplough during 5–7 January 1860 in between relieving duties at the Scotch Church in Ararat. At Lamplough he preached to a crowd of nearly 1,000 miners. There was also a passing reference to a 'disciple of that celebrated English fanatic Spurgeon' (a famous nineteenth-century Calvinist preacher) who spoke in front of the Warden's office. On Tuesday 27 December an unnamed 'Israelite with a serious cast of countenance' preached from opposite the United States Hotel but his audience of some hundreds deserted him when a foot race started nearby.[56]

Of the major denominations, there are intermittent references only to the subsequent activities of the Catholics, Church of England, and Wesleyans. The Rev. T.B. Garlick of the Church of England was responsible for both the Avoca and Amherst areas and although there was a report in February that arrangements had been made to provide a service once in the fortnight at Lamplough, one suspects that the Lamplough adherents were encouraged instead to go to Avoca where the Rev. Garlick had average Sunday congregations of 170 people during 1860. Despite a report of a meeting at Lamplough in July to get something started it seems that nothing much happened until November when Archdeacon Archibald Crawford of Castlemaine reported that a lay reader had been provided who officiated every Sunday and a Sabbath-school had been established. Bishop Charles Perry from Melbourne visited Avoca on 20 April 1860 but did not apparently divert to Lamplough.[57]

By contrast the Wesleyans were very active on the goldfields at this time. In 1859 they had more churches in Victoria than either the Catholic Church or the Church of England. At Lamplough during the 1860 the Wesleyans outgrew their accommodation in May and again in July. The Rev. J.C. Symons of Amherst preached on Sunday

20 May when the new Wesleyan Church was opened. Rev. Symons had originally been sent from Adelaide for six months to minister to the former South Australian residents who had followed the rushes but he ended up spending thirty-four years in Victoria. Before coming to Australia he had helped to establish the Y.M.C.A. in London and was the first secretary. Funds were soon pledged for the Lamplough building which was of iron with a canvas roof. There was a report that on one particular Sunday 120 children attended the Sunday School. By July the building was not big enough and an old store in Amphitheatre street was purchased. The Rev. William S. Worth was the Minister of the Circuit.[58]

The Catholics were the first to obtain a chapel at Lamplough and it was opened on 4 March 1860. It was an iron building of 60 feet by 30 feet with a canvas roof. Mass was celebrated by Father R.F.X. Fennelly who had pioneered the Catholic mission at Carisbrook where he was now based. He was a Tipperary man who had been ordained from All Hallows, Dublin, in 1855.[59]

There are references in the R.E. Johns diaries to Father Fennelly visiting Lamplough regularly at least during February to July. It is unlikely, however, that he visited weekly because in May there was a case in which Sgt. McDonald fined Constable Patrick Burke £1 for disobeying an order not to go to the Catholic chapel in plain clothes and in the course of Burke's appeal against the penalty he mentioned that the Catholic clergy attended only one a fortnight or three weeks.[60]

The Catholic chapel was blessed by Bishop Goold during a retreat he conducted at Lamplough between 10–12 August 1860. In his diary he reported that people came from Avoca, Back Creek, and Amphitheatre. There were 100 communicants on the Sunday, when he also confirmed four people.[61]

The end

In early December 1860, a little over one year after the Lamplough rush had helped to temporarily depopulate Back Creek, a new rush to Mountain Creek (later called Moonambel, meaning 'hole in the mountain') had an even more significant and lasting effect on Lamplough. The new diggings were at the northern extremity of the Pyranees ranges, twelve miles west of Avoca and fifteen miles from Lamplough, on McKinnon's property.

On Sunday 9 December 1860 the sound of hammers rang through Lamplough as stores and shanties were taken down for removal to the new rush. The Catholic chapel, which doubled as a school, and the Wesleyan chapel, built of galvanised iron, both found their way to Mountain Creek. Even George Cartwright of the 'Clare Castle' hotel followed the miners to their new location and attempted to establish another 'Clare Castle' there. 'Carts loaded with tents, stores, wives, and children, passed through Commercial street almost every quarter of an hour during the day ...', one correspondent wrote of the Sunday exodus.[62]

Other rushes to Navarre (Barkly), Hines, and Redbank, around the same time, sealed Lamplough's fate. Even the Avoca District Surveyor Richard English, who was generally conservative in his estimates reported a population of 35,000 at Mountain Creek in his December report to the Board of Science. The removal of buildings from Lamplough had turned the town 'into an emblem of a graveyard', according to the Lamplough correspondent of the *BS*; '... the mining Israelites have in a body left Egyptian Lamplough, and gone to happy Mountain Creek Canaan ...', he wrote and, indeed, within a fortnight he had transferred there himself.[63]

By the time of the Census on 7 April 1861 there were 469 people remaining on the Lamplough goldworkings, 110 people in the village itself, and a further 53 people living nearby – a total of about 600, compared to the thousands twelve months previously. The population of nearby centres included: Avoca township (518), Amphitheatre goldworkings (370), Inglewood town and gold areas (4,584), Navarre (875), Hines (2,401), Amherst and Back Creek areas (4,080). Mountain Creek and Redbank had a total of over 11,000 inhabitants.[64] The population of Lamplough hovered around 100 for the remainder of the century and dwindled to about 50 by 1905. Today there is only one family living on the site of the old town.

Ironically, just as the miners were preparing to desert Lamplough in December 1860 a tender notice appeared in the newspapers for the construction of a water reservoir. In February 1860, when water had been very scarce, 1,500 miners had crowded into a meeting at the Theatre Royal to petition the Government for a share of the money which had been set aside for water supplies to the gold fields. In this they were successful. A site was approved in October and by April

1861 a reservoir of six acres with a capacity of nine million gallons had been constructed at a cost of £1,232. This prompted the Back Creek-based *NWC* newspaper (jealous at its less favoured treatment) to suggest that it was '... an outlay of money neither warranted by the resources of the locality nor the number of its population ...'.[65]

The reservoir still stands today and is shaded by some large and attractive Australian native trees. It, the mullock heaps along the course of the lead, and a few rusted implements occasionally turned up by farmers, are the only material evidence that this was once the site of a busy rush on which the hopes and expectations of thousands of miners rested. Despite an appeal in the *Newsletter* of the ADHS, there are no known surviving photographs or pictorial sketches of any aspect of the Lamplough rush and so we have had to rely almost entirely on the chronicles of those mostly anonymous newspaper correspondents.

There has been the recent welcome appearance of a published history of the early days in Avoca, a history of Barkly, the story of Glenpatrick and Nowhere Creek, and a history of the adjoining Shire of Lexton.[66] There is plenty of room for further detailed studies of the gold rushes in the North Western region of Victoria. This particular essay about Lamplough illustrates the interrelationship between the rushes to Back Creek (Talbot), Lamplough and Mountain Creek (Moonambel). One day we will be able to weave these and similar stories together until they reveal the way in which the great tide of humanity which followed the rushes went from one part of Victoria to another, and even crossed into New South Wales, and also to New Zealand as they followed the gold, leaving small settlements in their wake, some to flourish and others, like Lamplough, eventually to perish and remain merely as a location sign on the main highway or a name on an ancestor's birth or death certificate.

Postscript

In the course of undertaking this research two interesting features of genealogical interest have emerged – the almost exclusively European origin, and the relative youthfulness, of those who were associated with Lamplough, however fleetingly. Scarcely any were over fifty years of age. Examples of the origin and age of some of these people in 1860 (some of whom are mentioned in this essay) are as follows: **John**

Mitchell Barr, Miner, Paisley, Scotland, 24 years; **Edward John Bateman,** Journalist, Hatton Garden, London, 28 years; **James Francis Bentley,** Restaurant keeper, Surrey, England, 42 years; **G.V. Brooke,** Actor, Dublin, 42 years; **Robert Clark,** Printer, Dunfermline, Fifeshire, Scotland, 34 years; **John Cooke,** Editor, *MADA,* Abingdon, Oxfordshire, 39 years; **Dr E.F. Dehane,** Devon, 54 years; **Rev. R.F.X. Fennelly,** Catholic priest, Tipperary, 40 years; **James Hugh Gearing,** Newspaper proprietor, Brompton, Kent, England, 39 years; **Mrs R. Heir,** Actress, England, 27 years; **R.E. Johns,** Assistant Clerk, Police Court, Crediton, Devon, England, 26 years; **Avonia Jones,** Actress, Richmond, Virginia, U.S.A., 21 years; **Dr F.M. Laidman,** District Coroner, Exeter, 28 years; **Frederick Lowe,** Storekeeper, Nottinghamshire, England; **M.T. McDonough,** Barrister, Parsonstown, Ireland, 34 years; **Thomas McHugh,** Journalist, Castlederg, Co, Tyrone; **John McPhee,** Coach driver, Fort William, Scotland; **John Matheson,** Landowner and banker, Lairg, Sutherlandshire, Scotland, 39 years; **Godfrey Morgan,** Newsagent, Bath, Somerset, England, 23 years; **Francis Knox Orme,** Police Magistrate, Ireland, 47 years; **Owen Owens,** (Brother of prospectors), Holyhead, Wales, 39 years; **W.H. Puddicombe,** Newsagent, Dartmouth, Devon; **Samuel Scarse,** Brewer, Sussex, 47 years; **Dr Alvara Lofthouse Slater,** London, 37 years; **Rev. J.C. Symons,** William Templeton, Gold fields Warden, Glasgow, 32 years; **William Macoboy Wise,** Property manager, Tulla, Co. Clare, 45 years; **Leonard Worsley,** Barrister, 41 years.

The writer was a member of the Avoca and District Historical Society (ADHS). His great grandfather, William Downing Strangman, came from County Cork to Victoria in 1853, was married at Ararat in 1859 and moved to Lamplough during the rush in 1860, where he operated a puddling machine for several years. The family remained in the Avoca district for eighteen years before moving to New South Wales.

Published in *Familia: Ulster Genealogical Review,* no. 3, 1987.

Notes

1 *Votes and Proceedings (V&P)*, Victorian Legislative Assembly, 1860–1861, Vol. 1, Paper A 35. Reply to question by Mr Hadley. Of the 306 post offices in Victoria in 1860, Lamplough rated number eighteen in terms of volume of letters.

2 Geoffrey Serle, *The Golden Age: A History of the Colony of Victoria 1851–1861*, p. 217.

3 The Avoca and District Historical Society (ADHS) was founded in 1984 and is dedicated to preserving, collecting and researching the history of Avoca and the surrounding district.

4 Microfilm copies of the *Age* and the *Argus* newspapers for this period are held at the National Library of Australia (NLA) where much of the research for this article was undertaken. Only a limited run of hard copies of the other major Melbourne daily newspaper, the *Herald*, where available for perusal but it also carried similar references to Lamplough. The writer wishes to thank Margaret Brennan and Bill Tully and their colleagues in the Newspaper Reading Room of the NLA for their assistance.

5 *Ballarat Star (BS)*, 6 Aug. 1860; Report from the Board Appointed to Consider Applications for Rewards for the Discovery of New Gold Fields; *(Rept. Bd.)*, 1864, pp Vi, xvi. Extracts from the *Mining Surveyors's Reports (MSR)* for November 1859; No. 7 published 19 Dec. 1859, Board of Science, Melbourne; Maryborough Mining District, Avoca Division, p. 13; *V&P*, 1862–3, Paper D 33; Report from the Select Committee on Gold Prospectors, Appendix. Minutes of Evidence Taken Before the Select Committee During Session, 1861–2.

6 Margaret Oulton. *A Valley of the Finest Description – A History of the Shire of Lexton* (1985), p. 337; James Flett, 'Gold Discoveries in Victoria Before 1851', *Mining and Geological Journal*, Vol. 6, No. 4, 1959–1960.

7 W.S. Jevons, 'Remarks on the Australian Goldfields', read 15 Nov. 1859. In the First Volume of the Third Series of *Memoirs of the Literary and Philosophical Society of Manchester*, Session 1859–60 (Manchester, 1861), pp 1–16.

8 *Maryborough and Dunolly Advertiser (MADA)*, 1 Dec.1857; *Argus*, 30 Jan. 1860.

9 *Ballarat Times (BT)*, 5 Dec. 1859.

10 Report from *Back Creek Advertiser (BCA)* reproduced in the *Bendigo Advertiser (BA)*,1 Dec. 1859.

11 *MADA*, 2 Dec. 1859; *BCA* report reproduced in the *Mount Ararat Advertiser (MAA)*, 6 Dec. 1859.

12 *BT*, 7 Dec. 1859; *MADA*, 12 Dec.1859.

13 J. Chandler, *Forty Years in the Wilderness* (1893); see also A.J. Hopton, 'John Chandler Goldfields Courier' in *Victorian Historical Magazine* (*VHM*), Royal Historical Society of Victoria, Vol XXIV, May 1951, pp 92–117. Information supplied by Yvonne S. Palmer to Jessie M. Cameron, Hon Secretary, St Arnaud and District Historical Society Inc. in reply to inquiry from writer, 23 Dec. 1985.

14 Report, Thomas Evans, 8 Dec. 1859, VPRS 937, Unit 6, Victorian Public Records Office (VPRO).

15 *BT*, 7 Dec. 1859; *MADA*. 7 Dec. 1859.

16 *BT*, 5 Dec. 1859; *MADA*, 7 Dec. 1859.

17 *Argus*, 15 Feb. 1860.

18 Telegram, Barclay to Chief Commissioner, Police, 3 Dec. 1859, VPRS 937, Unit 6, VPRO; *MADA*, 28 Dec. 1859.

19 BCA in *BA*, 30 Dec. 1859; *Victorian Government Gazette* (VGG), No 45, 11 Apr. 1860, p. 651; Return of the Distribution of the Population Within the Various Mining Districts of the Colony of Victoria on 31 Dec. 1859 published in the *Argus*, 24 Oct. 1860.

20 *MADA*, 30 Dec. 1859.

21 Copy of letter kindly supplied by Dr Brian Trainor, Director of the Public Record Office in Northern Ireland, D955/8, the Lawrence correspondence is also quoted in: Patrick O'Farrell, *Letters from Irish Australia 1825–1929* (NSWUP, 1984), pp 46, 225.

22 *MADA*, 4 Jan. 1860; *MAA*, 6 Jan. 1860.

23 *Victorian Parliamentary Papers* (VPP), 1862–3, Paper No. 33, Report of the Post Office Department, Victoria, 30 Sep.1862; Lorna Banfield, *Colonists of the Early Fifties: J.W. and S.A. Banfield* (1972), p. 31; J.W. Banfield, *Reminiscences of an Incident at Dunolly Goldrush and of Coming to Australia in 1852*, MS 1765 (Handwritten); Same, MS1723 (typed), NLA, Also published in *MAA*, 30 Dec. 1893; J.W. Banfield was an early partner of Nuthall and Gearing; 'Robert Clark, J.P.', *Ballarat and Vicinity*, Ed., W.H. Kimberly, (Ballarat, 1894), pp 64–6; 'Obituary. The Late E.J. Bateman', *The Australasian Typographical Journal*, No. 274, April 1893, pp 2,356–7, Identified in Biographical file, La Trobe Library, Melbourne.

24 Godfrey Morgan, Alexander Sutherland and others, *Victoria and Its Metropalis* (*VIM*), Vol. 2, 1888, p. 116; and Margery and Betty Beavis. *Avoca – The Early Years*, 1986, pp 64, 211. (I am indebted to the Beavis sisters for alerting me to the existence of the diaries of R.E. Johns.); Thomas McHugh: Summary of obituary in *Avoca Free Press* (*AFP*), 30 Jan. 1905, held by ADHS; and Miss Annie Mitchell, *Back to Avoca, 1921*; *A Brief History*, M. 3255, Australian Manuscripts Collection of the NLA), cited also in *Beavis*, op. cit, p. 63.

25 *BT*, 13 Dec. 1859; *BS*, 6 Feb. 1860.
26 *MADA*, 11 Jan. 1860; *BS*, 12 &17 Jan.1860.
27 *Bell's Life in Victoria and Sporting Chronicle* (*BL*), 4 Feb. 1860; *MADA*, 6 Feb. 1860.
28 *MADA*, 6 Feb. 1860.
29 *MADA*, 9, 11, 14 & 16 Apr. 1860; *Age*, 1 June 1860.
30 *BS*, 6 Sep. 1860; *MADA*, 30 July 1860.
31 *MADA*, 8 Aug. 1860.
32 Mark St Leon, *Spangles and Sawdust: The Circus in Australia* (1983), pp 31, 41–2; *MADA*, 1 Oct. 1860.
33 *North Western Chronicle* (NWC), 18, 25 Oct. 1860; *MADA*, 26, 31 Oct. 1860.
34 *BS*, 31 Mar. and 2 Apr. 1860; report from *Mount Alexander Mail* (MAM) in *MADA*, 4 Apr. 1860; *Table Talk*, 30 Sep. 1892.
35 Ms Helen Harris, Hon. Secretary of the ADHS, kindly itemised for me all the offences committed at Lamplough which were notified in the *Victorian Police Gazette* (VPG) between November 1859 and 25 April 1861. The major offences were: robbery of the person (35), robbery from the tent or dwelling place (31), horse stealing (29), robbery from the store (13).
36 *R.E. Johns Diary* (*REJ*) and associated papers, MS 10075, Australian Manuscripts Collection, State Library of Victoria; see also: Carol Cooper. 'Reynell Eveleigh Johns: A Rediscovered Victorian', *La Trobe Library Journal*, Vol. 5: No. 20, Oct. 1977, pp 90–96; Cooper suggest (note 5) that Johns could have had a museum at Lamplough, but his diary seems to suggest it was only a sitting room (*REJ*, 24, 25 Oct. 1860); Carol Patricia Cooper, 'The Beechwood Collection of Aboriginal Artefacts', BA (Hons.) thesis, Australian National University (ANU), 1975; *BS*, 7 June 1860; *Age*, 8 June 1860.
37 The Australian natives used to hunt and roast the possum. Mrs Isobel Massary (Elizabeth P. Ramsay-Laye) was offered a taste of roasted possum by members of the Avoca tribe when she visited the area in the early 1850s but found it to be 'very tough' with a disagreeable flavour, *Social Life and Manners in Australia*, 1861, pp 55–68. (The tribe had been virtually wiped out by the time of the rush).
38 *REJ*, 21 Oct. 1860; *MADA*, 2 Apr. 1860; *BS*, 3 Apr. 1860; *MAM*, 4 Apr. 1860; *Age*, 5 Apr. 1860.
39 *Argus*, 29 Oct. 1853; both J. L. Forde and Sir Arthur Dean claim that Henry Lawes in 1859 was the first 'colonial barrister' to be admitted. J.L. Forde, *The Story of the Bar in Victoria*, 1913, p. 235; Arthur Dean, *A Multitude of Counsellors: A History of the Bar of Victoria*, 1968, p. 26. The

Librarian of the Victorian Supreme Court Library was unable to verify the accuracy of the McDonough claim, letter to author, 24 Nov. 1986.

[40] *Herald*, 18 Jan. 1860; *Age*, 24 Jan. 1860; *Argus*, 30 Jan. 1860; *Argus*, 20 Mar. 1860; Inglewood correspondent of the *MAM*, 24 Feb. 1860.

[41] *VPP*, 1860–61; disputes on the Gold Fields, reply to a Question put by Mr Brodie, 30 Aug.1860; by June 1860 there was a greater number of disputes at Homebush (51) than at Lamplough (32).

[42] *Argus*, 30 Jan. 1860; *MAA*, 7 Feb. 1860; *BS*, 7 Feb. 1860; *Herald*, 9 Feb. 1860.

[43] *BS*, 6 Mar. 1860.

[44] *MADA*, 4, 7, 9 May 1860; *Argus*, 9 May 1860; *BS*, 10 May 1860; *NWC*, 11 Oct. 1860.

[45] Clara Aspinall, *Three Years in Melbourne*, London, 1872; chp. XII; entry for Butler Cole Aspinall (Clara's brother), *Australian Dictionary of Biography* (*ADB*), Vol. 3, A–C, 1851–90.

[46] *Age*, 12 June 1860; *BS*, 16 June 1860.

[47] The Lamplough correspondent of the *BS* reported that '... At Green Hill Flat I noticed many a poor fellow eating for his dinner nothing but dry bread, and the quantity so small that a child three years of age could manage double as much if accompanied with a slight snack of butter.', *BS*, 25 June 1860.

[48] R. Brough Smyth, *The Gold Fields and Mineral Districts of Victoria*, 1869, reprinted, Queensberry Hill Press, 1980, p. 100; *MADA*, 3 Oct.1860; *NWC*, 14 Oct. 1860.

[49] *VPP*, 1859–60, Paper No. 78, Statistics of the Colony of Victoria for the Year 1859; *VPP*, 1862–3, Paper No. 9, Statistics of the Colony of Victoria for the Year 1861 (Johns and O'Connor).

[50] *MADA*, 11 July 1860.

[51] *Argus*, 4 Apr. 1860.

[52] *MADA*, 28 May 1860.

[53] *BS*, 6 Sep. 1860; *NWC*, 6 Sep. 1860.

[54] Analysis of Lamplough interments undertaken by Ms Helen Harris, Hon. Secretary of the ADHS, during transcription of names from Avoca Cemetery Register to ADHS card index.

[55] *BS*, 10 May 1860; *Age*, 11 May 1860; *BS*, 6, 9 Aug.1860.

[56] J.J. Westwood, *Journal of 8 Years Itineracy in Australia as a Minister of the Gospel*, 1865, p. 90; BCA report in *Age*, 12 Jan. 1860; *MAA*, 3 Jan. 1860.

[57] *The Church of England Record for the Diocese of Melbourne* (Ch. Rec.), No. XLI, May 1860.

[58] *The Christian Times and the Australasian Weekly News* (CT), Vol. III, No. 4, 27 Oct. 1860; official return of the number of Churches etc, C of E

(163), RC (69), Presbyterian (74), Wesleyan (179), *CT*, Vol. II, No. 92, 7 July 1860; *A Century of Victorian Methodism* (ed.), Rev. C. Irving Benson, 1935, p. 98; *BS*, 20 July 1860.

59 *MADA*, 2 Mar. 1860; *From Abel to Zundolovich*, comp. by Cather T.J. Linane, p. 45; Rev. Walter Ebsworth, *Pioneer Catholic Victoria*, Melbourne 1973, pp 233–4, 428, 441–2, 445–8, 481, 497–8.

60 *REJ*, 27 Feb.; 2, 3 Mar. (Fr Fenelly: '… the best fellow here …'), 13, 21 Apr., 5 May, 16 June, 7, 28 July 1860; Report, Constable Burke to Inspector Barclay, 8 May 1860; VPRS 937, Unit 6, *VPRO*.

61 *The Diaries of Archbishop Goold*, Graphic Books, 1979, p. 78. This book appears to paraphrase the full entries. Slightly more detail of the Lamplough visit was contained in a transcription from the original Goold Diaries supplied by Mr Les McCarthy of the Diocesan Historical Commission Melbourne, Letter to author, 21 June 1986.

62 Ebsworth, Op. cit., p. 428; Benson, Op. cit., p. 452; *The Pioneer and Mountain Creek Advertiser*, No. 11, 16 Feb. 1861; sale notice for Moonambel 'Clare Castle' (only surviving issue reprinted by ADHS).

63 *BS*, 15 Dec. 1860.

64 Victorian Census 1861; *VPP*, 1862–3, Paper No. 1.

65 *NWC*, 20 Dec. 1860; *MAA*, 21 Feb. 1860; *MADA*, 26 Oct. 1860; *V&P*, 1862–3, Paper No. C21; reservoirs on the Gold Fields Return, Legislative Assembly, 5 Mar. 1863, 'Lamplough. This place is deserted and the Reservoir remains only useful for pastoral purposes'.

12

Family Migration to New Zealand The Bassett Family of Ballygawley, Downpatrick, County Down

John Bassett

In pursuing genealogical research on an amateur basis over many years, a number of features which I initially thought were unique to my own family I now recognise are part of a wider pattern involving a large number of emigrants from Ulster over a considerable period of time. Having lived in Inch parish, north of Downpatrick, Co. Down, for at least two hundred and fifty years, my family has provided its fair share of emigrants, particularly to New Zealand. The factors which contributed to this migration were the usual ones of large families; increased pressure on, and lower returns from, land at home; frequent advertisements in the local press offering cheap fares and sometimes free land; and encouraging reports concerning gold findings in Australia and New Zealand. These influences encouraged and persuaded the more entrepreneurial family members to emigrate in search of success.

Beginning in 1862, a number of members of my great-grandfather Bassett's family from the townland of Ballygawley, Inch, left Co. Down for New Zealand, to both the North and South Islands. The second eldest, Edward Bassett, born 1826, had married Miss Ann Leonard in 1849, and owned a grocery shop in Church Street, Portaferry for a number of years during which time he was a founding shareholder in the formation of the Portaferry Gas Co.[1] He and his family emigrated to Auckland on the *Indian Empire* arriving on 17 October 1862 along with 380 other passengers. A copy of a simple drawing of the ship made by their eldest son, William John, is deposited in the Public Record Office of Northern Ireland.[2] A small two line entry in the *Downpatrick Recorder* of 17 January 1863 notes 'the emigrant ships *Romulus* and *Indian Empire* are reported in New Zealand', no doubt to the relief of anxious relatives at home. In the book *Early Northern Waitoa*, published in 1916,[3] Edward is stated as having lived at Mangere, Auckland, but when gold was discovered at the Thames he was one of the first on the field. After some success he sold his claim in 1876 and moved to Aratapu where he farmed until he died in 1909. When Hobson County was separated from Otamatee in 1886 he was elected the first member of the Council for Aratapu by a considerable majority. His son, Thomas Bassett, born in Portaferry in 1856, became a successful farm and road contractor, represented his area on county councils and education and hospital boards for many years. After his marriage to a Miss Chadwick, the daughter of the storekeeper at Aratapu, he bought a river bank house, placed it on a raft and floated it to a site on the family homestead on the Aratapu-Sargaville road. Thomas was instrumental in forming its inception in 1902 until his death in 1928. He was also one of the early settlers on the Tatarariki flats region and, along with others, helped develop that region.

The eldest daughter of Edward and Anne married in New Zealand George Lendrum from Clogher, Co. Tyrone, who sailed with his brother Robert to New Zealand on the *Romulus* previously mentioned. The Lendrum family settled on the Tatarariki flat region and descendants still own extensive lands there. A copy of a map of the Lendrum family farm at Clogher was sent to relatives in Te Koparu recently.[4]

Edward Bassett's sister, Margaret, married in Inch Church Anne's brother, Thomas Leonard, the landsteward on the Maxwell estate at Finnebrogue, Downpatrick. After a period of seventeen years at Finnebrogue, during which time his progressive developments and sound organisation were widely acclaimed and he himself was described as 'the Finnebrogue Prime Minister',[5] in 1864 he too decided to emigrate to New Zealand to join his sister and brother-in-law. The *Downpatrick Recorder* records the presentation of a watch and chain to Mr Leonard by the tenants of the estate as a mark of their esteem.[6] The quality of Mr Leonard's stewardship is fully documented in the reports of the Finnebrogue Harvest Home,[7] as is Mrs Leonard's ability as a crafts-woman, winning the silver cup for several years for the most points collected for various craft skills. The Inch National School registers record two of the Leonard children after 5 July 1864 as 'gone to New Zealand'.[8]

The Leonard family sailed to New Zealand on the *British Trident* and lived near Edward and Anne Bassett at Mititoi. One of their children, Anne, married her double first cousin William John Bassett with unfortunate consequences for several of the ensuing family. Family postcards, showing forestry clearing, mention Thomas Leonard as being foreman at the sawmills at Te Koparu from where, I am informed, timber from the Northern Wairoa region was shipped to Australia for the rapid housing development in Sydney, New South Wales. Descendants from the Bassett and Lendrum families are to be found in a wide range of business, professional and political positions in the North Island, the most widely known being Dr Michael Bassett, the Minister for Internal Affairs in the present Labour government.

Another brother and sister also emigrated slightly later but this time to Christchurch, South Island. Samuel Kennedy Bassett, born 1840, left Inch National School at the age of twelve years and served his time to the grocery trade, with his older sister Sarah, in Church Street, Downpatrick. Sarah had married, at the age of 16, an older distant Bassett relative, Thomas Bassett, who owned the spirit grocery shop. Also working in the shop was David Morrow, a brother-in-law, whose wife Madeline Bassett died while giving birth to their first child and is buried with the child in Saul Graveyard. (The faded inscription begins 'Erected by David Morrow of Christchurch, Canterbury in loving memory ...').

In the late 1860s it is reported Mrs Sarah Bassett sent David Morrow to New Zealand with a cargo of Irish pork which sold so well that Samuel Kennedy Bassett decided to emigrate and go into business with him in Christchurch. The *Downpatrick Recorder* records the presentation of a bible by Ballygawley Orange Lodge to S.K. Bassett prior to his departure for 'Australia'.[9] A copy of a diary written by S.K. Bassett[10] records that he left Downpatrick with his wife and niece on 17 March 1869, travelled by the *Prince Patrick* to Fleetwood, by train to London and departed from Blackwall on the sailing mouth to load final stores. The diary records 'we went ashore to the rocks, which lay opposite the ship, to explore. I took the gun to get a rabbit or so but nothing worth shooting so that was our last walk on English soil'.

The celebration crossing the equator and the high standard of cleanliness of the ship are later reported and on 3 May it is noted 'passed a ship called the *Southern Cross* bound from London for Melbourne, she started two days before us'. By 22 May he reports the eggs and butter brought with them are nearly done while they have not only enough hams for their own use on board ship but enough to start housekeeping with when they arrive. They also supplied the cook with their own oatmeal which, when baked, 'eats nicely with the ham' and they had enough 'porter' (Guinness), which Sam had personally bottled before leaving Downpatrick, for the entire journey. The *True Briton* arrived at Melbourne on 22 June and Sam reports seeing the wreck of the *Hurricane* which left London some time before them only to be wrecked on the approach to Melbourne. Fortunately the passengers and crew were saved.

On arrival in New Zealand Morrow and Bassett went into partnership in the hardware and machinery business with depots in Manchester and Cashel Street, Christchurch. In 1875 Sam went to America to purchase McCormick reapers and binders and travelled on to Ireland. He waited in Downpatrick while sister Sarah sold not only her shop in Church Street but her late husband's 28-acre farm beside the river Quoile and two acres at Ballygawley.[11] A remarkable coincidence appears in the *Downpatrick Recorder* of 30 January 1875. The advertisement for the auction of Mrs Bassett's spirit grocery business in Church Street including stock, 'as Mrs Bassett is about to leave Ireland' appears directly above auction advertisement for the mansion house and extensive farm at Lisbeg, Co. Tyrone, of George Vesey Stewart, 'in consequence of his leaving Ireland', this being the George Vesey Stewart who established the settlement at Katikati. Also included in the same issue is the weekly advertisement by the Edinburgh agent for the Provincial Government of Otaho offering free passages to agricultural labourers, ploughmen, shepherds and single female domestic servants. Those paying their own way had the added inducement of being offered £20 of free land. Ballygawley Orange Lodge, to which Mrs Bassett had donated the land for the building of an Orange Hall, held a similar presentation to that which it had given her brother in 1869.[12]

Mrs Sarah Bassett with her two younger children set sail, with S.K. Bassett, on 26 May 1875 on the *Blairgowrie* a vessel of 1550 tons built by Thomsons of Glasgow, owned by Thomson and Gray and commanded by Captain Darke. The ship contained 430 emigrants as well as saloon passengers. Sam wrote 'among the saloon passengers were Mr Mander (late of A.J. White's), Mr Woodrough, Mr Sweet – coming to his sister's wedding. The Government emigrants included a lot of South of Ireland girls, who could only speak the Gaelic, under a matron. Mr Mander, who looked after the issue of food to the single emigrant girls, is believed to have married the matron's daughter and lived in Draper Street, Richmond'. Mrs Sarah Bassett employed one of the emigrant girls as a maid during the voyage: 'her name was Annie Munro and she became engaged to the chief mate, Norman McLeod – on arrival she never heard of him again'. During the voyage some of the emigrant girls were selected to help in the distribution of food to the other passengers. At the end of the voyage in Lyttleton Sam bought the oil painting of the *Blairgowrie* from the steward and this is still in the possession of the family.

The success of the Morrow Bassett company in importing agricultural machinery into Christchurch in the 1870s must have been considerable. Family anecdotes record that, such was the demand, they sold boatloads of reapers even before they had been unloaded. Sinclair writes 'the introduction of American reapers and binders led in the seventies to 'bonanza' wheat farming, which reached its peak in the early eighties when wheat accounted for nearly one-fifth of exports. For a short time parts of South Island looked like Eastern Australia or the American mid-west. As late as 1894 thirty-five reaping machines were to be seen on one farm on the Canterbury Plain'.[13]

Evidence of the Morrow and Bassett success in Christchurch must have become well known to relatives in Downpatrick over the next few years and was an encouragement to some at least to emigrate. James McClurg, a cousin of Mrs S.K. Bassett, put his 38-acre farm at Ballygawley on the market in January 1883[14] and emigrated in June 1884 on the *Florida*, an old transport ship which had previously taken troops to India and China, and landed on 1 September. He was provided with a rent free house by Sam Bassett, and Thomas Bassett (Mrs Sarah Bassett's son) got him a job as caretaker at Plumpton Park, a mile from Templeton, with the instructions he was to help himself to a sheep whenever he needed one. Later the Park was broken up and sold and the McClurgs lived in Richmond until Sam Bassett moved one of his Johnston Street houses to the corner of Redway Street where James cleared a section of several acres. Sam's two nephews, William and another S.K. Bassett, emigrated to Christchurch around 1890 and William married Minnie McClurg in 1894, a romance which possibly originated at home.

From the evidence of the two sections of the Bassett family in North and South Islands it appears they remained a closely knit group in their new homeland and inter-marriage between relatives, or immigrants from home, was quite common. Bellam's suggestion that significant numbers of Irish immigrants married outside their group from the earliest years is, I find, only partially true in the case of my relatives.[15] Similarly the Bassett families who went to Christchurch were not poor emigrants but had some financial resources: for example, Mrs Sarah Bassett received £127 for her two acres at Ballygawley,[16] £150 from her father's will[17] in addition to the proceeds from the sale of her business in Downpatrick and her twenty-eight acre farm.

A study of emigration could easily overlook the fact that emigrant ships also returned to Britain and therefore passengers also returned. Mr Thomas Bassett, son of Mrs Sarah Bassett, returned in 1894 to Ireland, is reputed to have had a genealogical search carried out in Dublin linking the Bassetts to the Tehidy, Cornwall family and had the family crest to Ireland with his brother Frank in 1900 and kept a diary of his visit. On visiting Downpatrick he mentions enjoying reminiscences with old friends of his father and calling in at Sam Martin's who had kept Aunt Sarah's place since she left. One of the duties S.K. Junior was asked to perform when at Ballygawley was to act as godfather in Inch Church in 1900 to his cousin and namesake, Samuel Bassett – my father.

Note: Ballygawley or Ballygally. I have checked a series of articles by J.W. Hanna in the *Down Recorder* in 1861 entitled 'Gossipings about the Parish of Inch'. He mentions the names and meanings of townlands and says: Ballygally – in old documents Ballivick-Negallie and Bally-Mucknegall (Bailie-Na-Cailleac – 'the town of the name'). I am unsure when or why the spelling Ballgawley began to be used. Locally both spellings are in common use.

FAMILY MIGRATION TO NEW ZEALAND: THE BASSETT FAMILY

Published in *Familia: Ulster Genealogical Review*, no. 5, 1989.

Notes

1. *Journal of the Upper Ards Historical Society:* Article on The Portaferry Gas Co. at the time of opening 139 shares of £5 each purchased by various people including 'Edward Bassett, grocer – Portaferry'.
2. PRONI, T3034/17.
3. John Stellworthy, *Early Northern Wairoa* (Wairoa Bell and Northern Advertiser Printing Works, Dargaville, 1916).
4. PRONI, D627/192A.
5. *Down Recorder*, 23 Nov. 1861, 'Ramblers by Road and by Rail County Down – Finnebrogue'.
6. *Down Recorder*, 23 July 1864, address and presentation to Mr Thomas Leonard land-steward by J.W. Maxwell of Finnebrogue on his departure for New Zealand.
7. *Down Recorder*, 28 Sep. 1861, report of Finnebrogue Harvest Home.
8. Inch National School Registers – in possession of the author.
9. *Down Recorder*, 27 Feb. 1869, farewell entertainment to Samuel Bassett prior to his departure for Australia.
10. Diary is in possession of Mr D.M. Bassett, 335b, Devon Street West, New Plymouth, New Zealand.
11. *Down Recorder*, 27 Mar. 1875, advertisement for sale.
12. *Down Recorder*, 23 Apr. 1875, address and presentation to Mrs Sarah Bassett on the eve of her departure for New Zealand.
13. Keith Sinclair, *A History of New Zealand* (Harmondsworth, 1959), p. 156.
14. *Down Recorder*, 7 Jan. 1883, advertisement – 'Farm for Sale'.
15. Michael Bellam, 'The Irish in New Zealand' in *Familia: Ulster Genealogical Review*, Vol. 2, No. 1 (UGHG, 1985).
16. PRONI, D366/979.
17. PRONI, D1145/8/2/1–168.

13

Sir Samuel McCaughey
Ulster Australian
Irrigator, Breeder and Benefactor

James Thompson

One of the most striking examples of that pioneering spirit which has been the mark of many an Ulsterman down through the ages is to be found in the life of Sir Samuel McCaughey. McCaughey, who possessed all the fine pioneering qualities in abundance, gave them generously to Australia, his adopted country. He was a true nation-builder, one of the makers of Australia, and one of the greatest forces in the development of the sheep-breeding and wool-producing industry of the country. It was largely due to his experiments (undertaken regardless of cost) and sound judgement that the average yield of wool from a single sheep was increased from about five to nine pounds, and much superior wool too, during his lifetime. His work in irrigation, and in opening up the outback, added to his princely benefactions, increase the great debt that Australia owes to him.

The name McCaughey is Irish Celtic; in that language Eochaidh (meaning Horseman) is the equivalent of Caughey. Some time after the Norman Conquest the family of Eochaidh migrated to the Scottish highlands (Aberdeenshire) to escape from feudal persecution. It was then that the prefix Mac (son of) began to be used in their name to distinguish the family as being of Celtic, rather than of Norse or Viking origin. Around the fifteenth century many members of the family returned to the north of Ireland, where a number of their descendants still live.

Sir Samuel was born at Tullynavey, near Ballymena, on 30th June 1835. He was the eldest son of Francis and Eliza McCaughey. Francis McCaughey was a linen merchant and a farmer. His linen business was apparently a solid and substantial one, and for more than thirty years he was in a position to give employment to a large area of the country. His Tullynavey farm was a sizeable property which was managed with great efficiency and it was here on his father's farm, and in the linen merchant's office, that young Samuel received his early business training. There can be no doubt that Francis McCaughey was at the time grooming his son in order that he might one day succeed him in the family career.

Samuel McCaughey's home life was a full and pleasant one, despite his father's strictness. His mother came from a family with a colourful history and her influence and heredity marked powerfully in her three sons. Eliza's father, Samuel Wilson, owned a farm at Ballycloughan, not far from Tullynavey, and there were close and affectionate links between the two families. Sir Samuel McCaughey was only three years old when two of his Wilson uncles emigrated to Australia. Thus from his very earliest years he had been accustomed to hearing talk of Australia, where his uncles were succeeding so remarkably. Charles and Alexander Wilson were later joined by their brothers John (1841) and Samuel (1852) and it was with the departure of the latter that young McCaughey began to grow increasingly restless. He had long been taking an eager interest in his uncles' letters from the 'new country', and his resolve to emigrate developed steadily. Finally, at the invitation of his uncle Charles, McCaughey left for Australia and arrived at Melbourne some 88 days later, in April 1856. Samuel McCaughey wasted no time in that thriving and increasingly busy port of his entry, but promptly made his way by foot to Charles's Walmer station, in the Wimmera. The twenty-year-old McCaughey had no great amount of money with him, as the earlier Wilsons had had. The trip, made with another who had also been invited by the Wilsons to emigrate, was long and arduous, but it taught Samuel many valuable lessons regarding the country and its climate.

After a warm welcome from the four Wilsons, McCaughey quickly plunged into his first regular employment in his adopted land, as a jackaroo on Kewell station, a property of 120,000 acres acquired in 1845. His starting salary of £30 per year was a modest one, and clearly the young man was going to have to prove his worth, in true family tradition. This he quickly did, and within three months McCaughey had been appointed overseer. He revelled in the various tasks on Kewell and was keen to learn every detail of station work and management. His unwavering confidence in his own abilities was confirmed when, at the end of two years, he was appointed manager of Kewell. In 1859, when Charles Wilson made another trip to Ireland, he left his young nephew in complete control of the property. Samuel McCaughey was well-fitted for such a grand responsibility. He had authority over men, worked extremely hard and never tolerated slackness. He possessed the ability to get the very best out of his men, who clearly respected him for his consistent example and fairness. The absence of his uncle presented McCaughey with a fine opportunity to put a few of his many ideas into operation. He showed much initiative, starting with the fencing. The property was subdivided into 4,000-acre paddocks, an innovation which cut down running expenses and greatly simplified management. He therefore started the era of fencing in the Wimmera district and probably Victoria. McCaughey undertook several other improvements too, in the knowledge that he had full authority and confident that his uncle would approve.

The time had already arrived, however, when managing others' properties was insufficient to satisfy him. He had served his apprenticeship and was fully competent to run his own place. Financed by his uncles John and Samuel, he purchased a third share of Coonong, in the Riverina district of New South Wales. His other partners were his cousin David Wilson and John Cochrane. The start was most inauspicious and soon David, having lost confidence in the place, sold out to Cochrane. A visit to England by Cochrane left McCaughey in sole charge of Coonong and once again he lost no time in putting his ideas into practice, which had previously been rejected by his two initial partners. He improved the water supply first, and then stocked up with sheep. Soon after Cochrane's return McCaughey persuaded him to accept an offer of £15,000 for his two-thirds share. Thus in 1864 Samuel McGaughey, having weathered the difficult and unencouraging beginning, became the sole owner of Coonong, just eight years after his arrival in Australia. Now at last, unshackled by partners and their divergent views, he pressed ahead, spending money wisely on improving the flow of water and initiating other improvements in order that the property become fully profitable.

From then on, McCaughey began to purchase further properties, in every case displaying sound judgement. He possessed boundless confidence and the courage to borrow to finance these increasingly weighty undertakings. Money was readily advanced by the banks, such was their confidence in their client. By 1871 McCaughey had his Australian interests so well organised that he was in a position to visit the place of his youth. He was now a man of wealth and assured position, having more than justified his position to emigrate. In 1880 Sir Samuel Wilson (knighted in 1875) left Australia to reside in England, and he induced his nephew to buy his huge lease-hold stations Toorale and Dunlop on the River Darling. At the time these two properties comprised about 3,000,000 acres, but Sir Samuel had complete confidence in McCaughey's capacity to carry on such immense undertakings. The new owner's brother, John, was made manager of Toorale and was given an interest in the station. James Wilson (no relation) became manager of Dunlop, and both stations made history in different ways. Toorale was the first shearing shed in Australia to be installed with electric light, while Dunlop has the distinction of being the first place to undertake a complete shearing with machines.

A mark of a successful man is his ability to choose his assistants and when and how to delegate a responsibility to them. Sir Samuel McCaughey certainly did not come short in this respect, consistently proving his worth when assessing character and capability. In 1881 he appointed his brother David (whom he had brought out to Australia in 1874) manager of his newly-acquired Coree station, with an interest in it. By the end of 1886 David McCaughey had become the sole owner of the property which he occupied until his death in 1899. John McCaughey left Toorale in 1897 to manage Yarralee, another of his older brother's purchases. Later on he became its owner. Certainly Samuel McCaughey, well-established and strikingly successful as he was, took great delight in giving his two brothers in particular opportunities to do likewise. However, they too had to prove themselves fully, and this they did in due course. Their appointments were well justified and they proved to be much more than merely sentimental ones.

At various times McCaughey was owner or part owner of twelve stations in New South Wales and three in Queensland. On a trip abroad in 1905 he had an interview with the great French bacteriologist, Louis Pasteur, to seek his advice on the destruction of rabbits: such was his eagerness to experiment with new ideas. Pasteur was rather optimistic of helping him in his war with rabbits until he learned of the size of McCaughey's property. The Frenchman apparently raised his hands and exclaimed, 'It's as big as the whole of France!' McCaughey claimed that if the total area of his land were cut up into strips of three-quarters of a mile and pieced together end on end, it would stretch as far as England, a distance of 12,000 miles!

From the time of his first arrival in Australia, McCaughey had realised the vital importance of irrigation and improved water supply. Ever since his purchase of Coonong in 1860 he had developed schemes for conserving and distributing water on his various properties. However it was at North Yanco, purchased in 1899, that McCaughey made his most important contribution to irrigation in New South Wales. His work was so remarkably successful that it was largely responsible for the Government undertaking the Burrinjuck reservoir and the northern Murrimbidgee Canal Scheme. Eventually more than 200 miles of channels were constructed on North Yanco and 40,000 acres could be irrigated as a result. He flooded 10,000 acres of grass land and grew 5,000 acres of lucerne and watered it, making five of six cuts a year. Wheat was sown and oats and potatoes soon followed. All this provided an object lesson from which developed the Murrimbidgee irrigation area. Such a vast scheme as that undertaken at North Yanco could only have been achieved by a man of vast financial resources, but it furnished proof that expenditure on irrigation could justify itself on economic grounds if it were carried out with boldness and wisdom. Although the Burrinjuck dam was not completed until 1928, work was begun on the reservoir in 1901 and water was available from the dam to farms on the Murrimbidgee irrigation area in 1917. McCaughey was therefore able to see some of the results of the vision he had had of the storage and use of the waters of the Murrimibidgee. The total storage capacity of the Burrinjuck dam is greater than that of Sydney Harbour, an indication of its immense size.

Sir Samuel McCaughey, besides being an irrigation pioneer, was one of the foremost sheep-breeders in the history of New South Wales. No man ever, perhaps, has conducted more extensive or expansive experiments in endeavouring to improve the popular type of sheep. He was always an experimentalist rather than a man who clings to one fixed type through thick and thin. Price was quite a secondary consideration with him when it was a question of getting a good ram. The first sheep bought for Coonong came from Widgiewa from a flock whose ewes were of a large frame and sported wool of an excellent type. He introduced rams from Harrilah and from Mona Vale, Tasmania; he also obtained a pair of Ercildonne rams, which were renowned for the lustre and fineness of their wool. But he bought the finest sheep he could acquire from any State that had them.

Coming to the conclusion that the white-yoked sheep were not all that could be desired on the hot Riverina plains, he decided upon another experiment. He came down to the Sydney stud sheep fair and bought ten Californian rams which were descendants of French merinos exported to California and bred there for a number of years. One of these rams had won the prize for being the best ram at the California fair. He paid 100 to 450 guineas a head for the rams. A few American ewes were also secured at the same time. The result exceeded his expectations, and he decided to visit America personally. He went through all the best studs and secured some of the best sheep obtainable in Vermont. His first shipment comprised 92 rams and 120 ewes and his second shipment totalled 312, all the sheep being from the oldest and most celebrated strains. He also bought large numbers of American sheep imported by the Sydney sales. Altogether McCaughey spent around £50,000 on Vermont sheep, and the Coonong stud was for many years invincible. Indeed, he had to stand down for several years to prevent the stud sheep show from becoming a one-man affair. He did not hesitate to discard Vermont blood, however, when he became aware that considerations other than weight of fleece were coming to the fore. When the large-framed Wanganella type became popular he bought heavily and bred for a large carcase, recognising that mutton was becoming an important factor.

On 11th April 1899 Samuel McCaughey was sworn in as a member of the New South Wales Legislative Council, an honour that was rather burdensome to so busy a man. It was regard for his friend, the

Married	Born	Died	
Francis McCaughey Elizabeth Wilson May 7, 1833.	Feb. 14, 1811	Nov. 12, 1887.	
Eliza Daniel Whitley	Feb. 23, 1834		
Samuel	June '35		6
Mary, Rev. Wm McCoy	Dec. 25, '37		1
Jane Hugh Alex Stewart	June '39		
Louisa Dr John McCay	Dec. 14, '40		
John	May 8, '43		2
Anna Robert J. Smith	May 2, '45		2
David L.L. Blanche Tell	Aug '48		
Margretta Thos. Smith	50		
Charlotte John McChesney	52		

(from the 'McKinney Note Book').

The McCaughey family births

Premier G.H. Reid (later Sir George), that led him to accept. Although he was never a politician at heart, McCaughey was to prove a useful member, and his practical advice on measures connected with the land and its problems was greatly valued. His speeches in the Upper House were few, but worthwhile, and always brief.

In the birthday honours of June 1905 King Edward VII conferred a knighthood on the Honourable Samuel McCaughey, M.L.C., in recognition of his labours for the wool industry in Australia and of his many philanthropic and patriotic gifts. But this apparently made no difference to the essential simplicity of the man. He displayed no pretence and no ostentation; his tastes and outlook remained simple and humble.

Sir Samuel had always enjoyed wonderful health (he had once claimed that he had never felt an ache or pain), but by his middle seventies a slowing down of his vigour had begun. He began to feel less inclined to continue the control of his many properties, and he started selling these off in 1911 when in his 77th year, a process which he continued until the end of his life when he did not own a single acre of land. It was only during the last two years of his long life that McCaughey's health began to deteriorate markedly and on 25th July 1919 he passed peacefully away at his North Yanco home from heart failure. He was buried at St. John's Church, Narrandara, on 26th July and a memorial service in his honour was held at St. Stephen's Presbyterian Church, Sydney, on 3rd August 1919.

Sir Samuel McCaughey was always a practical philanthropist. At the time of the South African War he subscribed £5,000 towards the cost of sending the Bushmen's Contingent to South Africa and made generous contributions to the Red Cross too. In 1912 he gave £10,000 to the Dreadnought Fund. With his brother John he presented a battle plane costing £2,700 to the Australian Air Force, as well as contributing liberally to the Red Cross and other First World War charities. When Sir George Reid was in London as High Commissioner for Australia, McCaughey sent him £10,000, asking him to donate it to a charity of his choice. Reid gave it to Dr. Barnardo's Homes, and it was used to bring out a number of children to Australia. Nor did Sir Samuel forget the country and the county of his birth. The Ulster Defence Fund found in him a ready and able financial supporter, and he intimated that more money would be forthcoming if needed. Further, he was always delighted to give work to Ulstermen, especially those from his own native county of Antrim.

Truly a generous-hearted man, he gave a great deal of thought to the matter of drawing up his will. Sir Samuel McCaughey never took the opportunity to marry (something he lived to regret) and so by far the chief beneficiary from his will was his adopted country, Australia. Not only was he a generous financial supporter of every good cause during the course of his life, but McCaughey's bequests to education, the Church, hospitals and other worthwhile interests were the greatest ever made by any individual in Australia. For example, more than £500,000 was made available to universities, £250,000 to the Presbyterian Church, and the same amount again for the widows and children of the Australian Imperial Force.

Sir Samuel McCaughey was not a great man by privilege. It is true that he had been given an extremely good start in life by his parents, but the greatness and uniqueness must have come from his own courage, effort and self-reliance. A great Australian builder, he was of the old school in his energy and drive; he was an example of the success of hard work, something he never shrunk from. Work was always his principal occupation; he gained tremendous satisfaction from it. Essentially constructive in his outlook on life, he was never happier than when wrestling with and solving business and pastoral problems, or devising and carrying out his schemes for land development. He used to spend a great deal of his time working in the blacksmith's and carpenter's shop on his property. In his address given at McCaughey's memorial service in Sydney, the Rev. R.G. Macintyre said this of him:

> Great wealth came to him, but not the most radical socialist could begrudge it, for it was not gained by unholy profiteering, not won at the cost of the community ... What prosperity came to him was not a title of the prosperity his labours of body and mind brought to the Commonwealth. This man added to the wealth of the state infinitely more than his own account!

Indeed, Australia has much to thank Sir Samuel McCaughey for, because that country's development could never have been so spectacular without the lives of such far-sighted pioneers as he unquestionably was.

Published in *Familia: Ulster Genealogical Review*, no. 3, 1987.

14

John King

An Ulster Explorer of Australia

William B. Alderdice

John King was the first person to cross the continent of Australia from south to north, from Melbourne to the Gulf of Carpentaria in 1860/61, and return alive. He was my great grandfather's brother and was born on 15 December 1838, on the Benburb Road, Moy, Co. Tyrone. The exact spot is still known by the local residents as "King's garden". A few hundred yards away stands the little cottage where his brother Tom lived all his life. This was the cottage John called "Home". Today it still stands, deserted and unnoticed behind a laurel hedge near to the Council Dump. Close by was 'Camp Park Hill', which received its name from being the site of Owen Roe O'Neill's camp before the battle of Benburb in 1646. A short distance away is Legar Hill graveyard, where many soldiers who died in battle were buried.

John's early days were spent with his mother and brother Tom, around the beautiful and quiet countryside of Moy. His father Henry, born and reared at Ballygawley, was a soldier in the 95th Highlanders, so was often away from home. After the Potato Famine, John went to the Royal Hibernian School, Phoenix Park, Dublin, to complete his education. This was a school for soldiers' sons and at the early age of 14 he joined the 70th Regiment. The following year it was ordered to India, arriving in October 1853. John went through the violence of the Indian Mutiny and, at Peshawar, he saw 40 mutineers shot away from guns. Later he fell ill and when convalescing at Karachi he met George James Landells who was in India buying camels for the

Burke/Wills trans-Australian expedition. King bought himself out of the army and was engaged by Landells to supervise the Sepoys in charge of 25 camels and off he went to Australia to join the expedition.

The Philosophical Institute of the State of Victoria had organised this expedition to explore the interior of the Australian Continent, under the leadership of another Irishman, Robert O'Hara Burke, from Galway. He belonged to a family that had given faithful and loyal service to the British Crown. For some time he served in the Australian Army but, in 1848, he returned to Ireland and served in the Royal Irish Constabulary. Later he emigrated to Tasmania and then crossing over to Melbourne became an officer in the police. There he was selected to lead the expedition, known as the 'Burke, Wills, King and Gray,' which left Melbourne on 21st August 1860 on its northward trek to the Gulf of Carpentaria.

Business in the city was practically suspended on that day as crowds flocked the streets to see this unique procession of horses, drays, camels, wagons loaded with provisions, and the seemingly light-hearted men going out into the unknown. What a sight this must have been! In spite of all the careful planning beforehand, they encountered many difficulties and problems before reaching Menindee in October. Here Landells, who had been greedy for money, resigned and King was put in charge of the camels. He was also chosen as one of the advance party which set out for Cooper's Creek. They reached the Creek, on 11th November, and set up camp LXV. Here the party split up again.

Burke, Wills, King and Gray decided to make a dash for the Gulf some 750 miles away while the depot was left in charge of Brahe. He was expected to wait for three months, as the rearguard, with further supplies, was to arrive in a few days. These 4 men with 5 camels and a horse managed to travel some 14 miles a day enduring unbearable heat and sand. On 4th February 1861 they reached their goal on the tide waters of the Flinders River.

John King was the only survivor of the final exploring party. He was originally brought out from India to look after the camels. Their return journey was disastrous to say the least. Rations were getting low, and in the course of the journey they were obliged to kill their only horse, 'Orange Billy', which caused King great sorrow, and also

3 camels. On 17th April, Gray died under rather mysterious circumstances but not as some diaries state. My grandfather gave me the true facts which he received from his father, John's brother. They seemed to be treated as a family secret, but revealing that Gray's death was due to Burke's hasty temper. Four days later the remaining 3 exhausted men made a superhuman effort and in one day covered 30 miles back to Camp LXV, arriving at 7.30 in the evening. To their horror they found that the depot was deserted. The only human sign was the word 'DIG' carved on a tree. (These 3 letters remain on this tree to the present day.) After digging they discovered a box of rations and a message from Brahe saying that the rearguard had not arrived, so he had decided that very morning to return with all his men to Menindee, having waited for four months.

King's sweating camels were too weak to follow Brahe, so Burke, against the wishes of King and Wills, decided to go to Mount Hopeless. A police station lay en route, and one has cause to wonder had Burke something else in mind when he chose the opposite direction. For 2 months they struggled through this inhospitable country, with food diminishing and bodies weakening every day. Late in June Burke and Wills died of starvation, and King was left alone. After burying his companions one wonders how a young man in his early twenties had the will and determination to live in such indescribable conditions in the interior of Australia.

Speaking from experience one could liken the outback in ways to the Sahara Desert, or to the barren wastes of Siberia, though the climate differs. It is a land of extremes – dry air, cold nights, incredibly high temperatures by day, dreadful thirst, the impression of empty land stretching away silently into infinity. Often these desolate wastes are visited by cyclonic thunderstorms and rainstorms which are unforgettable, as I experienced in Boulia on the Burke River when I had to abandon tent. A notice still stands beside that river which states – 'Burke and Wills filled their waterbags here. Would all travellers do likewise'.

In spite of all the seemingly insurmountable obstacles, King battled on. Had it not been for the kindness of the Aborigines, King too would probably have died. They befriended him until a relief expedition led by Howitt found him, almost half demented by starvation, and near to death. By this time the Aborigines had grown so fond of him that they wished to adopt him.[1] After being rescued by the Howitt party he revived considerably, and managed to bring them to the place where he had buried Wills, but the native dingoes had mangled the body, so only his bones remained. The skull was nowhere to be found, but they carefully gathered up the remains and made a new grave, where they buried them. Howitt read those familiar words from 1 Corinthians 15: 'O death where is thy sting? O grave where is thy victory?' King was heard to say, 'How strange to hear such words in such surroundings'. The grave was marked on a nearby Coolibah tree – 'W.J. Wills, LXV yards W.N.W.' The diary of Wills was found before they left the spot. Later Burke's body was discovered, as well as his Colt revolver which was lying on the sand corroded with rust but still cocked and capped. His bones were placed in a Union Jack and lowered into a new grave. Howitt read from John 11: 'I am the resurrection and the life: He that believeth in me, though he were dead, yet shall he live'. On a gnarled box-tree close by they carved 'R.O'H.B. 21.9.61 A.H.' After the funeral services Howitt tracked down the Aborigines who looked after King, and handsomely rewarded them for their kindness. Although King was still in a weak condition, it was agreed that all should travel homeward.

The news travelled fast to Melbourne and, by the time the sole surviving explorer arrived, his admirers were frantic. There were flags and bunting everywhere; he was greeted by the Governor, Dr Macadam, and taken to Government House. Meanwhile Howitt was commissioned by the Government to go back to Cooper's Creek to dig up the bones of Burke and Wills, so that they could be brought back to Melbourne. The funeral for the two courageous explorers was held on 21st January 1863. It was a tremendous affair, with an estimated 40,000 in attendance. The funeral car was a replica of the one in which the Duke of Wellington had been carried to his grave in St. Paul's Cathedral in London, ten years before. It was drawn by 6 black horses with plumes on their heads. King was one of the pall bearers, and the Governor was present. Soldiers, with reversed arms, were posted on either side of the street.

Today on the grave in the Melbourne Cemetery there stands a 34 ton monolith of undressed Harcourt stone, to their memory. It is inscribed:

> In memory of Robert O'Hara Burke and William John Wills ... comrades in a great achievement, companions in death, and associates in renown, Leader, and Second in Command of the Victorian Exploring Expedition, who died at Cooper's Creek, June 1861.

John King is also mentioned in the inscription as the sole survivor. Later a royal commission of inquiry revealed the mismanagement of the whole expedition. However, the last words in Burke's diary stated: "King behaved nobly and deserves to be well rewarded". In due time King was presented with an inscribed watch, which is treasured by my cousins in Larne, Co. Antrim and he also received £180 per year. The terrible ordeal through which King had passed took toll of his health, and he became a recluse at St. Kilda – a suburb of Melbourne, for the last years of his life. King died on 18 January 1872, aged 34, and was buried in the Quaker Area of Melbourne Cemetery, a short distance from Burke and Wills.

The following letter written by King himself, at 22 years of age, will let readers see something of his character, wisdom and early upbringing in Grange Quaker Sunday School, of this remarkable young man.

> To the Hon. John Macadam, &c., Hon. Sec. of the Victorian Exploring Expedition.
>
> Sir – In reply to the letter of the Hon. G. Coppin, handed to me by you, in which he offers me £1,000 in consideration of my exhibiting and describing a panorama of the route taken across the country to the Gulf of Carpentaria, I beg to say, first, that I do not consider myself at liberty to entertain any proposal from any private party in reference to making public any information in my possession as the only survivor of the late unfortunate exploring expedition, until authorized so to do by the Government or by the late Committee acting for it. Secondly, that such have been the physical and mental exhaustion through which I have passed, that I am totally unable to endure excitement much less to appear before crowded audiences – to mentally travel over scenes so full of distressing reminiscences. I require absolute rest, and if possible the diversion of my thoughts into other channels, that I may regain the mental and physical energy I enjoyed before I entered upon the exhaustive labours of the expedition. Thirdly, the remembrance of the melancholy deaths of

my late brave commander Mr Burke, and his noble associate Mr Willis, under circumstances which threatened my own life also, and my wonderful deliverance and ultimate preservation from death, is such, that I am a wonder to myself. The Almighty has been so gracious to me to present myself for exhibition under Mr Coppin's direction for any pecuniary advantage whatsoever. I beg, therefore, to leave myself in the hands of a paternal and just Government, to be rewarded by it as it may deem proper for my services, as one of the members of the late ill-fated expedition.

I remain, your obedient servant,

JOHN KING
St. Kilda, November 30.

His life was short. No one could ever imagine what suffering and anxieties by endured in this expedition. On 5 June 1861 Burke wrote in his diary at King's Creek 'I am satisfied that the frame of man never was more severely taxed'. Yet we never read of King complaining, though he was so weak at one stage that he crawled on his hands and knees to get a drink of water. In spite of all this, life had its crowning hours – from the green meadows of the Blackwater River in his native County Tyrone, to his academical attainments in Dublin, to the battles of the Indian Mutiny, and finally achieving what man had never done before – crossing, from South to North, the Great Continent and returning alive.[2]

Published in *Familia: Ulster Genealogical Review*, no. 3, 1987.

John King: Ireland's Forgotten Explorer – Australia's First Hero by Eric Villiers was published by Ulster Historical Foundation in 2012.

Notes

[1] Last year I fulfilled a lifelong ambition, by going on a camping tour from Melbourne to Darwin via the Gulf of Carpentaria, to trace as near as possible the tracks of King, and to meet the Aborigines. To my amazement, I discovered that John had an Aborigine daughter, known to

many as King's daughter, and to others as 'Yellow Alice' because of her ginger hair similar to her father's. She lived to be over 90, but never married. Today some around the Creek still remember her and it seems she was a highly respected lady. The Rt. Hon. Martin Cameron, leader of the Opposition in the S.A. Government, confirmed this with police at Birdsville. It is most unlikely that John even knew he had a daughter.

2 Although there are numerous memorials in Australia to this outstanding explorer (which I saw while visiting the country), in his native Ulster there is nothing at all to commemorate this Tyrone man who was a renowned scholar, soldier and explorer in a past generation. Perhaps this will be rectified in the near future. [In 2010, a blue plaque was erected to John King in Moy by the Ulster History Circle.]

15

John Ballance
New Zealand Premier, 1891–3
Irish Origins and Influences

Tim McIvor[1]

Introduction

On the 27 April 1893 the Premier of New Zealand, John Ballance, died in office after a long illness. When his death was announced the country stood still. Public servants were sent home, meetings were cancelled and court cases adjourned. Flags flew at half mast. After little more than two years in power Ballance had become one of New Zealand's most popular leaders. Thousands turned out at his funeral, watching in silence as the horse-drawn carriage and cortege moved slowly through the streets of central Wellington. The New Zealand native wood Kauri coffin was lowered into a simple grave at the public cemetery in Wanganui, the town Ballance had made his home.

Two years later Ballance's wife, Ellen, imported a block of Irish black polished granite as headstone for the grave. On it were the words 'John Ballance, Prime Minister of this Colony. Born in Glenavy, County Antrim, Ireland, 27 March 1839, died in Wellington, 27 April 1893. "To live in the hearts of those we love is not to die".' Ellen had been born in County Down, daughter of a British Army officer. Shortly after her husband's death she had returned to Ireland on a visit. There she arranged to have the granite shipped to New Zealand. The Irish roots of John and Ellen Ballance were vitally important to them.

John Ballance, son of a Glenavy tenant farmer, had made an enormous impact on the New Zealand political scene. Soon after arriving in the colony he established a newspaper in the North Island coastal town of

Wanganui. His activities as a journalist led quickly and easily into a career in politics. He first entered Parliament in 1875 and, with only a three-year break, remained in the House until his death eighteen years later. A Cabinet seat came early. Ballance was a young Colonial Treasurer (the equivalent of the British Chancellor of the Exchequer) when appointed in 1878. Between 1884 and 1887 he held three portfolios in the Stout-Vogel Government: Lands, Native Affairs, and Defence. His land legislation sought to encourage closer settlement and develop fully the country's potential; his Maori policy was, for its day, enlightened.

Ballance became leader of the liberal grouping in the House of Representatives (New Zealand's Parliament in Wellington) in 1889. In New Zealand at that time there were no formal, organised parties. Ballance led the liberals (including a small labour wing) to victory at an election the following year. It was a bitterly fought contest held against a background of high unemployment, worsening living conditions and strikes that in the extent and intensity were unprecedented in the country's history. The mild and gentlemanly Ballance faced a conservative government backed by landed interests and the professional and business classes. Conservative alliances had held office in New Zealand almost continuously since the colony's Parliament was established.

Though successful at the polls, it took Ballance about eighteen months to establish his government and party firmly in power. The conservative-dominated upper house (called the Legislative Council), reinforced with a batch of new members mischievously and hastily appointed by the outgoing Atkinson Government, rejected most of the Liberal Government's legislation. Only when the Governor, at the directions of the Colonial Office in London, appointed twelve additional councillors was Ballance finally secure.

By early 1893 the future of the Government looked bright. Legislation had been passed to encourage land settlement and to improve working conditions, the taxation system had been made more equitable and soon a bill would be presented to the House that would give New Zealand women the right to vote. At the same time the economy had turned round after long years of stagnation and depression. Ballance, dubbed 'The Rainmaker', was seen by many to have brought in a new era of hope and prosperity. Sadly, the illness that had plagued him for much of his premiership soon killed him.

The remainder of this article looks at Ballance's Irish background and examines the nature of its influence on the development of his political ideas and career in New Zealand. It argues that the Irish influences on Ballance were significant but largely 'negative'. That is, Ballance strove consciously to ensure that the problems of Ireland were not reproduced in New Zealand. He sought to ensure that for the mass of its people New Zealand would be a better place than Ireland to live in.

Origins

John Ballance was born in 1839 in Ballypitmave, four kilometres east of Glenavy village, in a stone house set back from the road to Lisburn. His father, Samuel, was a moderately prosperous 39-year-old tenant farmer. His grandfather had been one of many Orangemen recruited locally to the Yeomanry by the English authorities at the time of the 1798 Rebellion, and had been wounded in the fighting. The year prior to Ballance's birth, Samuel had married Mary McNiece, a woman in her early twenties who came from a well-known family. Her uncle Conway McNiece owned property in the area, including the nine-hectare Ram's Island in Lough Neagh.

The Ballances were of English Puritan stock rather than of the more populous Scottish Presbyterians who dominated counties Down and Antrim. Settling first in Lurgan, the Ballances later moved north to County Antrim townland of Ballypitmave; to an area where Anglicans, and English influence, remained dominant when elsewhere in east Ulster they gave way to the Presbyterian influx.

Glenavy Parish Church records reveal that Ballance was the eldest of ten children. After John came Jane, then Samuel, Isaac, James, Anna, Rebecca, Isabella, Robert, Henry and Mary. We know little of these people's lives. The family scattered to other parts of Ireland and much further afield. Some followed John to New Zealand, no doubt encouraged by his success there. Isabella became a teacher and (as did Mary) remained unmarried, while Rebecca died at the early age of eleven. Anna (born 1850) married a man called Knox and went to live in Lisburn. Jane (1841–80) married John McKnight at Magheragall Presbyterian Church in 1862. Their son Robert later settled in New Zealand. Isaac (born 1845) left Ireland also bound for New Zealand but was never heard of again. Family rumour has it that he died en route, in Australia. The fate of Samuel is equally mysterious. Of the remaining brothers James (1847–1927) took over the family land whilst Robert (1855–1936) emigrated to America. Today the farm at Ballypitmave is owned by James's grandson, John. Finally, Henry Ballance (1857–1932) succeeded to Crew Mount, the property of his grand-uncle Conway McNiece. Henry established himself as an influential local figure and was at various times Magistrate, Chairman of Lisburn Rural District Council and Chairman of the Board of Governors of Lagan Valley Infirmary.

The house the Ballances lived in was substantial for its day; a single-storey dwelling with a thatched roof, white mortar walls, small windows and a huge open hearth. It appears to have been located at right angles to a mid-nineteenth-century substantial two-storey addition. Both the original cottage and later extension are being restored by the Ulster-New Zealand Trust. There was plenty of room in the house when Ballance was born. Samuel's father, also called John, had not long died and the 1835 valuation noted that the family had more accommodation than was necessary. Samuel took over his father's tenancy of about eleven hectares of good land, most of which was given over to crops (predominantly wheat) with the remainder grazed.

The Ballance farm was well above average in size. The majority of holdings in the area were below six hectares. The region was agriculturally advanced in eighteenth- and nineteenth-century Ulster since English colonists had improved farming techniques and landowners were relatively progressive and liberal. And farm incomes, at least until the 1830s, were frequently supplemented by weaving. Thus the Ballances were comfortably off, even if there was not much left over for luxuries.

John Ballance attended a local national school from which he was rarely absent. His parents saw to it that all their children received a good education and all were avid readers. John was physically lazy and if at all possible avoided helping out at the farm. He much preferred to spend his spare time with his head in a book. Yet he was not a weak-looking child. The earliest photograph we have of him shows a well built boy for whom it would have been difficult to plead a frail constitution as an excuse not to contribute to the many tasks around the farm.

Ballance's father was an Anglican with 'strict evangelical tendencies'. Mary was a Quaker. On a Sunday the family would attend Glenavy

Parish Church (where John had been baptised) in the morning and the chapel at 5:00 p.m. The nearest Quaker meeting house was some distance away in Lisburn. Ballance grew up in a family and culture of tenant farmers whose greater security and relative prosperity placed them at a considerable distance from the majority of Irish peasantry. The famine which struck Ireland before Ballance was ten years old affected Antrim and Down least of all and his experience of the Hungry Forties would largely have been through newspaper accounts and stories passed by word of mouth, rather than first hand.

As eldest son, Ballance would have been expected eventually to take over his father's farm. Yet we have seen that he had not the slightest interest in farming and so it was agreed that John would go to Belfast to continue his education at Wilson's Academy there. He left home at the age of fourteen and went to stay with his uncle Robert McNiece who lived in the city. The academy had a good reputation and no doubt there were high expectations of John. However, despite his apparent academic bent he soon quit school and went to work for a hardware firm. We do not know the circumstances surrounding this decision but it must have been a disappointment to his parents. The job, in which Ballance remained until he left Ireland in 1857, held no real prospects.

Belfast was within easy reach of home and Ballance's parents continued to influence his development. From an early age politics fascinated him. His father, like his father before him, was an Orangeman and involved in local politics, often proposing the nomination of Conservative candidates for Belfast. John read, watched and listened. His knowledge and understanding of politics grew into a precocious keen political sense and awareness. By the age of sixteen he was helping Samuel write his speeches. Yet if it was his father who brought Ballance into early contact with political life, it was his much more liberal mother who influenced the direction of his own political philosophy.

When Ballance left Ireland he was only eighteen. In Birmingham – where he spent some time before emigrating to New Zealand – he came under the influence of liberals such as Cobden and Bright. He attended evening classes at the Midland Institute, studying politics, history and biography. These gave him a firm philosophical and intellectual base from which he would develop his political programme in New Zealand.

Influences

Ballance believed that New Zealanders had the opportunity to create in the 'new world' a society that did not suffer from the social, economic and political ills of the mother country. In this Irish influences on Ballance were important. They can be seen particularly in his views on land ownership, on religion and on education.

From the start land reform was central to Ballance's political platform. He argued vehemently that land should be made available to small farmers and new settlers rather than 'locked up' in the hands of large landowners and speculators. When Minister of Lands in the 1880s he implemented schemes to promote small farm settlement and passed legislation encouraging the leasing (rather than selling) of crown land. When Premier he introduced a land tax aimed, in part, to prompt the sub-division of under-developed land. The Government also passed a Lands for Settlements Act, under which the Crown could purchase private land for subsequent leasing to small farmers. Ballance's land reform programme was critical to his success in gaining the Treasury benches in December 1890.

In emphasizing the need for liberal land legislation Ballance had Ireland very much at the back of his mind. He regarded land monopoly as the greatest obstacle to progress in the country of his birth and its avoidance vital in the country of his adoption. Ulster, he wrote in 1889, had 'suffered just as much from landlord tyranny and from castle government as any part of Ireland'. Eight years later he moved to a resolution at a 'monster' meeting in Wellington in support of the Irish National Land League and its sympathy with evicted tenants, whom he described as 'victims of misgovernment, persecution and tyranny'.

The inequitable distribution of land in Ireland was intertwined with the position of the established Church. Ballance thought the Irish Church and the land laws 'the foremost evils to be grappled with'. He emphasized the alliance between clergy ('greedy land sharks') and landlords at the expense of the people, and warned of the 'evils of ecclesiasticism' being introduced into the colony. By the early 1880s Ballance was a convinced 'freethinker'. That is, he became a secularist, believing in rational thought rather than religious dogma.

Ballance's Irish experiences had made him sceptical of religion and vexed at the influence of religion on politics. In Belfast as a young man he had witnessed a succession of sectarian riots. He wrote later of a particular serious clash in 1857:

> Much bloodshed was caused by street preaching, and though the offensive practice of shouting on a highway that all papists were on the broad road to destruction was naturally objected to by those who were said to be doomed, the practice was persisted even after it was found that riot had ensued. One character, 'Roaring Hanna', the pastor of a Presbyterian Church, obtained much notoriety by his open air effusions in critical times, and found immortality in Punch. 'Allow', said this divine on one occasion vividly remembered, 'a small passage for the papists to pass along, and it shall be known hereafter as the Pope's Pad!'

Contrasting the rising prosperity of Belfast at that time with continued rioting he concluded:

> The truth is that the Protestants of the North have long considered themselves the dominant class and cannot to this day tolerate the religious or political equality of the Catholics. The remembrance of the days of the yeoman and the rebellion of 1798 are still faithfully preserved, and Protestant ascendancy is still a principle and a sentiment in the breasts of the descendants of those who put it in practice in many questionable ways.

Ballance rejected totally the Orangeism of his father. He saw the Orange Order as an anachronism, engendering a bitterness and violence that could only alienate the Catholic minority. He attacked the basis of religious and cultural sectarianism by denying the existence of an exclusive and pure Ulster race. Rather 'the men of Ulster, to their glory be it said', he wrote, 'are hybrids, and they possess the characteristics of the nations with whom they claim kindred. The industry and perseverance of the Saxon, the proud spirit of the Norman, the fervency and enthusiasm of the Irish, and the endurance and purpose of the Scotch, have been beautifully mixed up by nature in this race'.

It was not only from politics, but also from education, that Ballance sought to remove religion. He advocated a state system of liberal, secular education. Religion had no place in schools, though Ballance believed that religious liberty would permit Catholics to maintain instruction of their own children, if that was their wish. 'Every child of poor parents ought to have its education free, and of the best to be had in any country in the world', he wrote in his Wanganui newspaper. Obstacles to a non-sectarian, state system of education would have to be overcome. 'The intemperate opposition of religious partisans or the groans and grumbles of irritated taxpayers should not be allowed to impede the progress of education. At most, their grievances are inferior to the real interests of the State'.

Ballance was a New Zealand nationalist. But he was not an imperialist, nor a xenophobe. Rather his nationalism took the form of a belief that it was vital for New Zealand to establish its political and economic independence, particularly from Britain, if the country was to develop to its full potential. He argued that a political and social framework should be constructed to suit the needs of New Zealanders. He was open to external influences – he was a keen follower of John Stuart Mill, for example – but said that these should be adapted and tailored to New Zealand conditions.

It was particularly during the constitutional crisis on the Legislative Council appointments that Ballance's attitude to relations with Britain came to the fore. He politely but firmly criticised the Governor's approval of a new batch of councillors in the dying days of the previous ministry. He was equally adamant that this misdeed should be corrected by the Governor's agreeing to appoint twelve Ballance nominees to the Council. In arguing his case to London, Ballance stressed the principle of New Zealand's political independence from Britain. Constitutionally, he said, the Governor was a figurehead and was obliged to accept the advice of the New Zealand Government.

Ballance was not slow to suggest that an unfavourable decision by the Colonial Office could do serious damage to the relationship between New Zealand and Britain. It was partly because of this, and because of his refusal to accept a knighthood, that Ballance had something of a reputation as a republican. He undoubtedly had republican tendencies, but at the same time acknowledged that the constitutional monarchy appeared to work.

These views were consistent with Ballance's position on the relationship between Ireland and England. In the early days he had hoped that loyalty to the English Crown could be restored through removing rural poverty which Ballance saw as the basis of discontent.

But by the 1880s he was advocating Home Rule, arguing that Ulster Protestants were by no means solidly against the idea and pointing to their leadership of the rebellions against the English in 1782 and 1798. Growing up in Ireland Ballance had not suffered personally (nor had his family) at the hands of the English, economically or otherwise. His support for Home Rule came rather from a philosophical and intellectual belief in the right of people to govern themselves. Yet his own observations doubtless reinforced this. Belfast was in political turmoil for much of the time Ballance lived in the city. He would not have been unaware that English intervention in Ireland was a root cause of this conflict. Certainly his view of the early settlement of New Zealand recognised the wrongs of the British colonisers. There was barely a war in New Zealand, he said, that had not been prompted by settler greed.

Conclusion

Ballance's Irish experiences contributed significantly to the development of his political ideas and platform in New Zealand. These were major features of Irish society that he sought to ensure New Zealand did not replicate. Ireland provided Ballance with lessons to be learnt and principles to be pursued: the critical importance of the ownership and distribution of land, the dangers of mixing religion and politics, the right of people to govern themselves. Ballance's Irish background did not, of course, predetermine his later outlook. W.F. Massey, another Ulsterman who became a New Zealand Prime Minister, came from a similar background. Massey, however, was an arch-conservative and one who, for example, had no qualms about trying to break the New Zealand trade union movement by force. Clearly the difference between the two men must lie elsewhere than with their Irish origins. Ballance had a predisposition towards liberalism. This came from his family, from his reading, from the influences on him of people he met, and from his studies in Birmingham. It had to a significant degree an intellectual basis. But that is another story.

Published in *Familia: Ulster Genealogical Review*, no. 5, 1989.

Notes

1. Dr McIvor was a diplomatic officer with the Ministry of External Relations and Trade in Wellington, New Zealand.

   For a fuller account of Ballance's life readers should consult Dr McIvor's biography of John Ballance, *The Rainmaker: A Biography of John Ballance, Journalist and Politician, 1839–1893* (Heinemann Reed, Auckland, 1989) *Editor.*

Hume family headstone, Hillsborough, Co. Down, including references to Andrew Hamilton Hume of Humewood, New South Wales (d. 1845) and his son John Kennedy Hume who 'was murdered by the bushrangers Jan. 15 1848'.
The Hume Highway in Australia was named after Hamilton Hume, the eldest son of Andrew Hamilton Hume. Image courtesy of William Roulston

www.ingramcontent.com/pod-product-compliance
Lightning Source LLC
Chambersburg PA
CBHW041139110526
44590CB00027B/4071